Museum Masterpieces: The Metropolitan Museum of Art
Part II

Professor Richard Brettell

THE TEACHING COMPANY ®

PUBLISHED BY:

THE TEACHING COMPANY
4840 Westfields Boulevard, Suite 500
Chantilly, Virginia 20151-2299
1-800-TEACH-12
Fax—703-378-3819
www.teach12.com

ISBN 1-59803-391-3

Richard Brettell, Ph.D.

Margaret McDermott Distinguished Professor of Art and Aesthetics
The University of Texas at Dallas

Professor Richard Brettell is the Margaret McDermott Distinguished Professor of Art and Aesthetics at The University of Texas at Dallas. He received his B.A., M.A., and Ph.D. from Yale University. Prior to joining The University of Texas at Dallas, Professor Brettell taught at Northwestern University, the University of Chicago, Yale University, and Harvard University.

Professor Brettell's museum career began in 1980 with his appointment as Searle Curator of European Painting at the Art Institute of Chicago, where he oversaw the renovation and reinstallation of the European Painting and Sculpture Galleries in the Allerton Building. Since then, Professor Brettell has been the McDermott Director of the Dallas Museum of Art and has advised and consulted for museums such as the Dixon Gallery and Gardens in Memphis, Tennessee; the Portland Museum of Art; and the Amon Carter Museum in Fort Worth, Texas. Professor Brettell presently serves as the American coordinator of the French Regional and American Museum Exchange (FRAME), a coalition designed to promote the exchange of art and information between regional museums in France and the United States.

Professor Brettell's museum exhibition work ranges from intimate explorations of individual artists to broader surveys of particular periods and movements in art history. His exhibitions include *Monet in Normandy* (for the de Young Museum in San Francisco); *Gauguin and Impressionism* (for the Ordrupgaard in Copenhagen); *The Golden Age of Naples: Art and Civilization under the Bourbons* (for the Art Institute of Chicago); and *The Impressionist in the City: Pissarro's Series* (for the Dallas Museum of Art). He has given scholarly lectures at numerous museums, including The Metropolitan Museum of Art, the Musée d'Orsay, the Singapore Art Museum, and the National Gallery of Art. He is also the author of more than 25 books, including *19th and 20th Century European Drawings in the Robert Lehman Collection* and *Impression: Painting Quickly in France, 1860–1890.*

Table of Contents

Museum Masterpieces:
The Metropolitan Museum of Art
Part II

Museum Masterpieces:
The Metropolitan Museum of Art

Scope:

There is no city in America—and indeed, few cities in the world—with as many distinguished art museums as New York City. Yet of all these great museums, The Metropolitan Museum of Art is the most wide-ranging and ambitious. Visitors from all over the world flock to the museum to experience its collections, unparalleled in their global and millennial scope. Since its founding in 1870, The Metropolitan Museum of Art has evolved into an influential cultural institution and a central destination for both tourists and scholars.

But how does one approach the vastness of The Metropolitan Museum of Art without becoming overwhelmed? How does one enjoy the depth of its collections while continuously appreciating the thematic connections between galleries and individual works of art? To wander blindly through the halls of The Metropolitan Museum of Art is to risk missing out on a wealth of information and history. This course offers a way both to understand The Metropolitan Museum of Art and to make sense of the wide range of works, artists, styles, and cultures that populate its various departments. Twenty-four lectures explore each of the museum's departments in depth, selecting key works of art based on their historical importance, their unique position within their respective collections, and their connections to the museum's other departments (and, in some cases, to works in other museums).

The course begins with a brief overview of The Metropolitan Museum of Art's history, from a dream in the minds of Americans eager to create a national institution of art in the United States to the iconic and ever-growing museum of the 21st century. After laying the groundwork for the course, the lectures dive into the museum's individual departments and chart a roughly linear course that takes us from the influential civilizations of Greece, Rome, and Egypt through the burgeoning art movements that proliferated throughout Europe to the disparate art styles of 20th-century artists. The early lectures illustrate how the museum's vast collection of cultural works and artifacts creates the foundation for much of the subsequent history of art. Lectures that cover the museum's important Asian, ancient Near Eastern, African, Oceanic, and pre-Hispanic collections are designed to help visitors emerge from the museum with a sense of the historical range and aesthetic qualities of these disparate but influential cultures.

A series of four lectures explores The Metropolitan Museum of Art's most famous department: the Department of European Paintings. Starting with the stylistic experiments of the Renaissance and continuing through the 19th century, these lectures show how select masterpieces by history's most influential artists—including Bernini, Canaletto, El Greco, and Monet—fit into the larger historical framework of European culture and art.

Other departments in The Metropolitan Museum of Art are devoted to other forms of art, including sculpture, drawings and prints, photography, costumes and textiles, musical instruments, arms and armor, and decorative arts. Individual lectures take you inside period rooms and detailed galleries designed to transport visitors to a different time and place. Indeed, one sees that an unspoken goal of The Metropolitan Museum of Art is to serve as a time machine in which one can experience life as a medieval warrior, a Venetian intellectual, or a 20th-century American businesswoman without abandoning the comforts of the 21st century.

While The Metropolitan Museum of Art is a global museum, its collection of American art makes it an equally viable record of the nation's aesthetic evolution. A pair of lectures explores the museum's collections of American art from the colonial era through the fracturing period of the Civil War to the start of the 20th century. Additional lectures offer insights into American works from the 20th century (along with their European counterparts) contained in the museum's Department of 20th Century Art [Department of Modern Art].

Of course, a great museum is nothing without the donors who help supply its galleries with important works of art. Among the most important donations in The Metropolitan Museum of Art's history is that made by Robert Lehman, whose collection of Old Master drawings and Italian Renaissance paintings composes an entire wing of the museum and spans a period from 1400 to 1960. In addition to lectures devoted to highlights of the Lehman Collection, the course concludes with a lecture that covers the important role individuals play in the foundation and maturation of an institution as influential as The Metropolitan Museum of Art. Without the past and continued support of curators and donors, the museum would be an empty shell overlooking Central Park instead of what it is today: an art museum richly populated with both magnificent works of art and visitors eager for a rich cultural experience.

Lecture Thirteen
European Sculpture

Scope:

The collection of European sculpture from the Middle Ages through the 19th century is housed mostly among the period rooms and decorative arts galleries on the ground floor of The Metropolitan Museum of Art. Although not nearly as comprehensive as the museum's collection of paintings from the same period, it is of national significance and includes major medieval altarpieces, superb Renaissance sculpture in stone, bronze, and terracotta, and masterpieces of Baroque sculpture by artists such as Bernini, Foggini, Canova, and others. The collection strengthens considerably in the 18th and 19th centuries, and there is scarcely a major European sculptor during this time period who is unrepresented by a masterpiece. The lecture will consider the rise of sculpture in the 15th century as an independent medium in competition with painting and will consider the evolution of the sculptor's various materials through the work of Rodin and Degas.

Outline

I. The most important of the three-dimensional arts is sculpture.

    A. In many museums, sculpture is segregated from the decorative arts.

        1. At The Metropolitan Museum of Art, two-dimensional objects are on the second floor, and three-dimensional objects are on the first floor.

        2. The history of art suggests a battle between making something in three dimensions or creating an illusion on a two-dimensional surface.

    B. The sculptures at the museum are contained in a naturally lit space because sculpture looks best out of doors.

II. The Metropolitan Museum of Art has major masterpieces throughout the course of European sculpture.

    A. *Madonna and Child with Angels* (15th century) by Antonio Rossellino is a low-relief sculpture.

1. The combination of real shadows and illusionary lines gives a sense that one is looking at both a sculpture and a painting.
2. Unlike many marble sculptures from the Renaissance and early Baroque period, this sculpture maintains its original surface and original gilding.

B. *Virgin and Child* (15th century) by Andrea della Robbia reflects the artist's mode of working with glazed ceramic sculpture.
1. He would put pure colored glazes on various parts of a ceramic sculpture in a manner similar to the two panels of striding lions in the Department of Ancient Near Eastern Art.
2. This work is a high relief sculpture that creates the corporeality of the Virgin and Christ Child.
3. The sculpture creates a psychological bond between mother and child that makes the work tenderer than Rossellino's.

III. The collections at The Metropolitan Museum of Art have a huge shift in time from the 15th century to the beginning of the 17th century.

A. The greatest sculptor of the 17th century was Gian Lorenzo Bernini.
1. The only great full-scale marble sculpture by Bernini in America is at The Metropolitan Museum of Art.
2. *Bacchanal: A Faun Teased by Children* (c. 1616–1617) is a carved bacchanal like the drawn bacchanals of Poussin and Castiglione.
3. Unlike Egyptian, Greek, and Roman sculpture, this work is about motion; from every single viewpoint, the work is a different sculpture.
4. There is a sense in which there is change and transformation in the sculpted image in the 17th century, just as there is in the painted image.

B. Giovanni Battista Foggini was a Florentine artist who worked with Bernini.
1. As the official sculptor of the Medici family, he created *Grand Prince Ferdinando de' Medici (1663–1713)* around 1683 to 1685.

2. We think of busts as relatively inert, but here the drapery, hair, and lace collar seem in the midst of a rustling wind.

C. Jean-Louis Lemoyne was the most important French sculptor of the first half of the 17th century.
   1. *La Crainte des Traits de l'Amour* (1739–1740) is a life-size female figure clad in a Roman way so that we see her as a goddess.
   2. Unlike the Bernini sculpture, this work was meant to be seen only from the front; it has more of the qualities of a picture frozen in marble than a real sculpture that you move around.

IV. Portrait busts are the representations of people in sculpted form.
   A. Jean-Antoine Houdon was the greatest French sculptor of the late 18th and early 19th centuries.
      1. *Sabine Houdon* (1788) is a tiny portrait bust of the artist's daughter that measures 10½ inches high.
      2. The work is one of the earliest sculptural portraits of a child.
   B. *Madame de Wailly* (1789) was sculpted by Augustin Pajou, Houdon's rival at the end of the 18th century.
      1. The Roman style of dress is both Classical and erotic.
      2. This bust is the result of centuries of rethinking and reworking the traditions of European marble sculpture.
   C. Antonio Canova's *Perseus with the Head of Medusa* (1804–1806) is a life-size male nude sculpted in perfect white marble.
      1. With this figure, modern sculpture finally reaches a higher plateau of style and perfection than ancient sculpture.
      2. Canova hollowed the head of Medusa and contrived the elegant drapery to carry the weight of the outstretched arm, reflecting the attention paid to engineering.
      3. Looking at the heads of Medusa and Perseus, one sees a careful observation in the midst of all this idealization.
      4. The work was commissioned by the Pope to be seen with the Apollo Belvedere (c. 350–320 B.C.), the most perfect sculpture of antiquity.

D. Jean-Baptiste Carpeaux's *Ugolino and His Sons* (modeled 1860–1861; executed 1865–1867) is a sculpture taken from Dante's *Inferno*.

  1. Like Bernini's sculpture, this is a 360-degree sculpture; as one walks around it, one sees the relationship between each figure.

  2. Ugolino's pose was the source for Rodin's *The Thinker* (1880).

E. Edgar Degas made more than 100 sculptures in wax during his lifetime, only one of which he exhibited: *The Little Fourteen-Year-Old Dancer* (executed c. 1880; cast in 1922).

  1. The museum's piece is cast in bronze; the original was in mixed media.

  2. Everything we know about Degas's sculpture comes from Mrs. Havemeyer, who gave a complete set of bronzes to the museum.

F. Auguste Rodin's terracotta portrait *Honoré de Balzac* (probably 1891) helps us think about the way in which the embodiment of a particular individual in sculptural form can be more powerful than any painting.

  1. Rodin made studies of Balzac's death mask, of which this bust is one.

  2. The work makes one think about the head of a ruler in the museum's Department of Near Eastern Art.

Recommended Reading:

Pope-Hennesy. *The Study and Criticism of Italian Sculpture.*

Tinterow. *The New Nineteenth-Century European Paintings and Sculpture Galleries.*

Questions to Consider:

1. What medium of sculpture is your favorite? Explain why it is your favorite using one of the sculptures studied in this lecture.

2. Who is your favorite sculptor represented in the museum and why?

Lecture Thirteen—Transcript
European Sculpture

In the last lecture, we had a wonderful exercise in time travel. We wandered through a whole series of what are called period rooms, imagining ourselves dining with a lord in London, having coffee in Switzerland, having a cup of tea in the south of France, and we looked at beautiful objects of decorative art—not nearly enough. This is an area in which I'm being actually a little bit bad to the Met because there are great ceramics, and there's great, incredible silver. And so you'll just have to see that when you go. But this time, we're going to deal with the other three-dimensional art, the most important of the three-dimensional arts in a hierarchical term, and that is the collection of sculpture.

Now, in many museums, sculpture is kept with painting and is segregated from the decorative arts. But in the Met, there's a segregation of two-dimensional things and three-dimensional things. Two-dimensional things are on the second floor, and three-dimensional things are on the first floor. There is a sort of sense in the whole history of art—and this was very strong in the late 15th century—in which sculptors and painters were vying against each other to see who was the best, who was the most imaginative, who was higher in a kind of hierarchy of the arts, with Leonardo arguing for painting because he wasn't such a great sculptor and Michelangelo arguing for sculpture because he wasn't such a great painter. Actually, he was a great painter, but his big thing was sculpture. There was this sort of battle as to whether it was better to make something in three dimensions out of obdurate material, like stone or bronze, or whether it was better to create an illusion on a two-dimensional surface. It was an argument that sort of activated art theory for several centuries.

In modern museum time, what has happened is that paintings are put on the second floor under skylights, and sculpture is put on the first floor with side light in order to make the shadows work and the sort of illusion of the sculpture work perfectly. That's exactly what happens at the Met. What's wonderful when you go through the Met is you go through all of the little period rooms which we've talked about so far, and then you kind of wander into this big space. This big space is extraordinary because it's naturally lit from above.

Suddenly, you're almost outside of the building, with clear natural light. You see two great façades, one a Classical façade with a limestone facing and the other a façade of brick and limestone, which is an extraordinary thing because it is the original façade of the Met. And what one does is one comes out of the old front door of the Met and goes into this place where there is sculpture. And, of course, sculpture looks great in natural light; sculpture looks best out of doors. This is a room in which you see major works of monumental sculpture out of doors.

Now, the Met's collection of sculpture is not as important as its collection of painting, and that must be said at the beginning. But it has major masterpieces throughout the course of European sculpture, and I'm going to take you, as usual, on a little tour of my favorite of those masterpieces. We begin in the middle of the 15th century with a sculpture which is a low-relief sculpture; that is, there's an element of illusion in the relief. The figure isn't carved as if coming completely out, three-dimensionally, of the flat surface of the back of the relief. But there's a sense in which the relief is illusionist, and if you get far enough away from the sculpture, the combination of real shadows and the sort of illusion of lines that are carved into the space give one a sense that one is looking at something that is both sculpture and painting. It's by a very great sculptor who was a student of the most important early-15th-century Florentine sculptor, Donatello, and his name was Antonio Rossellino. In the middle of the century, in the 1450s, he made this *Madonna and Child with Angels*.

Now, when you see it at the Met, it's absolutely beautiful. Her [the Madonna's] eyes are sort of lidded, and she looks off to the side, and the little baby, the little Christ Child, also has these sort of coffee-bean eyes, eyes that almost look pre-Columbian in a way. It's almost as if they're squinting because the light is so bright. They're surrounded with wonderful little *putti* who are beating their wings, and [the] little angel *putti* [are] having a happy time, sort of showing how wonderful this maternal bond can be. The deepest carving of the sculpture is behind the left hand of the Virgin, and it reveals the legs of the Christ Child and gives a sense of the real solidity of the figures. Both of them are looking off to the side, as if to suggest that maybe there was another sculpture that was a donor, or something else that paired with it, but one doesn't know that.

What's extraordinary about this is that it's in between painting and sculpture. It has an element of illusion because the figure doesn't emerge enough from the background to be actually real, but it emerges more than it would, obviously, if it was a painting. And so this idea of the paragon—of which is better, sculpture or painting—is resolved in this because it's a little bit of both. Now, the really most wonderful thing about this is that it is perfectly preserved. Many marble sculptures from the Renaissance and the early Baroque period, when they get old, they get dirty. And when they get dirty, oftentimes they're over-cleaned or scrubbed to make them look very clean. This sculpture was spared that, so it has its original surface. And because it has its original surface, it also has all of the gilding that it would have had and that you see in her halo and his halo. If you get very close to the sculpture and look at details of their clothing, you can see that the sculptor has inserted little bits of gilding in order to give a kind of luxurious feel and another level of reflection of light in the sculpture. This perfect masterpiece of mid-15th-century sculpture is downstairs in the sculpture galleries, and you could easily run up the stairs, if you were feeling athletic, and go into the paintings gallery and see equivalent paintings by both northern and southern artists, some of which we've talked about.

Fewer than 20 years later, this marvelous sculpture was made by an artist named Andrea della Robbia. Andrea della Robbia was the nephew of one of the greatest artists of the 15th century, whose name was Luca della Robbia. Luca della Robbia figured out this mode, made a kind of career out of doing glazed ceramic sculpture. He would make a ceramic sculpture, and then he would put pure colored glazes in green, yellow, blue, and white on various parts of it, sometimes with garlands, with green and yellow fruit and blue backgrounds, and bring [in] extraordinarily brilliant color, almost like the color of those lions from the ancient Near East that we saw in an earlier lecture but even more brilliant, as one sees in this.

This is a Virgin and Child, very much like the last image, made in the 1470s. Here, there is no sculpture-versus-painting [question]; this is sculpture. This is not a relief, not a sort of low relief, but a high relief. One believes in the corporeality of that Virgin and that Child. One believes, actually, in the corporeality of the little group of angels, of [the] *putti*, above—little, tiny baby angels above—which are sort of equivalent to the baby Jesus. Here, there's this marvelous psychological bond between mother and child, which makes the work of art much more tender than the Rossellino, in which each of them seems kind of distracted by something else. It's as if they're together, but they're not together psychologically. Here, they're together, and of course, the infant Christ looks at the viewer in a way which is very touching. So this is an object which we can imagine ourselves—if we were fervent Catholics—worshipping this because the little Christ Child is beckoning directly to us.

Now, we're going to have a huge shift in time, and that's because the collections at the Met have this huge shift in time, and we go from the 15th century to the beginning of the 17th century, a big leap forward. We're doing it because there are very few masterpieces at the Met in the middle of those two dates. But we've gone from two outright masterpieces of Italian sculpture to another outright masterpiece of Italian sculpture, and this is by the greatest Italian sculptor—probably, actually, undoubtedly, the greatest sculptor of the 17th century, the age of Velázquez, and Rembrandt, and Frans Hals, and Rubens, and Poussin. The artist who was the greatest sculptor, *nonpareil*, without a rival, in the world was Gian Lorenzo Bernini. Bernini was born in 1598, two years before the turn of the century, and died at the ripe old age of 82 in 1680.

Bernini's sculptures are common when you go to Italy. You see actually quite a lot of it, and they're spectacular, when you go to Italy, but they're very rare in the United States. We have several works of terracotta sculptures, of his sort of studies for larger sculptures, which are at the Fogg Museum at Harvard and the Kimbell Art Museum in Fort Worth, but the only really great full-scale marble sculpture by Bernini in America is at the Met, and you're looking at it now. It's a bacchanal, and we've seen bacchanals by Poussin and by Castiglione in drawn form, but this is a carved bacchanal, *A Faun Teased by Children*. It's wonderful because, as you'll recall when we went through the paintings galleries, we saw a number of works of art which were amongst the earliest masterpieces by their artists, and this is a work of art like that. When Bernini made this sculpture, he was either 18 or 19 years old, even though he lived until 82. So as a very young artist, he made this extraordinary sculpture.

When you stand in front of it, it's absolutely extraordinary. It's not quite life-size. The figure of the faun is a little bit smaller than life-size; it's as if he's a sort of "faunette." He's climbing up this tree, and there are these marvelous children at the top of the tree that are pushing at him and teasing him. Everybody seems to be having a marvelous time. There are all these holes in the sculpture, and this is something that we actually haven't seen before. When we looked at sculpture, whether Egyptian or Greek or Roman, before, the sculpture is more or less inert and whole, and it doesn't have all these perforations to it. Here, you have air going everywhere. There's as much lack of substance as there is substance in this sculpture.

What's really remarkable about it in terms of everything that we've seen is that it's absolutely about motion. Here, nothing stands still, even though it is totally inert. One sees this very beautiful, highly polished marble body of the satyr rushing up, with drapery going through his legs and this sense of urgency to the sculpture. He's being pulled by these two charming little children, and there's a tree trunk and a lizard, and there are all these things happening around it. And as we begin to look at it, we almost feel drunk with our own motion. And what we do in looking at this sculpture is not to stand and find the best angle, as one often does with sculpture, [but] we find ourselves drawn to it by looking around it.

As one does go around it, you find that it transforms itself utterly. From every single view, it's a different sculpture, and it has a kind of tumbling sense of play. It's as if everything is in motion, and everybody has been arrested at this moment in time. And as you move around it, or as we move around it, we activate it. We reactivate it as we move. There's this sense of the moving viewer, the representation of motion in sculpture, which of course, goes along with what I talked about in the Baroque period in painting, in which Rubens and all these artists represent motion in painting. The clouds run through the sky; the little children turn around. There's a sense in which there's change and transformation in the painted image in the 17th century, just as there is in the sculpted image.

Now, let's go to Florence. Bernini was at work in Rome, and Bernini was patronized by the pope and was the most famous sculptor in the world. He was brought to Paris to sculpt Louis XIV. They didn't have a great time. He did a design for the Louvre in Paris. Louis XIV didn't like it, and he [Bernini] didn't like France, and so he went back to Rome. We have now an artist named Foggini, who was

Giovanni Battista Foggini, who was a Florentine artist, and who had to go, ignominiously enough, from Florence to Rome to learn to be a great sculptor, and he worked, of course, with Bernini. He goes back to Florence, and he is the official sculptor of the Medici family. This is a bust of the Grand Prince Ferdinand de'Medici, a wonderful portrait bust from the 1680s. Essentially right after the death of Bernini, Foggini makes this. It's hilarious. He did both father and son, and the Met owns both busts.

Of course, we think of busts as being relatively inert; I mean, the figure stands still. The figure is dressed in clothes. There isn't much of an opportunity to represent motion. But here, the drapery seems windswept, and the hair seems disheveled, and his lace collar seems to be moving. It's as if he is in the midst of kind of rustling wind, looking out. We can see that he's a rather foppish prince, and he turned out to be quite a foppish prince because when he was married, he wasn't able to produce issue, and so, therefore, there were no heirs to his reign. When you look at the bust of his father, also at the Met, you can see a rather stern and strict ruler. Foggini, in marble, could sort of get at the characters of both father and son.

Now, let's go to France, and we're going to go out of doors here. This is in that wonderful space out of doors in front of the old Met. This is by Jean-Louis Lemoyne, who was the most important French sculptor of the first half of the 18th century, of the age of Watteau and early Boucher. This is a sculpture called *The Fear of the Arrows of Cupid*. One sees here Venus, and Cupid is down below, and Cupid is threatening to give her a little arrow and make her fall in love. And, of course, she's terrified of this and doesn't want to be committed to, and is terrified of, the arrow. And so the relationship between this little, tiny figure of love and this very large woman is extraordinary. This is a life-size female figure. This is not for the faint of heart; it's a sculpture that is six feet tall. She's bending down—and, of course, there weren't too many women who were six feet tall in the early part of the 18th century—and she's clad in a kind of Roman way so that we see her as a goddess rather than a real woman; the little child [is] below her.

There's this sense, again, of motion, and we know of the visit of Bernini [to France]. We know that Lemoyne went to Rome. We have a sense that there is a kind of transference of this interest in sculpture as being pictorial and as representing motion. If you kind of wander around to the back of this sculpture, though it's finished, it's very different from wandering around to the back of the Bernini, because the back of the Bernini is just as interesting as the front, and the side of the Bernini is just as interesting as the front. This is a sculpture that was meant to be seen in a plane, and the back of it is completely boring. It has more of the qualities of a picture frozen in marble than a real sculpture that you move around and around.

Now, I want to talk about portrait busts because it's so much fun to talk about the representations of people in sculpted form. This is one of my favorite sculptures in the Met. You'll have a hard time finding it because it's really small, and it's not so important that it's out on a pedestal by itself. It's by Jean-Antoine Houdon, who was the greatest French sculptor of the late 18th and early 19th centuries. He was born in 1741 and died in 1828. He's very much a republican, by which I don't mean Republican like in America, but republican as meaning anti-aristocrat. After the French Revolution in 1789, he was very much accepting of the new government, and he believed in individual rights, and he was—in late-18th-century terms—a left-winger. He loved Benjamin Franklin. He was interested in the rights of man. He was a new individualist.

Here, we see him [at work] in 1788, the year before the French Revolution, and he makes a portrait of a little girl. Who is this little girl? Well, this little girl is his daughter; *Sabine Houdon*. When we look at it, it's this tiny bust. It's really tiny. The whole thing is 10½ inches high. When we look at her, we think, well, maybe she's five or maybe she's four and a half. It's the size of an infant. She turns her head on her little chubby body, and she looks up, and she's both charmingly accepting of our glance and also [has] a little bit of her own—she has her own mind. When one thinks about this, you think, you know, how can one make a marble sculpture of a child because what five-year-old, even the daughter of the artist, is going to sit for a long enough time for the father to get it, to get every angle of the head, and to make it work right, and to move around her, and make all the models, and measure her in all the ways that you have to do in order to do a proper portrait bust?

What's glorious about this is, of course, that she was his daughter, and so he could look at her all the time. What he did was work on this sculpture for quite a long period of time until he captured her sort of ineluctable youth, and the sense of her charm, and of her character, and of her individuality. This is one of the earliest great sculptural portraits of a child. If we think back to that wonderful Roman young man and the children that we've seen in our earlier lectures, this is the first child we've seen who really is a child, even if she is a child in white marble.

How different she is than this *Madame de Wailly*, a very important lady, as we can see, and a lady who was sculpted by Augustin Pajou, who was the rival of Houdon as the greatest sculptor at the end of the 18th century. He was older than Houdon, and had developed his success earlier than Houdon, and died, in fact, in 1809. This is a rather large bust of a rather grand woman, *Madame de Wailly*, done in the year of the revolution. We see her, and what's interesting about this is that if you were so inclined, and if you had a member of the staff at the Met, and you took her off her pedestal, and put her on a cart, and took her down the corridors and into the great entrance hall and into the galleries of Greco-Roman art, and took her to the gallery where there are all the Roman portraits (of which the Met has many), you would think that she would look very much like a Roman portrait. She has a rather Roman headdress. She's dressed in a toga rather than a dress. She's wearing no underwear because you can see her nipple underneath the rather thin fabric of the toga, so there's an element of eroticism in it. It's both correct and Classical and a little bit erotic at the same time. You think he's trying to make this modern citizen, this *Madame de Wailly*, into a Roman woman. But if you'll remember the Roman woman that we do know, Cominia Tyche, who was born and died in the end of the first century A.D., we can see there are certain similarities. They each wear togas, and they each have rather stern heads, and they each have rather elaborate hairdos. But there is something much more individualistic, much more human, much more real, and much more erotic about *Madame de Wailly*, showing that she is the result of literally centuries of rethinking and reworking the traditions of marble sculpture that had gone on in Europe continuously from the first millennium A.D. all the way to the French Revolution in 1789.

Now, let's look at a very large and very grand male nude. This is by, undoubtedly, the most important sculptor in Europe in the late 18th and early 19th centuries, and his name was Antonio Canova. He was born in 1757 in a small town in the Veneto, and he died in 1822. There is a great museum in his hometown, and if you really like his work, I advise you to go there because you'll learn about his working processes. In 1967, with the Fletcher Fund, the Met bought one of the greatest works of art he ever made, which is this larger-than-life-size Perseus holding the head of Medusa, whom he's just killed, in one hand, and holding the sword with which he has beheaded her in the other hand, in perfect white marble. There's a sense of perfection of form. There's a sense in which no Classical figure we have seen is as perfect as this, that finally, modern sculpture has reached a higher plateau of style and perfection than even ancient sculpture.

When you walk around it and you see the beautiful back, you can see the way in which Canova is also an engineer. Marble is very heavy, and if you have limbs that hang out, they're like cantilevered forms in a building. One of the limbs is holding the head of Medusa, and if that head of Medusa was solid, it would break because the arm would be too thin to support it. And so he [Canova] has done two things. He has hollowed the head of Medusa, and he has contrived this very elegant drapery that goes in a beautiful sinuous rhythm down the back of the form, but which actually carries the weight, almost like a flying buttress in a Gothic building, of that arm and of that hollow head. And so the sculptor is thinking about engineering as much as he's thinking about sculpture.

One of the wonderful things to do is to look at the two heads and see how they confront each other; [note] the sort of perfect-formed, rather androgynous Perseus, who's staring with a kind of steely stare at the dead Medusa, and he's holding her by the snakes of her head. She's obviously dead. Her face is slack, her lips are slightly open and slack, and there's a sense of very careful observation in the midst of all of this idealization. What's interesting is that this sculpture was first commissioned in 1790 by the pope, and it was commissioned by the pope so it could be seen with the Apollo Belvedere, the most perfect sculpture of antiquity, a Roman copy of a Greek original which was unearthed in Rome in the late 15th century and which was the exemplar for art. Here, you see them both together, and here, you can see Canova winning this kind of contest between antiquity and the modern.

Now, we go later to Rome, to a wonderful and rather ghoulish, at the same time, marble sculpture, bought also in 1967 by the Met, by the great French sculptor Jean-Baptiste Carpeaux. Carpeaux, like all great French sculptors, like Lemoyne, like all of them, learned to make sculpture in Rome, in the fountainhead. When you look at the base of this sculpture, even though it was carved in Paris, it says "Carpeaux, Rome" because the figure, and the plaster for the figure, was made in Rome. It's this wonderful white marble, and its [subject is] taken not from Classical antiquity but from canto 33 of the *Inferno* by Dante. It represents Ugolino, who was a count from Pisa who went over to the Florentine side traitorously in 1288 and was consigned to starve to death with his family in prison. One sees him surrounded by his children, and of course, the thing to ask is, when will they start eating each other? It's this horrible, ghoulish subject, and there are young children and old children. They're all male children, so you don't have to feel excessively sorry. There's not a female amongst them, and one thinks that if males eat each other, it's okay for some odd reason or, at least, that's what he [Carpeaux] seems to have thought.

But Ugolino is sitting there, and when you look at this today in the Met, you have to walk around the entire sculpture because it changes every single degree. This is like the Bernini; it's a 360-degree sculpture. As you walk around it, you see the relationships between the children and each other, and the children and the father, and the sort of mythic calm and melancholy of the father. And then when you look very carefully at the father and the father's pose, you'll think immediately of Rodin's *Thinker* because this is the source for Rodin's *Thinker*. This was carved before Rodin made any of his great sculptures, and Carpeaux was the great French sculptor before Rodin.

I have two more sculptures to show you, one of them a very bizarre sculpture indeed by Edgar Degas, the great Impressionist, who made more than 100 sculptures in wax during his lifetime, only one of which, this one, he exhibited. But he didn't exhibit it in bronze—and this is in bronze—but in mixed media. The figure was made of wax. The bodice was fabric. The shoes were real. The cloth was real. The hair was hair. The bow on the hair in the back was real. It even had eyelashes made of actual hair. One sees this figure; she's a little bit more than three feet tall, so she's not quite full-scale, and she's called *The Little Dancer of Fourteen Years*, or *The [Little] Fourteen-Year-Old Dancer*. She looks like this strange little model from a scientific museum rather than like a sculpture. She looks like nothing we've seen.

When she was first shown in the Impressionist Exhibition of 1881, everyone was terrified of her. Everyone thought she was ugly. She was called the little rat—she looked like a little rat—because lower-class dancers in the corps de ballet were oftentimes thought of as rats and were oftentimes prostitutes for the great men who were the subscription holders. But this little rat has a kind of beauty and melancholy about her. As you walk [by] her in the gallery, you have to think about the importance of New York for her because all of the wax sculptures of Degas were cast into bronze after his death in 1917 because Mrs. Havemeyer from New York gave the foundry the money to do it. So everything we know about Degas' sculpture comes from Mrs. Havemeyer, and Mrs. Havemeyer got a complete set of the bronzes, which she gave to the Met before she died in the late 1920s.

I want to end the lecture with a person and to think about the way in which the embodiment of a particular individual in sculptural form has something that is more powerful than any painting. This is Auguste Rodin's terracotta of Honoré de Balzac, the great French novelist of the first half of the 19th century, who was the first great French Realist novelist, who wrote about the life of Paris, the life of the provinces, the printers, the ordinary people, the shopkeepers, the people who came from the suburbs to the city, the people who came from the country to the city. He sort of laid bare all of French society in his great series of novels.

In the early 1890s, Rodin, then the greatest living French sculptor, was asked to make a memorial to him [Balzac], and he made a series of studies which ended up in a great caped memorial of Balzac wearing a kind of robe and walking out into space. But he also made studies of Balzac from Balzac's death mask and brought Balzac back to life. This terracotta is one of them. And when you look at it—it's from 1890–1891—it's made of terracotta. It's exactly life-size, and when you look at it, you think that Balzac is still alive, and you think that this was made directly from him. And then when you look at it and you think about your earlier time in the Met, you remember that ancient Near Eastern ruler in copper, the first portrait that we have seen in bronze or copper (it's an alloy of some sort, and we don't need to be technical) and the force of this individual. We know that this is a king who lived and ruled more than 4,000 years ago. And when we look at Balzac, we have an even more exact sense of what a man who has been dead now for almost two centuries looked like. That is the power of sculpture.

Lecture Fourteen
The Arts of Africa and Oceania

Scope:

The Metropolitan Museum of Art was, like many other great art museums, rather late in accepting the arts of Africa, Oceania, and the Americas into its representation of world art. It was only with the merging of the independent Museum of Primitive Art with The Metropolitan Museum of Art that a major department was formed which combined The Metropolitan Museum of Art's scattered holdings with the major collections established at the Museum of Primitive Art by the Rockefeller family. When the Department of the Arts of Africa, Oceania and the Americas opened its galleries in the Michael C. Rockefeller Wing in 1982, years of aesthetic prejudice were wiped away, and New Yorkers could consider the diverse tribal and highly urban art forms of these three continents as a major contribution to world civilization. There is no doubt, however, that the collections of this single department are more diverse than those of any other in the museum, making it all the more difficult to boil them down to a manageable number that is a fair sample of the whole. For that reason, this lecture is devoted to the fundamentally tribal cultures of Africa and Oceania, with some attention paid to the highly developed urban cultures of north-central Africa (particular that of Benin); the next lecture will be devoted to art from the ancient New World. It is no accident that the galleries for these cultures are located adjacent to those for 20th-century art—in the late 19th and early 20th centuries modern Western artists were inspired by the arts of Africa and Oceania.

Outline

I. The cultures of Oceania, Africa, and the ancient New World are brilliantly represented at The Metropolitan Museum of Art.

   A. These cultures came to the museum rather late in its history.

   B. In traditional fine arts museums, the idea was that these cultures did not produce art at all but instead artifacts that belonged in natural history museums.

C. In the 20th century, artists began to discover the great riches of these cultures; these discoveries began to be communicated through modern art to many people around the world.

D. The arts of Oceania and Africa came to the museum in 1969 through the Rockefeller family.

    1. The Rockefellers started their own private museum called the Museum of Primitive Art.

    2. In memory of Michael Rockefeller, the family gave their collection to The Metropolitan Museum of Art; in 1982, the Michael C. Rockefeller Wing opened.

E. The collection's galleries are dimly lit because its holdings (made of various woods, pigments, and feathers) would fade in bright sunlight.

II. The region of Oceania spans Papua New Guinea to Australia and includes the tip of New Zealand and island groups including the Easter Islands and the Galapagos Islands.

A. The Maori feather box (c. 18th century) is a very rare carved-wood object that reflects the magical powers many of the collection's objects were made for.

B. The mask (19th century) is a turtleshell mask from the Torres Straits.

    1. Many of these objects were destroyed when Westerners came to the islands; this is one of only two surviving masks of this type.

    2. When you look at an object with unknown origins like this, it allows you to interpret the work in extraordinary ways.

C. I want to contrast an object from the western Pacific Islands and an object from the eastern Pacific Islands.

    1. The standing male figure (Tiki) (18th–early 19th century) is a rare object from the Gambier Islands, correctly carved in terms of anatomical detail.

    2. The Moai Tangata (early 19th century) was made on Easter Island; its realism, perfect proportions, mysterious meaning, and physical power are extraordinary.

D. The Solomon Islands produced wonderful objects like a ceremonial shield from the early to mid-19th century covered with thin pigments and inlaid with fragments of shell.

E. The helmet mask (mid–20th century), represents one of the early mythical female cannibals of the Mbotgote island group; the great form that the woman gives birth to is the mask itself.

F. The museum contains works from the island of New Guinea.

    1. The skull hook, or Agiba (19th–early 20th century), was used to hold the skulls of enemies from another village.

    2. Bis poles (mid-20th century) were a type of memorial pole carved like a boat; boats frequently appear in work from these water-based cultures.

G. Almost all of these objects were made to be used.

III. The urgency of form (e.g., exaggerated facial features, exaggerated proportions) expressed in the work of non-Western cultures gave early-20th-century artists the idea that they did not have to follow the Greco-Roman forms of the Western tradition.

IV. The museum's collection of African art has a greater depth of time.

A. The seated figure (13th century) has a formal originality that makes us look at it in a new way.

B. The 16th-century pendant mask, made by the Edo people, was given to the museum by Nelson Rockefeller in 1972.

    1. The museum has many Benin bronzes.

    2. The mask's headdress is a series of Portuguese soldiers (who traded with the Benin people).

C. The seated couple (16th–19th century) was made by the Dogan people. One can imagine a whole series of works of modern art that stem from this couple.

D. The 19th-century prestige stool was made by an artist called the Buli Master, possibly an artist named Ngongo ya Chintu.

E. African art scholarship in Europe, America, and increasingly in Africa is able to identify particular artists whose work can be studied in relationship to artists before them.

    1. The department has a library formed by Robert Goldwater.

2. Knowledge has incrementally increased during the time these objects have been in the museum because the works are able to be seen by scholars.

F. The male power figure (19th–20th century) wears the particular sufferings and problems of its owner. There are many objects of this type in America, many of them forgeries.

G. The museum has two masks that are important for modern art.
   1. The mask made by the Senufo people between the 19th and 20th centuries is the kind of head found in works by Modernists like Modigliani.
   2. The reliquary head, made between the 19th and 20th centuries by the Fang people in Gabon, reminds one of Brancusi's work; its purity and form made Modernists want to change art forever.

Recommended Reading:

Douglas. *Art of Africa, the Pacific Islands, and the Americas.*

Kjellgren. *Oceania: Art of the Pacific Islands in The Metropolitan Museum of Art.*

LaGamma. *Art and Oracle: African Art and Rituals of Divination.*

Questions to Consider:

1. How was the Rockefeller family influential in the development of the museum's galleries of African and Oceanic art?
2. How were early 19th- and 20th- century artists influenced by the arts of Africa and Oceania? What work in the museum's collection illustrates this connection?

Lecture Fourteen—Transcript
The Arts of Africa and Oceania

You would think that we've exhausted the Met already with the lectures that have dealt with the three great avenues, to the left, to the right, and in front as one comes into the great hall on Fifth Avenue, but the Metropolitan Museum is so complex and so interesting and it has grown both architecturally and in terms of its collections so much over time that now we're going to sort of spill out into the great rectangle that gradually came to take over acres of space in Central Park. We're going to go, first, to the left and look at cultures which are usually not represented in the great art museums of Europe but which are brilliantly represented in the Met. These are the cultures of Oceania, Africa, and the ancient New World, and they're cultures that came to the Met rather late in the Met's history. But they came to the Met with such confidence, and with such brilliant installations, and with such an enormous number of works of art of major quality, of major international quality, that the Met went from being a museum with almost no non-Western art to being a museum with one of the greatest collections of non-Western art of any encyclopedic art museum in the world.

When you go to the Louvre, or the Prado, or the National Gallery in Washington, or the National Gallery in London, or the Kunsthistorisches Museum in Vienna, you wouldn't ever think of walking up to the information desk and asking where the African art was, or where the pre-Columbian art was, or where the Oceanic art was because it's not there. In fact, in those museums, which are called fine arts museums, the idea was that these cultures didn't produce art at all. They produced artifacts, and they produced artifacts that were interesting in natural history museums, museums of ethnology, and museums of anthropology. Well, the 20th century changed all of that, and as artists began to discover the great riches of the cultures of Africa, Oceania, and the ancient New World, those discoveries began to be communicated through modern art to many people throughout the world. Suddenly, one realized that artists who were in villages in royal cultures in Africa, who were on remote islands in the Pacific, who were artists from the dim, distant past of the Americas were just as much artists as were Assyrian artists, Greek artists, or European artists who made works of furniture, works of sculpture, or works of painting. So the Met was an extraordinarily important institution because it brought the work produced by these men and women, most of whom are nameless, into the large international context of an encyclopedic art museum. We're going to begin by looking at the arts of Oceania and Africa, which came into the Metropolitan Museum with a very munificent gift from the Rockefeller family in 1969.

The Rockefellers had been collecting so-called primitive art. That's what it was called in the [19]40s and [19]50s, when they first started to collect it with real enthusiasm. They, in fact, even started their own private museum called the Museum of Primitive Art, the director of which was a brilliant man named Robert Goldwater, who wrote a great book called *Primitive Art and Modern Art* which we still read today. And [this] museum was the only collecting place in New York that dealt with so-called primitive art, the arts of Oceania, Africa, and the ancient New World, and in fact, folk art of the New World, as well.

What happened is that one of the great scions of the Rockefeller family who was a collector who was really interested in the arts of these people, named Michael Rockefeller, was killed on an expedition looking for works of art and looking to document cultures in Oceania. In his memory, the Rockefeller family decided to give the collection of the Museum of Primitive Art, founded in New York in 1954 with its own building, to the Metropolitan Museum in 1969. The Metropolitan Museum put those collections together with the scattered objects in its own collections, created a major curatorial department, hired a major architect, built a large wing, and opened the Michael C. Rockefeller Collection of African, Oceanian and Ancient New World Art in 1982. It forever changed the Met, and I remember actually very well going and looking at the profusion of objects not only from the Rockefellers but from other collections because, of course, in memory of Michael C. Rockefeller, many great New Yorkers who were friends of the Rockefellers, who admired what they had done, gave their collections of African art, or pre-Columbian art, or Oceanic art to the Met to create something that was really great. There is no general art museum in America with such distinguished collections shown so magisterially as the Metropolitan Museum.

Now, the collections, you get to them—you come into the museum into the great hall. You turn left, and you go through those fabulous galleries of Greco-Roman art. Then you turn right, and you go into a series of galleries which are, in contrast to the Greco-Roman galleries, very dark. They're dark so that these collections, many of which are light-sensitive—the objects in them are made of various woods, pigments, and feathers which would fade in very bright sunlight, and so there's a very low light level, and the objects themselves are beautifully selected and lit. I'm going to take you on a little tour of a few of the objects that you will see when you go into these galleries. Now, the galleries are unlike any of the other galleries, even the Egyptian galleries, in that you see a sea of glass cases. In those glass cases are many objects beautifully organized, beautifully displayed, beautifully lit, and beautifully labeled. If you're like me—I've never myself been to Africa in my life; I've been to Tahiti and New Zealand but not to most of the other islands in those groups—you learn from going and picking out your favorite objects, reading the information about them, and looking at them. So one should not be afraid of one's own ignorance in going into these galleries because the riches are there, and they're very well explained.

Now, we're starting with Oceania, and I show you a map to show you the sheer extent of it. I call it a continent of water, and it has these little sort of eruptions, literally eruptions—volcanoes that come up in it—and it goes from Papua, New Guinea, over on the side and Australia. You see the little tip of New Zealand and all of these island groups, all the way over to the Easter Islands and the Galapagos up here. The Galapagos didn't produce works of art, but we're going to look today in this lecture at works of art from this whole enormous territory, which would swallow up three United States' or five United States' in its sheer vastness and which has such a small amount of land and such a large amount of water that one always has to think about that in looking at the objects.

Now, the first object is from New Zealand, and I remember very powerfully going to New Zealand for the first time myself and being introduced to the Maori culture. Maori culture is one of the latest of the Polynesian cultures. The people didn't get there until the 16th century, and the Met owns a very rare carved-wood feather box. And you think, what is a feather box? Well, this feather box is carved with all of these extraordinary masks. The eyes are inlaid with shell—all of the eyes of the masks. They ward off evil spirits. It has two knobs on the end, and what it did was to hold the feathers of the king of a particular Maori group, feathers that were so powerful that if you looked upon them, something horrible would happen to you. So they had to be kept away from the sight of people unless they adorned the king. They went into this box. Ropes were tied around the knobs on the end. The box was pulled up into the rafters of one of the great houses of the Maori so that no one could see them [the feathers], and the eyes warded off all of the evil spirits. So you can see that these objects are full of magical powers, and that's what you feel when you go into the collection.

Here's another object that is from the Torres Straits, which are between Australia and Papua, New Guinea. It's a group of islands that produced a few rare objects that are made of turtle shell. This is a turtle-shell mask from the 19th century. A lot of these objects were destroyed when missionaries came and when Westerners came and the tribal cultures on these fragile islands were gone. This is, in fact, one of only two surviving masks of this type. It's all made—the structure of it is the shells of various-sized turtles which are cut out to form this kind of eyed bird on the top, flying across the head down below; the long hair [is] made from cords or strands of material from the beach. This would have been worn on top of the head. One knows very little about the origins of this object, but it was made in the 19th century. It's one of the rarest objects in the museum because, as I said, only two survive. When you look at an object like this, you don't know yourself how to interpret it, which frees you to interpret it in extraordinary personal ways. You can look at the label to see if you're right.

Now, I want to contrast two objects, one from quite far west in the Pacific Islands and the other from the far east in the Pacific Islands. This is an object from the Gambier Islands, and this is another really rare object because the missionaries came to the Gambier Islands in 1836 and essentially destroyed everything, all the graven images, that the peoples there were worshipping. So very few survive, and they have a kind of quality of incredible power. They're human beings. This is a male figure, correctly carved in terms of his anatomical detail, with normal legs, normal torso, normal head, and this tiny, sort of strange shrunken arm. Because so little is known about the cultures that produced this, this is a mute survivor from another age, and one looks at it longingly, hoping that he will tell you what he means.

Then, one sees in another case, if one walks around these galleries, an object that was made on Easter Island. Of course, we all know Easter Island from those huge stone figures which line the island and which are great mysteries. There are many theories as to when they were made, why they were made, and why they were put where they were put, but the great rarity of Easter Island sculpture is wooden sculpture. This is an ancestor figure, an extraordinary figure of the Rapa Nui people, made in the late 18th or early 19th century. So it's something that wasn't made for the tourist trade, which was discovered early on when Easter Island was first discovered. It's polished beautifully. We get a sense of its realism, the sense of its perfect proportions, and the strange thing about it is that we know very little about what it means, but its power—its sort of sheer physical power—is extraordinary.

Now, let's go to Santa Isabel Island, which is in the Solomon Islands. The Solomon Islands produced these wonderful objects that are inlaid with shell, and it's as if the artists carved things from wood or made structures from wicker and other materials and then used shells so that they would shine in the light. They would draw with lines of shells, and this is, in fact, a shield with a humanoid form in the beginning, and these marvelous sort of boat-like forms on either side, and at the top and the bottom, something that looks almost like a maze that one goes through and enters. This is a ceremonial shield which is so light that if the Met would allow you to get into the case and pick it up, it would weigh almost nothing. It's made of wicker. It's covered with very thin pigments made of earths and then inlaid on the top with very carefully cut-out fragments of shell.

Now, if one wants to see an object that's really profoundly and extraordinarily scary, it's this one. It's a mask, or a helmet mask. You put on the lower part. And it represents an extraordinary woman who is said to be one of the early mythical female cannibals of this island group. I don't know quite if I can say this properly, and I'm sure the curator would murder me if I did it badly, but it's a Mbotgote. You'll have to read the label carefully yourself. I have no idea how to pronounce it, but I love the object. One of the great joys of going to the museum is that you can love an object about which you know very little, read the label, and the label tells you that this is a mythical cannibal figure. It's a she. She's a woman, and you see her giving birth to a great form. That great form is the mask itself, and you can imagine this not sitting in a case but riding on a figure, a costumed figure writhing around in a fantastic dance, in a dance in which all of the gestures and the sort of demonic, almost witch-like quality of this figure would have even greater intensity because it moved.

Now, this is a work of art and the title of it is rather grim. In fact, it is rather grim. It's a skull hook. The island of New Guinea is divided into two parts, Papua, New Guinea, and Irian Jaya. I'm going to show you two objects, one from each part. This one is from Papua, New Guinea. It is a skull hook. It's made of a very sort of complicated series of materials. It's wood, but the pigments are ground from various vegetable objects and earth, which are [pressed] around it, pressed into the form. It is in the form of a mythical ancestor whose arms come out extraordinarily, with these long, strange forms that come up from the bottom. What this object was for was to house the skulls of enemies in another village. So one village would go to another. There would be a war. The heads of the victims from the other village would be brought back. The skulls would be extracted from the heads, and they would be hung in rows like this from each of these protuberances and be hung in the men's house. In villages in Papua, New Guinea, the men are sequestered from women, live away from women, guard their power very carefully, and the power of their enemies and of their ancestors [is] very carefully kept for them so that they can keep this power. You can feel in these enormous eyes and these huge protuberances the power of the men, the power of the tribe, the power of control over land which this figure itself expresses.

Now, the final objects are objects that are extraordinary because they survive. They are from Irian Jaya, the other side of the island from Papua, New Guinea, and Irian Jaya is a place where there are extraordinary rituals of warfare and where these amazing, very tall objects are made, which are called "bis poles" or "mbis poles" or "memorial bis poles." Many of them are 19 feet high, 21 feet high, 17 feet high, and they are, of course, carved from a single tree with another tree carved to add to the sort of object that sticks off of them at the end, a sort of strange phallic object that goes into place. They're essentially carved like boats, and boats in most of these cultures are, of course, used because they're water-based. They're near the sea. They're near rivers, and so one goes into the sea frequently. The boats bring one's ancestors, who were stacked one onto the other in the boats of life, with these huge phallic forms that come off of them.

The people who made these objects made them with an idea that there is no such thing as a natural death, and this is something that is very strange for us, but in the cosmology of the people who made these objects, every death is caused by an evil spirit, whether by disease, whether by murder and war, whether by childbirth. Whatever it is, there is something else that causes the death, and so whenever there's a death in a tribe, that death has to be avenged with a death in another tribe. These objects are made—the skulls are collected from the other village, mounted on the objects, and then the objects are put into the forest and go back into nature. They're not meant to survive, and what we have to understand when we look at objects, almost all of these objects were not meant to survive. They are very different from European paintings and marble sculptures and granite sculptures by the Greeks and Romans or the Egyptians. They were made to be used. They are made of perishable materials, and the fact that they survived has more to do with the collecting interests of the West than it does with the tribes themselves. It is actually a miracle of civilization that so many of these materials were collected, from the discovery of these islands all the way through to the present, so that we can understand cultures that are fundamentally perishable and understand the wisdom of these cultures and their amazing, amazing formal gifts.

Now, if you were Max Beckman, or Matisse, or Picasso, or any of the other great artists of the early 20th century, and you saw material like this for the first time and you had been to schools of art just like all European artists, looking at Greco-Roman art, and looking at Egyptian art, and looking at things that were sort of for the ages, [in the non-Western objects,] there was a kind of formal urgency, a new vocabulary of forms, exaggeration of facial features, exaggeration of proportions. All sorts of things that were anathema to the Western tradition were permitted in non-Western traditions. And it was this kind of urgency of form in these [non-Western] artists that gave early-20th-century artists, who were the first to have access to so-called primitive art, this liberation, this sort of sense that one can make forms that do not have to look realistic, do not have to look like Greco-Roman forms, do not have to look as if they come out of a great Western tradition, are rejuvenated by a kind of global interest in all cultures, which the Metropolitan Museum is very clear about.

Now, let's go to Africa, and what's interesting about the collection from Africa is that it has a greater depth of time, and that's, of course, for several reasons. This is one of the earliest objects in the museum. It's an object probably from the 13th century. So it's an object co-equal with the late cathedrals in France, and it's from when Giotto was working, when this object was made. One sees a clay figure of a sort of humpbacked man, lying all entwined in himself. It's a beautiful form. It's a kind of form that really has very little precedence in anything else that we've seen. We will see other objects that look like it when we look at ancient Mexican objects, but you can see that it has this kind of formal originality which is non-European and which makes us look at it in a new way. Its date—there are thermal luminescence tests in which we actually can know when these objects were made, and what's fascinating is that it has this extraordinary depth of time. Civilization in Africa is an ancient thing. It's, of course, the origins of all mankind, and the Met has a few objects of this very early type so that we can understand the depth of time in Africa.

Now, probably my favorite object in the African collection is this Benin ivory mask, which was given by Nelson Rockefeller in 1972, 10 years before the wing opened. It represents a queen, or the mother of the *oba*. The *oba* is the king of the Benin people. The Benin people had a very hierarchical society, almost like a European royal society. They traded with the Portuguese. They cast bronze. They had a very elaborate social stratification, and when one looks at the great Benin collections in the Met—and the Met has many Benin bronzes—you feel as if you're in the presence of a culture that's every bit as great as most of the cultures that we've been talking about in all the rest of the world, in the ancient Near East, in Egypt, and in the ancient Mediterranean. This *oba* queen with her downcast eyes is carved, of course, out of ivory. It's a head that's almost but not quite life-size, and it's both charming and serious at the same time. The seriousness of it is [in] the beautiful proportions of the head and the scarifications on the head, which indicate that she is royal. There is, in fact, the figure of a mudfish, which can live both on land and in water; therefore, it's able to live anywhere. And if you look very carefully at her headdress, you can see that it [shows] a series of Portuguese soldiers who traded with the Benin people already in the 16th century. There's a connection here in this object between a royal woman—and this is a pectoral, or breast object, worn by her son, the *oba*, or the king—it shows her power, her fertility, her sense of being long-lived, and her wealth because, of course, the Portuguese were symbols of wealth.

Another great object and an object of real quality shows the touching relationship of a couple, of a man and a woman, who are next to each other. It was made by the Dogon people. Its date, according to the Met, can be from the 16th to the 19th century, so we can see how little one really knows, and of course, it's difficult to take a piece of wood and compare it with another piece of wood because one would ruin the object. Dating it scientifically would be a difficult thing to do, but one sees here these two long, fantastic figures with their long, thin torsos; their long, thin arms; their breasts, hers slightly larger than his; their heads turned at odd angles. The male figure has his arm wonderfully, possessively around the woman, sort of pinching her breast rather charmingly. They're each seated on a sort of stool, which means that they're a royal couple because if you were able to sit on anything other than the floor, then you're an aristocrat or a high-level member of society. This object, which is very large— space goes all the way through it, and you can imagine it being looked at by Giacometti. You can imagine it being looked at by Noguchi. You can imagine a whole series of works of modern art that come from it.

Now, this is a stool, a royal stool like the stools they were sitting upon, and it's fascinating because it was carved by a particular artist. The Met actually thinks that they know the name of the artist, and it's another one of these names that's hard to say. Ngongo ya Chintu is the way that I would say it, but your guess is as good as mine. He is a Buli artist, an artist from the Buli peoples, and it's a royal stool. It represents, again, the mother of the king or a female ancestor of the king. The power of the king comes not from his father but from his mother, and she has these huge hands, which are, of course, necessary to support the weight of the king. This stool on which the weight of the king rested gave him power. It lifted him off the ground with the spirit of, and the physical nature of, his mother or his female ancestors. You can feel the energy in her knees. You can feel the way that her face pushes forth, her extraordinary hairdress in the back, and what's fascinating about this is that its style is particular. Scholars who now are looking very carefully at African art are able to—looking at the collections in lots of museums—identify the *oeuvre*, or the life work, of a small group of artists whose names are beginning to be known to us. Finally, African art scholarship in Europe, in America, and increasingly, in Africa is able to identify particular artists whose work we can study and whose work we can study in relationship to artists who came before them. So the adventure of the primitive art museum and the Department of Africa, Oceania and the Americas at the Met is that because the works of art are for us to see, scholars see them. There's a great library in this department formed by Robert Goldwater, and there is a sense that knowledge has, in fact, absolutely incrementally increased during the time that the objects have been in the Met because they've been able to be seen not only by people like us, the general public, but by scholars.

Now, all of us in civilization are terrified of things that can go wrong, of things that we can't control, of disease, of injury, of depression, of anything that could happen to us. We read ads in newspapers and see them on TV that will sort of help us cure our ills, and this is a power figure that did that for a particular person in the Congo; the Malai people in the Congo produced this object, which is a kind of power object. It is a figure that wears or takes the particular sufferings and the particular problems of its owner or user, whether that owner is a group of people, a family, or an individual. What it does is it begins to wear those problems. They are expressed by being made and by being individually nailed on him, or placed around his neck, or pulled down upon him. The more objects that he has upon him, the greater the weight that he takes off of you, the user of this object. There are many objects of this type in America, many of them tend to be forgeries because we like them so much that the Africans made a lot of them and we bought them. This is, obviously or I wouldn't be showing it to you, not a forgery. The body was made in the very late 19th or early 20th century, and the amulets, offerings, and expressions of the problems were put on it later.

I want to end with two masks, and they're masks of the people who probably made the masks that are the most important for modern art.

This is a Senufo mask, a mask made by the Senufo people, and what's extraordinary is that most Senufo masks that survive, survive only with the mask itself—this part—and without the elaborate dressing, the headdress, the feathers at the top, all of the objects that were put on it when it was worn in a ceremonial dance. When you take a course on modern art, you oftentimes look at something like this, just the head, and you look at heads in artists like Modigliani and you find a head like this. But when you look at the real object with all of its profuse ornaments, you realize that the impassive, calm, wonderfully ordered head with its coffee-bean eyes, its sunken cheeks, its small sort of mouth that seems to be going "ooh," its scarification and headdress at the top—that it was part of an assembly that was of extraordinary power. The Met is lucky to have a mask that is not just the mask but an adorned mask, which would have then had fabric flowing out of it, the body of the person who wore it, and would have been moving, with all of the rustling that you can imagine when you look at this object.

The last object is a reliquary head made by the Fang people in Gabon. Fang masks are the masks that most people think about when they think about modern art. The purity of the shapes; the sense that the head becomes a shape; that though it is related to the shape of the skull, the head is more of a geometric, pure shape that comes down to its small point; this wonderful geometry of the nose; the way that the eyes sit near the nose; the stylization of the hair on either side; this long, thin neck—it really looks almost as if it's a sculpture by Brancusi, and it, too, was made in the late 19th or early 20th century. Its purity of form and its extraordinary power of form was what made modern artists want to change art forever.

Lecture Fifteen
The Ancient New World

Scope:

The Rockefeller donation, rich in the arts of Africa and Oceania, lured other collectors who specialized in art from the ancient New World. By 1982, The Metropolitan Museum of Art had important works from all the major civilizations of the pre-European New World. From the cultures of what is now Peru through the village-based, metallurgy-producing cultures of northern South and Central America to the successive urban civilizations of ancient Mexico, Guatemala, and the southwestern United States, these collections comprise the most comprehensive display of ancient New World art in a general art museum anywhere in the world. This lecture will explore the work of ancient Mexico's Olmec, Maya, and Aztec cultures, works from cultures with markedly less urban grandeur such as Costa Rica and Peru, and rarities from the museum's collection of work from Caribbean and Eskimo cultures.

Outline

I. Most art museums have very few works of pre-Hispanic (formerly pre-Colombian) art. The museum is fortunate enough to possess a collection of works that lay bare the depth of civilization in the Americas.

   A. The Department of Africa, Oceania, and the Americas has a series of galleries devoted to the Americas.

   B. These galleries have mostly portage objects; there are very few monumental objects that give one a sense of the grandeur of these civilizations.

II. We are going to look at a few masterpieces by the major cultures of the ancient New World, starting with Mexico.

   A. In the 1920s, there was a reform in Mexican education under Minister of Education José Vasconcelos that stressed a respect of Mexican history by making a connection to the ancient Mediterranean.

   1. The equivalents to the Egyptians were the Olmecs.

   2. The equivalents to the Greeks were the Maya.

3. The equivalents to the Romans were the Aztecs.

4. The museum has examples of Olmec, Mayan, and Aztec art.

B. The Olmec "baby" figure (12th–9th century B.C.) is made of white slip ceramic and is one of the most complex ceramic objects we have seen.

1. The figure's mouth is oftentimes interpreted by scholars as the mouth of a jaguar.

2. This work is part of a population of white hollowware ceramic babies.

C. The jade carvings of the Olmecs, including an Olmec mask (10th–6th century B.C.), are of extraordinary quality; however, we know little about where they come from and, hence, what they mean.

D. Both Olmec objects show that the people of the ancient New World were as technologically proficient as any ancient people.

E. The "smiling" figure (7th–8th century) is a hollowware ceramic object made by the Remojadas people.

1. All their ceramics are made with a slip over the costume elements and a red pigment over the skin.

2. Objects like this were tomb burial objects.

3. This is one of the first objects we have seen that represents humor or mirth convincingly; you have to go to Frans Hals's *Young Man and Woman in an Inn ("Yonker Ramp and His Sweetheart")* to find a similar expression in Western art.

F. The Maya, like the Greeks, had no centralized authority but were composed of various city-states with its own scribes, artists, and architects.

1. Only a few wooden sculptures, such as the Mirror-Bearer (6th century), survive. The Maya had the ability to convey emotion through physiognomy, an important ability in the history of art.

2. The Maya were the first and only people in the ancient New World to develop a system of writing; deciphering this writing has made it possible for scholars to understand what objects mean.

3. The Maya were great painters of vessels, including a vessel depicting a mythological scene (8th century).
4. Many pots were signed by the painters who made them, suggesting that painters were appreciated as artists.

G. The Aztec people came from the north of Mexico into the central valley, creating their capital of Tenochtitlan (modern-day Mexico City); because the city was destroyed by the Spanish, few elements survive.
1. One of them is a seated standard bearer (second half of the 15th century–early 16th century) which recalls the sandstone sculpture produced in ancient Egypt.
2. Almost all of Aztec sculpture is rare outside of Mexico; seeing a sculpture of this level and scale at The Metropolitan Museum of Art is almost impossible anywhere else in the United States.

III. We are going to look at a number of objects that do not come from civilizations with the same urban grandeur as the ones we have previously looked at.

A. The frog pendant (11th–16th century) was produced in Costa Rica and is part of a population of pendants depicting a certain type of tree frog used as a hallucinogen for vision quests.

B. A lime container (*poporo*) from 1st–7th-century Colombia held crushed seashells used to produce hallucinogenic reactions in shamans.

C. The seated figure (1st century B.C.–A.D. 1st century) is a figure from Colombia or Ecuador that represents a sense of motion and urgency.

D. The Peruvian collections at the museum divide themselves between ceramics and metals.
1. The single-spouted feline-head bottle (9th–5th century B.C.) from the Tembladera culture has an incredibly sophisticated originality of production unlike anything we have seen in China or other parts of the world.
2. The feline incense vessel (6th–9th century) from the Tiwanaku culture may be a family symbol.
3. The Nazca culture produced multi-spouted pots like the double-spout bottle (2nd–4th century).

4. Gold metallurgy in Peru was extraordinary, and the museum's collections include a Sicán funerary mask (10th–11th century).

5. The collection also has extraordinary silver objects, including a deer vessel (14th–15th century) from the Chimú region; silver was associated with pre-Hispanic Peruvians.

IV. A small part of the collection deals with works of art from the Caribbean Islands, the Eskimo regions of the Arctic, and Native American civilizations; the museum has a few rarities.

   A. The 15th–16th-century deity figure (*Zemí*) is made of ironwood inlaid with shell. It was produced by the Taino people, who lived on the islands around the Dominican Republic.

   B. It is no accident that the Surrealists loved Eskimo masks like the early-20th-century dance mask; American sculptor Alexander Calder took his impetus from Eskimo objects.

Recommended Reading:

Douglas. *Art of Africa, the Pacific Islands, and the Americas.*

O'Neill. *Mexico: Splendors of Thirty Centuries.*

Questions to Consider:

1. Based upon the objects studied in this session, what pre-Hispanic culture of the Americas attracts you most and why?

2. What object in this lecture has given you a new appreciation for the people of the ancient New World and why?

Lecture Fifteen—Transcript
The Ancient New World

We've looked at a lot of works of art made by people from ancient worlds—whether they be in Asia, whether they be in the ancient Mediterranean, or in the Near East—and those works of art have given us a sense of the extraordinary power of the civilizations throughout the world in ancient times. When we come to the United States, most of us came to the United States from Europe; now, we're coming to the United States from all over the world, and very few of us have a sense that there were people here way before Europeans came and that there were urban civilizations, and very complex urban civilizations, and entire histories about which most people in the United States are largely ignorant.

Most of our art museums have very few works of art which we used to call pre-Colombian and now we call pre-Hispanic, for a series of reasons that don't need to be explained, but those works of art tend to be small. They're in little rooms here and there, and they don't have the same kind of power as works of art produced in Greece, or Rome, or Egypt, or ancient Mesopotamia, or ancient China, or ancient India. The Met is fortunate, actually, to possess a collection of works of art which lay bare, in a powerful way, the depth of time of civilization in the Americas and with objects of the very highest quality. It's still necessary, if one is an American, to go to Lima to see great pre-Colombian Peruvian art, to go to Colombia to see the great riches of gold, and to go to Mexico to the great archaeological museum to see works of art which are not movable and which give a sense of the sheer power of the early arts, the archaeological arts, of the ancient peoples of the Americas.

But having said that, it's actually possible to take a kind of crash course in early American art by going to the Metropolitan Museum. You do the same thing. You enter on Fifth Avenue, you walk through the Greeks and Romans in their huge galleries with monumental sculpture, and the bedroom from Boscoreale, and the huge sarcophagus. And then you go a little bit to the west, and you go to this part of the Department of Africa, Oceania and the Americas, and you're in a series of galleries devoted to the Americas. Now, those galleries have mostly portable objects, objects that are small enough to carry in your hands; the Met has very few monumental objects, objects that give one a sense of the power of the cities and the grandeur of the civilizations that produced these small objects. But the small objects are powerful enough that they may make you want to get on a plane, and take a trip to one of the countries where the culture that you admire the most came from, and go to the national museum there, and get a sense of the sheer power of the ancient New World.

Now, I'm going to talk about the ancient New World, and the ancient New World has a lot to do, like the African and Oceanian collections at the Met, with the Rockefellers. The Rockefellers were very interested in the ancient New World, and they collected quite extensively, and part of the Museum of Primitive Art that came to the Metropolitan Museum in 1969, opening in 1982 in the Michael C. Rockefeller Wing, was devoted to the art of the ancient New World. But other collectors and the Metropolitan Museum staff have made that collection a good deal larger. We're going to look at a few masterpieces by the major cultures of the ancient New World, starting with Mexico and working our way south.

Now, even if you were a Mexican, if you were a schoolchild in Mexico early in the 20th century, and you were interested in learning about your archaeological past and the past of the people, the various peoples, who had lived in the territory that's now called Mexico, it would have been very hard for you to learn. But in the 1920s, there was a sort of reform in Mexican education with a new Minister of Education, whose name was Vasconcelos and who figured out a way of seducing the parents and teachers of Mexico to think about, to really respect, their own past by making an analogue to the past of the ancient Mediterranean. His idea was that there were the Egyptians in the ancient Mediterranean, and the equivalent to the Egyptians were the first people who built pyramids in the ancient New World, and their names were the Olmecs. Then, there were the Greeks who built city-states, had very advanced art, who were very interested in philosophy and all sorts of areas and human knowledge, and their equivalent in the New World were the Maya. And then, there were the Romans, who were a fundamentally military, organizational, and administrative people, who brought under their control huge territories in the ancient Mediterranean and, in fact, a good deal beyond the Mediterranean. And they, according to Vasconcelos's idea, were the Aztecs, who were the equivalent military power in the New World. And then, of course, Vasconcelos's joke was the Europeans were the barbarians who came in and ruined the whole thing, and we needn't go there. What's interesting is that the Met has supreme examples of Olmec, Maya, and Aztec art, and I'm going to take you on a little tour of the great works of art in those collections now.

We begin, maybe not accidentally, with a baby, a baby who is made of white slip ceramic, a hollowware baby, a work of art of incredible technical complexity. If you think about making this object—we've talked a little bit about how you make a vase, and if you don't have a wheel, and you can't sort of make the vase on a wheel, then you have to put it together with coils, and you have to make various parts, and you have to do this. Imagine this: Look at this baby and think of making it. Think of making it with clay, which is wet, and think of making the various parts, having the various parts fit together, having the joints be clearly worked out so that they fit together and can be smoothed, and then firing the whole thing, and then putting on a slip and some color on the little helmet that the baby is wearing.

You can see that this is one of the most complex ceramic objects that we have seen, and it was made by the Olmec people sometime between the 12th and the 9th centuries B.C. Now, in the last lecture, we were talking about how old African art is. And if we leave out the Egyptians and the Nubians, the earliest object that we had was from the 13th century. Well, this is an object which is more than 2000 years older than that and is an object that was made by peoples in one of the most remote parts of the world with no known contact with Europeans or Asians. It's of such a level of sophistication, formally and technically, that we marvel at it. You can see that it has been broken and that it has been reassembled, but that does not in any way lessen its power.

This little sort of chubby baby has these long slit eyes and a mouth which is oftentimes interpreted by scholars as looking like the mouth of a jaguar. I have my doubts about that association, but they are my doubts, and you can have your doubts, as well. It's a baby with feline features, possibly, and it may be a portrait of a particular ruler. It may be a god. What's riveting is that we have absolutely no idea what it really is. But it is beautiful, and it is part of a population of white hollowware ceramic babies that are amongst the marvels of the history of art, and the Met has one of the finest ones. It's not large.

It's smaller than an actual baby, and it has, because of its reduction in scale, an extraordinary power.

Now, the Olmecs did make pyramids. The first pyramid in the New World is in a place called La Venta [in Veracruz]. It was a kind of symbolic mountain. It's the same people who made this small hollowware baby who created that gigantic pyramid. [Those] people also [were] very adept at carving one the hardest stones known to man, which is jade. In fact, the jade carvings of the Olmecs are of extraordinary quality, and the Met has one of the most beautiful Olmec jade masks. It's a sort of deep-green jade with veins in it. You can see those same sort of feline eyes, those long eyes that look as if they might be the eyes of a jaguar or a cat; a mouth which is opened and sort of slightly oddly formed with a little rectangular part above the lips, suggesting that it's about to utter something; and a wonderfully formed nose. It's hollowed out in the back as if it was a mask, and yet you can't see through the eyes, and you can't breathe through the nose, but the mouth is hollow. It's almost but not quite life-size. It's 6 ¾ inches tall, so it's a little bit smaller than any of our faces, and it has flanges; it has little holes on the side, so it could be pulled around a form, maybe at death—we don't know. The problem with objects like this is not that they're beautiful, which is not a problem at all, but that we know remarkably little about where they come from and, hence, what they mean. So this is an object of mystery. You look into those eyes, and you have no idea what to think, and you see that mouth wanting to sort of say something to you. You don't even know what language would come out of that mouth.

Now, these two powerful Olmec objects—one in ceramic, one in stone—show that the people of the ancient New World were technically as proficient as any ancient people anywhere in the world. They're not quite as ancient as the ancient Near East, or ancient Egypt, or ancient China, but they're not so far behind—a millennium and a half behind—and already the level of skill is extraordinary, which indicates, to me at least, that we ought to know a good deal more about them and that we ought to say Olmec just like we say Chinese or Egyptian.

The next object that I'm going to show in the collection is not from one of the three civilizations that I was discussing, but it's so wonderful and charming and amusing that I want you to see it anyway. It's another hollowware ceramic object made in the 7th or 8th century A.D. by people who were called the Remojadas people. All of their ceramics have this same kind of quality, and they're beautifully incised, wonderfully done, with a sort of slip over the costume elements and a red covering, a red pigment, over the skin. You can see the same sort of coffee-bean eyes, and all of the Remojadas figures have this enormous laugh or smile. It seems as if mirth fills their lives.

And one has, again, absolutely no idea what they mean, why they were made. They were found in tombs, so they're tomb burial objects, but the people who made them left no written language, and they only exist in archaeological contexts, so we have to interpret them ourselves. To me, this is an object which is one of the first objects that we've seen in the entire class that actually represents humor or mirth convincingly. You have to sort of go forward a bit to the Frans Hals of *The Jolly Toper* and his girlfriend in the bar in Haarlem in the 17th century to find a similar expression in Western art. There's a sense that the people of Remojadas were onto something. They could represent an emotion, a sort of state of being, which has to do with happiness.

Now, we go from that amusing figure, that figure who can make us laugh, and makes us feel good about being human, and makes us realize that the people who lived way before us also had mirth, also told jokes, also enjoyed themselves, just as we do on occasion. This figure, which is much smaller—it's only 14 inches tall—is one of the rarest and most powerful objects in the collection, and it is from the second of the great cultures that Vasconcelos taught his schoolchildren about in the [19]20s and [19]30s and [19]40s in Mexico, the Maya culture. The Maya culture, to Vasconcelos, was like the Greeks. There was no centralized authority. There were various city-states that fought with each other just like the Greeks. Each had its own king or rulership. Each had scribes, and artists and architects, and a priestly class. Each of them flourished, in a way, as intellectual centers, and so they were very much like the Greeks.

This is a mirror-bearer made by the Mayans in the 6th century A.D. It's a tiny bit earlier than the Remojadas figure. But what's extraordinary about is that it's made of wood and that it survives. If you think about the Maya, most of them come from the lowlands in southern Mexico and Guatemala and Belize, and the later ones come from the Yucatan, which is, though a little bit drier, still a jungly culture. The two things that do not survive well in those cultures are fabric and wood. The idea that this little figure, this powerful little figure, survives tells us that there were many other wooden sculptures produced by the Maya, and only a very few survive. Of those that do survive, this is the very finest, given by Nelson Rockefeller after his death, in his bequest in 1979.

It represents a mirror-bearer, and he's holding a mirror at his chest. One knows that it's a mirror. I could explain it to you, but it would take me 20 minutes, and it's boring, but one knows that it's a mirror. That mirror would be reflecting something in the sky, and possibly, this figure was seated at a particular place for a particular astronomical or astrological event, like the solstice, or the sunrise on a certain day at a certain time, or the rising of the moon because the Maya had a lunar calendar. This extraordinary man is performing a rite, and we can only begin to understand that rite. He is mostly naked in the torso. He wears very elaborate jewelry and [holds] the mirror up here. He has got a very simple sort of skirt, lower on, which is knotted around him.

His face, which is the least well preserved part of it, is in this sort of powerful grimace. It's an expression which is unlike really any expression that we've seen so far in the class, and it gives us a sense that the Maya had an ability to convey human emotion through physiognomy, which is a very important ability in the history of art. And the quality of this figure indicates that there were major sculptors. In the West, we think of Tilman Riemenschneider and the major masters of wood sculpture in the Gothic period. This artist, who is nameless and we have no other works by him, was definitely at that level. When you stand in front of him at the Met, in spite of his diminutive size, he has an extraordinary power. He sort of leans back on his haunches. He leans probably to receive the sun or the moon or the light of something at a particular moment and to cast it across a big space in a spectacle or ceremony with intellectuals, beautifully dressed aristocrats, and the people of the city from which he came.

Now, the Maya were the first people, indeed, the only people, in the pre-Hispanic ancient New World to develop a system of writing, and it has taken most of the 20th century for scholars to figure out the writing. It has been the figuring out of the writing, the glyphic texts of the Maya, that has made it possible for scholars to really understand what objects mean. I want to show you a vessel because the Maya were great, great painters of vessels. They were at the level of the Greeks [as] painters of vessels, and like the Greeks, there are many Maya pots which are signed by the painters who made them, not this one but others. There is a sense that they were appreciated as artists and that their names were known. Many of them, we suspect, were aristocrats, were very highly born.

Now, this is a complex cylinder vase, and a lot of them are cylinder vases so that you can tell a story or sort of have a whole series of scenes going on. We see this sort of skinny god over here, this sort of strange, comic, silly god, who's communicating to a beautifully dressed figure gesticulating and moving on another point. If you had this in your hands and turned it around and if you had the benefit of having one of the great Mayanists who can read glyphs with you, then you could come to a full understanding of this work of art. Only in the last 20 years has it been possible for works of art like this to be understood, and it is, again, largely because they're open to the public. They're at the Met. They're in major museums now. They're beginning to be photographed, and scholars in Russia, in Germany, in France, in the United States, in Mexico, and Guatemala are beginning to decode them. The adventure of this decoding is part of the adventure of going to the Met because every time you go, the labels get better, and there is more of a sense that one has learned something since the last time you went.

Now, the last of the three great civilizations listed by Vasconcelos in his triumvirate—of Olmec, Maya—is Aztec. The Aztec peoples came from the north of Mexico, swooped down into the central valley where Mexico City is, and created their capital city at Tenochtitlan, which is modern-day Mexico City. It was the city that was conquered by Cortes and the Spaniards. It's the city that lies underneath Mexico City. But the Aztecs were a great military power, and they built a city that was one of the largest cities in the world in the 14th, and 15th, and early 16th centuries, when it was at its peak. At that time, it had canals. It had hundreds of thousands of people. It was a city that was the equivalent of Beijing or London or Paris in its scale and sophistication. Because it was destroyed and largely buried by the Spanish, very few elements of it survived, and this is one of them.

It's a standard-bearer figure from the late 15th or early 16th century; that is, [it is] right before Cortes descends into the valley of Mexico in 1521 that one sees this figure. He would have held in one hand a standard. He is a captive. The Aztecs were rather bloodthirsty people, and I'm not going to go there because it would take me another lecture. But this is a guy who was captured, who was nude except for his loin cloth, who is sitting down, who is in subjugation to the Aztecs. The Aztecs were a military empire that extracted their booty in blood and that created a kind of system of renewing the world through human sacrifice.

This is a figure who was a standard bearer who would have become a human sacrifice, but we see him here in this beautiful stone. It's sandstone, and you think for all the world, except for the expression on the face, that we're looking at something that could have been produced in Egypt. It has this marvelously smooth surface. Almost all of Aztec sculpture is very rare outside of Mexico, so to be able to go to the Met and see a sculpture of this level and of this scale is something that is almost impossible in the rest of the United States. It's only when you look at this object that you can get a sense both of the eloquence and of the power of the Aztec people.

Now, we're going to go further down and look at a number of objects a little bit more quickly because they don't come from civilizations of the same kind of urban grandeur as the ones we've looked at so far. This is a glorious frog pendant made of gold. It's Chiriquí, and it's from the 11th to the 16th century, as you can see, produced in Costa Rica. What's marvelous about it is it's part of a whole population of these frog pendants in which the frogs have these little sort of bubbles coming out of their mouths. What scholars have learned, is that actual frogs—and it's a certain type of tree frog in Costa Rica—produce these bubbles around their mouths, and it was a hallucinogen. It was taken as a drug to produce visions by a human population. So this pendant represents a vision quest, a quest into another world, made possible by the frog. It's cast gold, made before the Spanish arrived, of wonderful quality. If you go to the Met, you'll see cases full of objects like this, so this will tempt you as one out of many.

My favorite gold object is from Colombia, and it's a rather large cast gold container; very sophisticated if you think of casting technology and the creation of a hollow cast figure. You can see it in a case. It's dominated by this figure. You could have put cords around it in different ways and carried it with you. Its function is to be a container for crushed seashells, which form a kind of lime, which were chewed with leaves to produce hallucinogenic reactions. And so, again, one has a kind of vision quest object, an object which kept something which was necessary for the visions of shamans or priests who went into other worlds so they could predict the future. So this humble little object is an object which is really incredibly holy because it contained substances that produced hallucinogenic responses.

Now, the most powerful figure of all the pre-Colombian figures in the collection of the Met is this extraordinary seated figure from Colombia or Ecuador. It's a Tolita figure. It's from the 1st century B.C., so it's quite early. It's rather large. It was found broken. What you see is a sort of crouching male figure. He seems ancient; there are wrinkles, or lines, or scarification on his face. His eyes and cheeks are sunken. His nose sort of sticks out, and he seems to be emerging from a cave or emerging from the underworld. When you see him in the Met, the representation of the sense of motion and urgency of age is something that makes him clearly a major work of art. We have nothing else that's really quite like this in the Met, so it's very difficult to measure whether this was the greatest artist of this material at this time or not. But it doesn't matter because this object, when you see it, you'll rush up to it because it has such power. This whole wing is filled with power objects.

Now, we go down to Peru. The great thing about Peru and the Peruvian collections at the Met is they divide themselves between ceramics and metal. I'm going to show you some ceramics. This is a figure that is now called Tembladera, from a Tembladera culture. When I learned about it, it was Cupisnique, and when I learned about it the first time, it was Chavin. So you can see that knowledge changes frequently in this period. It's ancient; it's [from] the 9th to the 5th century B.C., and it's a kind of vessel, the originality of which, in terms of its making, its firing, its shape, is something unlike anything we've seen in China or anywhere in the world. It has this incredible sophistication. We see a feline, the tail of a feline, here, and the head of the feline over here. But what this thing is in the middle, I don't know. When you go, perhaps you can look at it, and walk around it, and theorize for yourself.

The next ceramic object is a wonderful feline incense vessel from the Tiwanaku culture around Lake Titicaca, the highest lake in the world, between Bolivia and Peru. This is a culture that existed in the 6th to the 9th centuries A.D., and this marvelous incense burner would have sort of a resin in it, and smoke would have come out of it. One sees the head of a feline and then the elaborate tail of the feline in the back. And then, if you look carefully at it, you can see a painted representation of the feline, so [we see] every embodiment of this feline, some sort of cat, a magical cat. The smoke from this incense burner would have carried the power of that cat with it. Oftentimes in the pre-Hispanic cultures of Peru, families were organized—had their emblematic animals. So this actually may be a family or a royal family symbol; it's a wonderful vessel.

One of my favorite objects is this wonderful Nazca double-spouted pot. There are a lot of pots in Peru, pre-Hispanic Peru, that have two and three spouts and that were either shared or they were used in various kinds of ways. This is one of the most charming ones. It's got a masked being on a white ground that goes all the way around it. It was produced by the Nazca culture, [which] not only produced beautiful ceramics of this sort—completely original, looking like nothing else produced by any culture—but [also had] major urban complexes and [left] a series of incised lines in the earth called the Nazca Lines, which we still today have no idea of their meaning.

Peruvian metal is equally original. This is a wonderful Sicán mask, and it was a funerary mask put upon a ruler; [it is] made of gold inlaid with turquoise and painted with copper and copper and cinnabar, so that it has this incredible quality of frightening away whoever comes to find it. The gold metallurgy was extraordinary in Peru, and the Met's collections are superb. They have hoards of cups, large-scale cups, cups with frogs on them—and you'll know what that means when you see them. Everything that has to do with gold has to do with the sun. They also have other cases with extraordinary objects in silver. Silver was associated, [in the cultures of] the pre-Hispanic Peruvians of all types, with the moon. And so the cool light of the moon and the warm light of the sun come out of the earth as symbolized in silver and gold. This is a Chimú vessel from the north coast of Peru—it's a deer vessel. Again, families or rulers with certain identities had objects of certain types, which they had, and this is an animal of that type.

Now, I want to end rather quickly, a little bit too quickly, because it's part of the collection that's very small, [with] the works of art produced from the islands in the Caribbean, all the way up to the regions of the Eskimo in the Arctic, in the north, by Native Americans who did not have big cities, and were peoples who were fundamentally tribal people, and oftentimes nomadic people; [some of these objects] are very great. The Met, though it doesn't have great collections, has a few rarities. This is a deity figure, a god who we think is called Zemi, which was made very early on in the 15th or 16th century, right when Europeans came. It's made of ironwood inlaid with shell. It's a work of art produced by the Taino people, who were in the islands all around the Dominican Republic, all in the Caribbean, and they made extraordinarily powerful objects, but we know almost nothing about them, except their objects. This is a rare ironwood object from [these people].

We have to end with the Eskimo, and this is a dance mask of the Eskimo people. It was produced in the early 20th century, and it's one of my favorite objects in the Met. When you stand in front of it, you can feel nothing but good. There is a sense in which it projects a kind of humor, a sense of acceptance of the world as it is, an inventiveness, an ability to put together forms that don't necessarily belong together. We see a bird with its feathers, a fish with its body, a seal with its flippers and arms, and then all sorts of other protuberances around this object's eyes, and mouth, and nostrils. It's a kind of combination of every possible animal with which this people interacted combined into a mask. It is no accident that people like the Surrealists loved masks like this and that people like the great American sculptor Alexander Calder—who produced works of art which were light and airy, which moved, which had appendages added to them—took their impetus from Eskimo objects.

When you see the objects of the pre-Hispanic people of the New World in the Metropolitan Museum, you'll want to go on an intellectual journey; you'll want to travel. And I assure you that your intellectual journey and your travel will be worth it.

Lecture Sixteen
Musical Instruments and Arms and Armor

Scope:

Few great European national museums have collections either of musical instruments or of arms and armor—the former tend to be in palace museums or separate museums of the decorative arts, the latter in royal or military museums. In a nation without a medieval or Renaissance military, however, there are few better places to place armor than The Metropolitan Museum of Art. Hence, the museum's great collections of both these areas of "the useful arts" (the arts of war and the arts of the hunt and of peace) are housed in a suite of galleries directly adjacent to the Department of European Sculpture and Decorative Arts' galleries. The collections are highly specialized and important in their own right and deserve the separation maintained by The Metropolitan Museum of Art. The lecture will deal with major masterpieces in the Department of Arms and Armor and the Department of Musical Instruments, treating swords, pistols, pianos, and guitars as important works of art worthy of study and admiration.

Outline

I. Two of the most fun, glorious, and educational parts of The Metropolitan Museum of Art to visit are the Department of Arms and Armor (on the museum's ground floor) and the Department of Musical Instruments (on the museum's second floor).

II. The Department of Arms and Armor contains a specialized collection of global arms and armor, with an emphasis on Europe and Japan.

   A. The galleries make you want to go into the rest of the museum and think about the arts of war as represented in other collections.

   B. The Metropolitan Museum of Art has one of the great curatorial departments of arms and armor, though the Philadelphia Museum, the Art Institute of Chicago, and the Cleveland Museum have collections.

C. The sallet (1470–1480) is an extraordinary helmet made of steel and covered with copper gilt.
  1. People in Renaissance Italy wanted to look like the ancients, just as they wanted to paint and sculpt like the ancients.
  2. The helmet's representation of the mythological Nemean Lion makes it a symbol of the wearer's power.

D. Burgonet with Falling Buffe (c. 1555) was made in the great armory of the Louvre.
  1. All the major imperial European powers had their own armorers who competed with each other to make their rulers look the best.
  2. Armorers of the late 14th and early 15th century employed the same techniques used to engrave and etch metal prints.
  3. Helmets like these would have very little effect from a distance; up close, it is just as complex as any engraving.
  4. This helmet was given by the king of France to Cosimo II; the museum has in its permanent collection a portrait of Cosimo II in which this helmet sits as an imperial gift.

E. The museum has wonderful examples of full suits of European armor. In certain parts of the museum you will see a whole set of armor and, around it, the various parts that compose that set.
  1. The armor of George Clifford, Third Earl of Cumberland (c. 1580–1585), shows how pervasive was the advanced technology of armor-making and weapon-making in Europe during this time.
  2. There was a whole group of artists who only decorated the armor.
  3. There are a lot of paintings in the European galleries of 14th- and 15th-century painting that show men in armor (such as Cranach the Elder's *The Judgment of Paris*, possibly from around 1528).
  4. It is interesting to compare the collection of armor in the museum with the armor in the galleries of painting.

F. The Department of Arms and Armor has one of the best collections of Japanese armor in the United States.

1. One sample of armor (*gusoku*) from the 16th and 18th centuries shows how different Japanese armor is from European armor: it is lighter, designed to encourage the movement of the knight underneath, and designed to shock and awe the enemy.
2. Japanese armor could be adapted as technology changed.
3. One can learn an enormous amount about the Japanese mind and military technology by looking at a Japanese suit of armor and comparing it to a suit of European armor.

G. The museum has a fantastic collection of swords.
  1. Presentation Smallsword (1798–1799) by James Morisset was meant to be an object not of violence but of power.
  2. The 19th-century saber was made in the Ottoman Empire to be the equivalent honor of a royal crown in Europe. The blade came from an Iranian sword and the jade handle was Indian, suggesting the depth of time and reach of the Ottoman Empire.

H. The museum also has a unique collection of pistols.
  1. Double-Barreled Wheellock Pistol of Emperor Charles V (c. 1540–1545) by Ambrosius Gemlich and Peter Pech is so detailed that one could view it with a magnifying glass.
  2. The Samuel Colt revolver (c. 1853) has very American designs (including George Washington and American mammals) crafted by Gustave Young.

I. There are wonderful shields as well, including a tournament shield (*targe*) from around 1450 and a symbolic shield (c. 1535) painted on wood and never meant to be used.

III. The gallery of musical instruments, located upstairs, is equally fun.

A. The double virginal (1581) is one of the earliest keyboard instruments that survives. Though made in Antwerp for the king of Spain, it was found in a country house in Peru and acquired by the museum in 1929.

B. Michele Todini's harpsichord (c. 1675) is a modern instrument that uses ancient and mythological prototypes.

One can imagine this harpsichord in the museum's Venetian period bedroom.

C. One of the museum's most important instruments does not look like a great work of art: Bartolomeo Christofori's grand piano (1720). The piece is the earliest surviving pianoforte and displays an extraordinary use of the technology of sound rather than physical beauty.

D. The museum has other kinds of string instruments as well.

    1. Matteo Sellas's guitar (c. 1630–1650) is strung as it would have been at the time of its creation.

    2. One of the rarest instruments in the world is a 1693 violin by Antonio Stradivari, which is still in the condition it was when it was made.

E. The museum's musical instruments are not all European.

    1. The 19th-century *mayuri* is an Indian instrument probably made for a Hindu court; it is from the Crosby Brown collection—the great collection of musical instruments that came to the museum in 1889.

    2. *Rag-Dung* was a Ming Dynasty (1368–1644) instrument used in Tibet for important rituals at Buddhist temples.

    3. This s*ho*, a 19th-century Japanese flute played laterally, depicts a charming lacquered scene of a spider and a cricket below its bamboo pipes.

    4. Charles Joseph Sax's Clarinet in B-flat (1830) is made of elephant ivory.

    5. *Bondjo* (c. 1915) is an African transverse flute meant to embody sound; the shapes are also the same as those on the crown of this particular tribe's king.

    6. *O-daiko* (c. 1873) is a Japanese drum made to be sent to the 1873 World's Fair in Austria, where Japan displayed its prowess to the great European nations.

Recommended Reading:

Dean. *Helmets And Body Armor In Modern Warfare: The Metropolitan Museum Of Art.*

Libin. *Our Tuneful Heritage: American Musical Instruments from The Metropolitan Museum of Art.*

Nickel, Pyhrr, and Tarassuk. *Art of Chivalry: European Arms and Armor from the Metropolitan Museum of Art: An Exhibition.*

Questions to Consider:

1. Should art museums have a department for musical instruments? Why or why not?

2. Is there a need for all encyclopedic art museums to have a gallery of arms and armor? Why or why not?

Lecture Sixteen—Transcript
Musical Instruments and Arms and Armor

We're about to begin an adventure, an adventure [into] a kind of museum within a museum at the Metropolitan Museum, which is one of the most fun, and one of the most glorious, and one of the most educational parts of the museum to visit. It is in one building on two floors, but it consists of two different departments; one of them, the Department of Arms and Armor, which is on the first floor, and secondly, the Department of Musical Instruments, which is on the second floor. You can get to them in not too circuitous a way. If you go into the Met, and you go around the grand staircase into the galleries of European Decorative Arts and Sculpture, and hang a right, and go through a series of galleries with wonderful furniture and things to look at, you find yourself in a courtyard right here, open to the sky, two stories tall, filled with horses—armed horses with riders wearing armor on them—that's one of the most glorious parts of the Met.

Around it on that floor are a sequence of galleries that are a specialized collection of arms and armor, global arms and armor, with an emphasis on Europe and Japan but with other interesting things, as well, that comprise all of the facets of arms and armor. I sort of fancy myself a pacifist, and I think well, why should I be interested in pistols, and rifles, and swords, and armor if I fundamentally don't believe in war? But it doesn't matter if you believe or don't believe in war; what's riveting is to go to the galleries, and read the labels, and look at the objects because they're fascinating, they're beautiful, and they're a good deal of fun. You can learn an enormous amount about history.

And, of course, what it then makes you want to do is to go into the rest of the museum and think about war and the arts of war as they are represented in other collections in the museum. There are many paintings in the Metropolitan Museum that represent war. You'll remember the great Edo screens of the battles that we saw through the gilded clouds in the Asian Art department, and you can look at the Japanese armor collection, and run into those galleries, and look at those screens, and see virtually identical suits of armor and weapons that you see in the galleries. It's a sort of an entrance into a good deal of the rest of the museum. It's difficult for us to believe after the sort of bloody wars of the 20th century that war could be beautiful, and that incredible costumes and pageantry went along with war, and that there were all sorts of symbolic wars and symbolic shows of power in which objects were really never used to violent purposes but were made to look as if they could be and made to look as if they embodied power.

Now, we're going to do it floor by floor, and I'm going to take you first into the arms and armor floor. I'm just going to show you a few of my favorite things, as the song says, which are probably not the most important things, but they're things that very much appeal to me when I walk through the collections. Now, the horse armor is spectacular, and it's a kind of, in a way, visual extravaganza. You walk into the great room; you see banners hanging from the walls; you see horses; you see knights in shining armor going toward you. It's almost like an army is rushing through the middle of the museum, and it's as if you're back into the Late Middle Ages and the Early Renaissance when people wore armor like tanks wear armor now and when horses wore armor like tanks wear armor now. You almost look at the sort of proto-Humvees going down, striding down, the center of the Metropolitan Museum. Now, you can look at these objects. They have fabulous labels; they're very well published. The Met has, actually, one of the great curatorial departments of arms and armor. It's not the only museum in America with arms and armor. The Philadelphia Museum has got a great collection. The Art Institute of Chicago has a great collection. The Cleveland Museum has a great collection, but the greatest collection is at the Met, and the sort of assembly of it is extraordinary.

Now, I'm going to sort of take parts and look at various kinds of things because that's the way that they're presented at the Met. We're going to turn first to this extraordinary helmet. It's a kind of helmet called a "sallet," made in the 1470s in Italy. It's made of steel, and then it's covered with copper gilt. It represents, of course, a lion. It's armor in the antique mode because it was thought that the ancients had these animal helmets, which they wore into battle, and so the moderns, the people of the Renaissance in Italy, wanted to look like the ancients, just like they wanted to paint like the ancients and make sculpture like the ancients. So they created battle armor and these extraordinary helmets, which look like what they imagined ancient armor to be. Now, this isn't just a lion but the representation of a mythological lion, the Nemean lion, who was killed by Hercules. So, therefore, the wearer of this is the wearer of the trophy of that lion. If you were Hercules and you killed the Nemean lion, then you wore the head of the lion on your head as a kind of symbol of your power. This [is a] charming lion; it's sort of almost a circus lion in its way, and it's one of the most delightful objects in the Met. Its glass eyes glint in the spotlights as you go around it. The hair is beautifully chased, and [we see] its beard and nostrils; it's as if it's shouting out to you. It's as if it's just about to eat you, though you have killed it.

Now it's a delightful form, and if one wants to see a sort of serious helmet, one has to go a few cases down and look at a helmet that was made in the great armory of the Louvre in 1555. All the major imperial powers of Europe had their own armorers, and the armorers competed with each other, whether they were in Spain, in Madrid; or in Paris, in the Louvre; or in Greenwich, outside of London for the English; or the great armorers of Italy or Germany. All of these people competed with each other to make their rulers and their most powerful lords and aristocrats look the best. This is a particularly important helmet. It's called a Burgonet with Falling Buffe, made in 1555, as I've already said.

As you can see, it's a work of art in itself. What you see when you look at armor, particularly armor of the late 14th and into the 15th centuries, is that the same kind of techniques that were used to engrave and etch metal to make prints, as we've seen in our lectures on prints, were applied to metal to make decorations on the sides and surfaces of steel armor. Then they were blued, which is a kind of technique in which you affect the steel in a certain way—and I don't know exactly how—but it turns this kind of vivid, brilliant blue, so it's called "bluing." And then you gild other parts, so you've got the steel, the bluing, and the gilding to create a chromatic effect on the surface. Then you engrave various designs. You can do fleur-de-lis, and coats of arms, and double-headed eagles, and battles of the Centaurs, and battles of the Lapiths and the Centaurs. You can do Hercules. You can do all sorts of things.

What's interesting about these helmets is that they would have very little effect from a distance. When you look at this helmet from even three feet away, you have no idea what's on the surface. But when you get close to it and examine it as an object, it's just as complex as any engraving would be. Now, this helmet is a particularly important helmet because it was given by the king of France to the grand duke of Tuscany, the great Medici family. It was given to Cosimo II. What's riveting is that the Metropolitan Museum has in its permanent collection in European Paintings the portrait of Cosimo II, in which this helmet sits as an imperial gift from one great figure to another. One can see that this has almost the status of a work of art. It's not completely a work of military might, but it's also a work of art, and it's a gift from one great sovereign to another. Of course, as we all know, there were many marriages between the Medici family and the French court.

Now, full suits of European armor, the Met has really wonderful examples of. I like a lot of them, actually. It's one of the most fun things to do to compare how they're joined, and how the elbows work, and how they're detailed, and the sort of knee details, and where they're broken, and how the skirts work, and how they're assembled from parts. Because there are certain parts of the Met in which you'll see a whole set of armor, and then, around it, the various parts that compose that set, so you could actually understand the construction technology of a suit of armor, and [at] other times, you see the whole suit, like this.

This is a particularly important suit of armor. It was made in England, which shows really how the advanced technology of armor-making and weapon-making were pervasive in Europe at this period of time. It was made in the 1580s, in the first half of the 1580s, at the Royal Armory in Greenwich. There was the great palace of the queen in Greenwich, and the Royal Armory was in Greenwich; in fact, the Imperial War Museum is in Greenwich. So if you want to see lots of suits of armor in England, you have to go to Greenwich, where this suit of armor was made. It was made for George Clifford, who was the third earl of Cumberland, who was one of the favorites—one of the many favorites if lore is any indication—of Queen Elizabeth I, Elizabeth the Great, the first great woman ruler of England. She loved this guy, and she knighted him, and she gave him favors in 1590 after this suit of armor was made.

You can see that it is a suit of armor made for an enormously powerful, rather lithe man who was young at the time. It's both blued and etched, and gilded in all of its parts. It's an object of real luxury. In a way, these suits of armor are more luxurious than a standing full-scale bronze because you don't just have to chase or finish the surface when it comes out of the foundry, but you have to etch and blue and gild the surface. So the technology of making these things is extraordinary, and the artifice of making them is extraordinary. There was a whole group of artists who didn't make the armor but decorated the armor, who were called artists of etching and engraving, and who made prints, and who also made suits of armor.

Here, one can see it in all of its glory. This is a case in which you can actually go into the Met in the paintings galleries, not so far away— just climb up the stairs and go down the hall—and you see this marvelous knight. This is Paris, dressed as an early-16th-century knight. This is a painting by [Lucas the Elder] Cranach of the 1520s; [Paris is] all suited up in glorious armor and also wearing this fantastic cape. So one can see there are, in fact, quite a lot of paintings in the European galleries of 14th- and 15th-century painting and early-16th-century painting which show armor and men in armor. It's really interesting to go back and forth and compare the great collection of suits of armor and parts of armor and helmets in the Met with those on the paintings in the galleries.

Well, now, we're going to completely flip continents and go to Asia because the Department of Arms and Armor is not just European arms and armor, but it, in fact, has a very important collection of Japanese armor, one of the best collections in the United States of Japanese armor. You can see arranged in these marvelous cases many suits of armor. This is a suit of armor which dates from a wide period of time and which shows really how different Japanese armor is [from] European armor. It's much, much lighter. It is made of steel but of small, thin pieces of steel, which are lacquered, and the gilding is applied to the lacquer. They're very light, and they're applied in little parts, almost like the scales on a lizard or on a snake, rather than like these big, heavy pieces that cover whole parts of the anatomy.

They're designed as much to encourage the movement of the knight underneath the armor as they are to protect the surface of that [knight]. They're also designed, as you can see from this, to sort of shock and awe the enemy because you appear in this armor, and you have this incredible headdress. You have these sort of gilded horns, and you have feathers coming out of the top, and you've got this strange mask that covers your face. You're kind of complicated.

You're at once insect and bird and man, ready to come over the hill. You look a little bit like a character from *Star Wars*, a prototype of a character from *Star Wars*, rather than like the lumbering giants of European arms and armor, who could never move very deftly.

This guy, the guy who would wear this armor, which was made between the 16th century and the 18th century—the helmet is the oldest part, and underneath are parts that were made throughout the 18th century. The last dated part of the armor is 1735, and so it was made from parts over a period of time. That also shows that Japanese armor was more flexible in two senses. You could adapt it as technology adapted. You didn't buy the suit and were stuck with it. So one can learn an enormous amount about the Japanese mind, about Japanese military psychology, and about Japanese technology by looking at the one suit of armor in Japan, [then] running across the hall and looking at another suit of armor produced in Europe.

Now, the Met has a fantastic collection of swords, and there are so many of them that just picking out favorites is a hard thing to do, but I have two. This one was made in England, and it was made in 1798–1799. It was made by a jeweler rather than by a sword maker. The sword maker made the sword itself, and the jeweler made the handle of the sword, which you see here, which is enameled, and then [it has] semiprecious stones; and gold and silver, gilded silver; and steel. So one has a kind of complicated work of art which is as much jewelry as anything else.

It was produced to honor a particular person, and that particular person—[there is a] whole inscription on it, and it's very interesting to read. Of course, it's in English, so we can read it today. It says, "The Committee of Merchants of London presented this sword to Lieutenant John Burn for his active and spirited conduct on board H.M.S. *Beaulieu* during the late mutiny at the Nore in 1797." So this is colonial Britain [and] a man who performed extraordinary services. He obviously saved a merchant ship that was loaded with cargo owned by the merchants of London, and managed to get that cargo ship back, and therefore, was rewarded by the merchants by being given this extraordinary sword, which of course, he never used. He just had it; it was in a case, and it was presented. It was an object not of violence but of power and of power that was so beautifully made and so expensive that its power was all the greater.

Now, my other favorite sword is a sort of tragedy story, and it's a wonderful story. It's a saber that was made in the Ottoman Empire, and in fact, it was completed in 1876, and it was made for the investiture of the sultan of the Ottoman Empire, and it was the sultan whose name was to be Murad V. What you do in the Ottoman Empire—you don't get a crown put on your head. You're given a sword; you're sworded rather than crowned. It is the presentation of the imperial sword that makes you the emperor. And so this sword is the equivalent of the crown of Queen Elizabeth II or the late crowns of the kings of France, and it is extraordinarily beautiful. The blade was old, and it came from an old Iranian sword. The wonderful jade handle was Indian and came from the 18th century. So the parts of it suggest the depth of time of the Ottoman Empire and the reach of the Ottoman Empire.

Those parts are put together by a jeweler in Constantinople, or in Istanbul at that period of time, in the 1870s. The craftsmanship is phenomenal [in] both the hilt and the sword itself, and they're displayed in all of their glory at the Met. It's really worth looking at. It's one of the most beautiful pieces of jewelry in all of New York. Unfortunately, Murad V had a nervous breakdown before the investiture and was declared unfit to rule, was forced to abdicate, and died in prison in 1904. This sword came to the Metropolitan Museum in 1923. He had only been dead for a few years. This is one of the most important pieces of imperial Ottoman jewelry, but it's in the Arms and Armor Department at the Met.

This is the pistol of Charles V, the great emperor of the Hapsburg Empire, the Austro-Hungarian Empire, who ruled Spain, who ruled Flanders, and who split them into parts. This is his wonderful personal pistol; light, extraordinary, made both of metal [and] of cherry and of burl woods. Every detail of it is amazing. It has inscriptions in it. You could actually look at it with a magnifying glass if you wanted to.

This is an American pistol made by Samuel Colt in the 1850s. It's a charming thing because it's very, very, very American. You can see George Washington on it, American mammals all over it. It was the work of a German-American craftsman named Gustave Young. It was made in this hilarious story. Samuel Colt, for a publicity stunt, gave one pistol to the Ottoman sultan and one pistol to the czar of Russia, who were fighting each other in the Crimean War. This is the pistol that was given to the sultan, who lost. The pistol that was given to the czar is in the Hermitage Museum in Saint Petersburg. So one's in New York, and one's in Saint Petersburg.

Now, there are wonderful shields, as well. Here's one that I love. It has got this sort of beautiful woman holding a shield with a rampant animal, this sort of strange being, in the background. And then she is holding a marvelous little scroll, on which is written in German, "*Hab Mich als Ich Bin*" ("Take me as I am"). You can imagine the sword sticking out of it, this beautiful woman looking at you, and [a warrior] rushing down on a horse, and this glorious shield says, take me as I am, and he is obviously carrying with him his loved one and his power. The most beautiful shield is a shield that was made in Italy in the 1530s, and it represents a Roman battle. It's so beautifully painted. It's painted on wood, and when you look at it, you can tell that it was never used. It's a symbolic object rather than an object that was used.

One can spend hours in those galleries, and I'm showing you only a few things. But I'm going to take you up the stairs and take you into the musical instruments gallery, which is equally fun. And being a pianist, it's very frustrating for me because there are all these great keyboard instruments that you're dying to play, but of course, the Met covers all their keyboards with little devices, and so you can't, even if you're bad, leap over the barriers and play them. This is one of the earliest keyboard instruments that survives. It was made in 1581, probably for a Spanish market in Flanders. It was made in Antwerp in 1581 for the king of Spain. On it is a scene of the king of Spain on the top, of Philip II and Anne of Austria, his wife. There are two keyboards, so that two people could sit and play simultaneously, sometimes reinforcing each other and sometimes going away from each other. It would be enchanting to hear a concert played on it. [It is] one of the earliest and one of the rarest musical instruments in America, made, as I said, in 1581 and found not in Spain and not in Flanders, in Antwerp where it was made, but in Cuzco, Peru, in a country house, when it came out to the Met, and the Metropolitan Museum acquired it in 1929.

Now, if you want to see the harpsichord to end all harpsichords, you have to go to the Met, and it is this harpsichord. It was designed and made by a great instrument maker in Rome whose name was Michele Todini, and it was made about 1675. What you're seeing now is actually not the whole thing but a part of the whole thing, because it wasn't made on commission to a rich person but for the shop of Todini in Rome. In back of the keyboard instrument and these sculptures was a gigantic mountain, a faux mountain, in which was embedded an organ. There were concerts in the afternoon and in the evening at this place, where the harpsichord and the organ were played simultaneously.

Well, what is this instrument? We see the Triumph of Galatea, all these Tritons, and the Triumph of Galatea all around down here. One has a sculpture of Galatea, a full-scale sculpture of Galatea over here. Galatea is playing a lute, and this is Polyphemus over here, who is playing a pipe. Of course, the whole composition would have included the organ, and of course, the organ would play the pipe of Polyphemus, and the harpsichord would play the lute of Galatea. So the modern instruments take their ancient and mythological prototypes. The whole thing is gilded, incredibly elaborately carved, hilariously funny, very serious, and it would look great today in the Venetian in Las Vegas.

If Todini made the most elaborate High Baroque harpsichord and its accompaniment ever seen in Europe—and you can actually run and look at the wonderful Venetian bedroom that we saw several lectures back and see a place where it would look great—one of the most important instruments in the Met is, in fact, not complicated at all and doesn't, in fact, look like a great work of art. It is a grand piano made in 1720 by an instrument maker named Bartolomeo Cristofori. You see it here, very plain, very simple, on simple turned legs. It has no grace, no elegance whatsoever. Why is it in the Met, and why is it important?

Well, it's important because it is the earliest surviving pianoforte. It is the ancestor to every piano that's in everybody's house, that you see in the concert halls of Carnegie Hall and Lincoln Center. This is the earliest surviving piano, and that means that it has hammers that strike strings rather than pluck them, like the harpsichord. If you had to list the five great musical instruments in New York, this would be one of them. The reason is technology and date, not beauty. In this case, it's the technology of the sound, the way in which the sound is conveyed to us, rather than the physical beauty of the musical instrument, that's extraordinary.

Now, there are other kinds of string instruments, as well, and there are wonderful sets of lutes, and guitars, and ukuleles, and various and sundry kinds of string instruments, and you can learn the difference amongst all those kinds. This is a guitar made in the 17th century by the most important maker of stringed instruments in Venice. His name was Matteo Sellas. It's of incredible beauty. It's inlaid with ivory. The frets are perfect. All of the wood is perfectly inlaid. There is not a single aspect of this instrument which isn't extraordinary. It was made in the 1630s or 1640s, so it's a very old instrument. It's strung as it would have been at the time, and we know that whoever bought this instrument was incredibly rich. We only hope that he was as talented as he was rich.

Now, this is another instrument which is one of the rarest instruments in the world because it is a violin by Stradivarius, by Antonio Stradivari. Of course, there are many violins by Stradivarius that survive in the world, and they're used by many of the great violinists in the world, but this is the only one that has not been modified in the 19th or 20th century to make the big sound that we like in our concert halls. So this is an instrument that is still in the condition that it was when it was made in 1693. It would be wonderful sometime to be in the Met when Midori or any of the great living violinists came to the Met, and they opened the case and took out this Stradivarius and allowed them to play [the] instrument, letting it sound as it would have sounded in the 17th century rather than with the big sounds that we have in concert halls today.

Now, the instruments are not at all only European, and that's the fun thing about it. This is a *mayuri*, which is a 19th-century Indian instrument. It's a real beauty. It represents, of course, a peacock, and it has real peacock feathers coming out of the end, which have obviously been changed since the 19th century when it was made. It's made of wood, and parchment, and metal, and feathers, and it was played rather like a lute, sitting down. It has wonderfully beautiful sounds. It's a fascinating object because the peacock is the attribute of the Hindu goddess Sarasvati, who is the goddess who is associated with music, which means that this was probably made not for one of the Mogul courts but for one of the Hindu courts in India. It's a very rare surviving Indian musical instrument from the Crosby Brown collection, the great collection of musical instruments which came to the Met in 1889 and started the whole thing.

Now, instruments that you blow in, they go from this extraordinary Ming Dynasty brass, copper, and cloisonné *Rag-Dung*, which is a more than six-foot-long, glorious instrument which makes these low sounds and which is used in Tibet for important rituals at Buddhist temples. Again, if we could hear the sound of this recorder, there would be this deep, low, sonorous sound that would resound through the mountain valleys of Tibet. Or this wonderful *Sho*, a Japanese laterally played flute, which has all of its beautifully gathered bamboo pipes attached to it. And then below, in a little lacquer part, one sees this little, charming lacquered scene of a spider in its web and a cricket, which we associate, of course, with the summer and the heat of the summer, and this little drama, this little dance of death of the cricket and the spider, is on this beautiful musical instrument.

Or this delightful clarinet made by Charles Joseph Sax, who was the father of Adolphe Sax, who created the saxophone. This is a clarinet made of elephant ivory, one of the most beautiful instruments in the world, made about 1830. Again, how one would love to hear one of the great clarinetists play this instrument. [We also see] an African transverse flute that you play from the side; and the idea is that out of the horn part of it is this thing that seems to look like embodied, visually embodied, sound, but those shapes are precisely the same shapes as the crown of the king in this particular Congolese tribe. So one would have seen these projected sounds out of a whole host of musicians associated with the crown of the king, who walked behind them. The final musical instrument is a drum, and the Met has wonderful drums, but none of them can outshine this one. It was made in the early years of the 1870s in Meiji Japan. It has every technique that you can imagine, mostly cloisonné enamel, and it was made not to be played. It may, in fact, never have been played, but it was made to be sent to the World's Fair of 1873 in Austria, where Japan was showing its prowess to the great European nations.

When you go to the Met and you see this variety of musical instruments, and you imagine their sounds, and you see the arts of war embodied so superbly and in such various ways in different kinds of form downstairs, you're in a world of wonder, a world that very few people know a lot about, and a world, therefore, in which you feel free to read the labels, to look, to imagine that you're listening, and to learn.

Lecture Seventeen
Costumes and Textiles

Scope:

Although every great universal art museum collects textiles, few museums extend their collections to fashion or costume art. Because of New York City's international prominence as a center for fashion design and retail, however, The Metropolitan Museum of Art created a separate department called the Costume Institute in 1937, which united the museum's various holdings in Western costumes from the late 16th through the early 21st centuries. The institute is treated as a resource for professionals, retailers, costume designers, and other experts who consult its files, library, photo-archive, and storage collections. In the 1980s, the Costume Institute inaugurated a permanent space for its exhibitions, some based on their collections and others curated by the staff to expand knowledge of costume art to the larger public. What once had been a scholarly department for specialists has become one of the most visible centers for the exhibition of fashionable clothing in the world. The Costume Institute, however, contains a minority of the vast collections of textiles controlled by other departments at The Metropolitan Museum of Art. These textiles—from immense Flemish tapestries and Islamic carpets to small samples of Venetian velvets and French silks—are catalogued and conserved in the Antonio Ratti Textile Center.

Outline

I. This lecture is devoted to two departments at the museum, one of which has gallery spaces and the other of which only has a study center: the Costume Institute and the Antonio Ratti Textile Center, respectively.

   A. These are among the most important collections of textiles and costumes in any museum in the world.

   B. In 1937, the Lewisohn family started its own independent costume institute in New York City. The collection became so widely used and so important that the institute came to The Metropolitan Museum of Art in 1959.

C. The textile collection includes more than 30,000 objects such as shoes, belts, buckles, dresses, trousers, and hats. It is to be used by people who need to be inspired by the past: clothing designers, retailers, set designers, and costume designers.

D. The Costume Institute's galleries are located on the museum's ground floor. You will not see the galleries' permanent collection but instead an exhibition derived from the collection along with loaned objects.

II. We will review a sample of objects from the Costume Institute, mostly European and American, to illustrate the range and quality of The Metropolitan Museum of Art's holdings.

A. A doublet from the early 1620s was made in France and painstakingly embroidered so that it has, for us today, a decidedly feminine quality.

1. What makes it possible to date this object are the slits of contrasting silk in the sleeves and bodice, called pinking; male garments were pinked for only a five-year period in the early 1620s.

2. There are only two garments of this type in the world that survived: this one, and one in the Victoria and Albert Museum in London.

B. Early shoes are rare; one sees them more in paintings than in real form.

1. The collection includes a pair of 17th-century men's shoes made for silk-stockinged legs.

2. The cantilever suggests that men kept the weight of their body on their toes.

C. The court dress (c. 1750) is the type of dress worn in European courts in the mid-18th century. The dress, with its metallic threads and panniers that push the skirt out to the sides, has a symbolic courtly purpose.

D. A coat from 1833, with its faux waist and lengthened trousers, provides a sense of elegance and height to the man wearing it.

E. In the mid-19th century, there was a desire to have skirts (generated by the Paris fashion) that were as large as possible.

1. Women wore a slip, then an enormous whalebone and wood contraption that supported acres of fabric and a long train.
2. The military braiding along the top and sides of an American dress from 1855–1865 suggests that it may have been made during or immediately after the Civil War.

F. A fancy dress was designed by Paul Poiret in 1911 for an elaborate party in which everyone dressed as if they came from an *Arabian Nights* tale.

G. Caroline Reboux was one of the great French designers who made simple, elegant clothes. Toward the end of her life, she created modern costumes like a 1920s cape which combined unprecedented designs with a sense of antique fashion from the Old Testament.

H. The museum has great collections of work by Coco Chanel, the most famous fashion designer of the first half of the 20th century.
1. Her coat (c. 1927) falls like a Grecian costume, creating a sense in which costumes are not structured anymore (like Reboux's work).
2. Chanel's most famous design is her 1938 business suit; its modesty suggests that the wearer is not meant to be an object of sexual desire.

I. The shoe collection at The Metropolitan Museum of Art contains thousands of fascinating shoes. Salvatore Ferragamo's sandals (1938), with their colorful layers of pillowed leather, remind one of late-1960s fashion.

J. *"L'Eléphant Blanc"* (spring/summer 1958) by Yves Saint Laurent—which shimmers as one walks—and *Ensemble* (1967) by Rudy Gernreich—with its strips of fabric and exposed flesh—look like nothing in the pervious history of art.

K. In *I Love New York* (2000), Miguel Adrover combines the two things New York City does so well: street art and incredible refinement.

III. The Antonio Ratti Textile Center was established in 1995 and represents a great need on the part of The Metropolitan Museum of Art.

    A. The original problem with the textile collection at The Metropolitan Museum of Art was that no one was in charge of it; none of the curators in individual departments with textiles knew how to conserve them.

    B. In 1995, the museum established the Antonio Ratti Textile Center to keep, catalogue, conserve, document, photograph, and make whole the textiles from all departments.

    C. A sheet of royal linen from c. 1466 B.C. is one of the most ancient pieces of surviving textile.

        1. It is very difficult to find ancient textiles except in dry places (such as Egypt).

        2. Though unadorned and simple, the linen is so fine that it would be impossible to make today.

    D. The Peruvian mantle from the 2nd or 1st century B.C. is both woven and crocheted (to bring out the feline masks). For the mantle's complex techniques to be understood, the Ratti Textile Center had to use a computer.

    E. The museum has very rare early textiles. It is fascinating to look at textiles that survive as long as paintings on panel or sculptures made of immutable material.

        1. The linen fragment from the late 3rd or 4th century is a Coptic fragment probably produced for funerary purposes; it is in perfect condition.

        2. The fragment of printed Islamic textile from the 10th or 11th century was also probably a funerary fabric; the piece's block prints of lions project a power that we have seen in the arts of the ancient Near East.

    F. An imperial textile made between 1330 and 1332 in China is made of silk but has gilded paper woven in to represent clouds.

        1. There is no Chinese textile that survives in any collection in the world that is of this quality and date.

        2. The piece, like other old textiles, is almost never shown because it is light sensitive.

G. A beautiful length of Venetian velvet was woven in the late 15th century by a series of craftsmen who learned their craft from the Ottoman Empire. An almost identical piece of velvet, woven in the same time period, can be found painted by Raphael in *Madonna and Child*.

Recommended Reading:

Druesedow. "Celebrating Fifty Years of the Costume Institute."

Stauffer, Hill, Evans, and Walker. *Textiles of Late Antiquity.*

Questions to Consider:

1. Choose your favorite costume item presented in this session. What attracts you to it and what is "art worthy" about this piece?

2. The museum's textiles have been collected from a diverse selection of cultures. How have textiles influenced other art forms (e.g., painting, sculpture) in these cultures?

Lecture Seventeen—Transcript
Costumes and Textiles

There are 3 lectures amongst the 24 lectures devoted to the Metropolitan Museum that are, for you at least, exercises in frustration because they're lectures about collections which have little or no viewing space, and they are collections which are really gathered for the use of specialists and scholars by appointment. But they're such great collections that it's almost impossible not to talk about them. If I want to give you a really complete idea of the Metropolitan and all of its richnesses, I need to deal with the collections that are closed, or hidden, or for specialists only. You've heard one lecture on the Department of Drawings and Prints. You've heard another lecture on the Department of Photography, and those departments have enormous holdings and very tiny gallery spaces.

This lecture is going to be devoted to two departments in the Met, one of which has gallery spaces and the other of which only has a study center. They are the Costume Institute and the Antonio Ratti Textile Center. They are amongst the most important collections of textiles and costumes in any museum in the world. Now, it's hardly surprising that the Metropolitan Museum in the city of New York has such great holdings in costumes and textiles because it is, of course, the number-one city in America for the theater, for opera, for set design, for plays, for the rag trade, for retailing, and for clothing sales and manufacturing. And the professionals, the thousands of professionals in the city of New York who want to be inspired by the human past, want to be inspired by real things. They don't want just to go into the galleries and look at costumes, and paintings, and chairs, and rooms. They actually want to know how people dressed, how [clothes] fit on you, and how they looked, and what the shoes were like, and how belting was done, and all of these things.

For that reason, in 1937, a family called the Lewisohn family started its own independent costume institute in New York. They had their own collection. They acquired other collections from notable people in New York City. What happened is that the collection became so widely used and so important that they approached the Met—or the Met approached them; I'm not sure which—and in 1959, the costume institute of the Lewisohns came into the Metropolitan Museum, just like the Museum of Primitive Art came into the

Metropolitan Museum 10 years later, in 1969. That kind of merger of a great collection and a great museum created a collection that is, without question, the most important collection of costumes in any American art museum and one of the great global collections, being rivaled only by the Victoria and Albert Museum in London.

Now, the textile collection has over 30,000 objects. It's only a little bit smaller than the collection of Egyptian art, and so you can imagine the sort of storage needs of such a collection. The objects are shoes, belts, buckles, dresses, trousers, hats, every form of clothing that you can imagine from all of human history. And so if you were doing a set for a Donizetti opera about Elizabethan England, you can go and see what the Italian costumes that are Elizabethan look like in the Met, and you can look at books, and drawings, and other works of art that support the collection of costumes. And so it's really to be used by people who need to be inspired by the past, whether they're clothes designers, whether they're retailers, whether they're set designers or costume designers, literally thousands of whom live in New York.

Now, the Costume Institute has galleries, and I'm going to show them to you because they're famous in New York. When they do exhibitions of Balenciaga, or of France in the 18th century, or of Chanel, all of New York goes, and the openings are extraordinarily glittering. But the galleries are in the basement, which is called politely the ground floor. You enter them down a long staircase. Here they are, this little, teeny blip in this gigantic plan of the underground part of the Met, and these are the galleries of the Costume Institute. When you go to them, you won't see their permanent collection. You'll see an exhibition derived from their permanent collection and with loans from other [collections]. But I'm going to show you a kind of sample of glorious objects, mostly European and American, from the Costume Institute to show you the range and the quality of the holdings. This is like a summary of a huge collection in a tiny bit.

Now, I'm starting with men because in most of human history, men had cooler clothes than women. Only in the last sort of four centuries have men had boring clothes and women had cool clothes. And so we're starting with a male doublet made in France in the early 1620s. It's a marvelous object in which every single part of the surface of this very elaborate and complex doublet is very painstakingly embroidered, mostly with flowers. It has, for us today, a decidedly feminine quality, except for these sort of protruding geometric forms in the front. [Note] this wonderful series of ruffles on either side. But what makes it possible to date it very precisely [are] these little slits, both in the sleeves and in the bodice at the upper part. These are called "pinking."

For literally a five-year period in the early 1620s, male garments were pinked. That is, they were cut through the center [and] lined with a contrasting color of silk. This is white, so it's very subtle in this particular one. It's white silk that sort of peeks through these little slits that are called "pinks," and so this is a pinked garment. Pinking, like all fashions—even the 17th century had fashion—was in fashion amongst aristocrats for only five years, which means that if you owned this garment in 1630, you wouldn't have worn it. You would have put it away. The fact that it survives is miraculous. In fact, there are only two garments of this type in the world that survive—one in the Victoria and Albert Museum in London and the one in the Metropolitan Museum.

The second object is also French and also [from the] 17th century and isn't an object but two objects. It's a pair of shoes. Now, early shoes are rare. One sees more of them in paintings than actually survive in real form. It's absolutely fascinating to look at them. When we look at these shoes today, we think, what glorious and original women's shoes. One can imagine somebody wearing them today to a sort of fancy dress party. But, of course, they're not women's shoes; they're men's shoes. If you think about it for a few minutes, these are shoes that are made in such a way that they move up the ankle into the leg, and they're for silk-stockinged legs. Of course, the only people who showed their legs in the 17th century were men, not women.

Those of us who know our French history [know] that the best legs of the 17th century in lore are the legs of Louis XIV, which were painted and which were—if they could have been insured, like Marlene Dietrich's legs, they would have been, though, of course, Louis XIV didn't need insurance. So if you have beautiful legs, wonderfully dressed in tight silk hose, and they come down to the floor, and these embroidered shoes with pointed edges, and these extraordinary cantilevered heels, then the sort of lightness of your body and the lightness of the legs would come down to points. So it wouldn't feel as if the weight of your body was being carried by them. The cantilever of these is extraordinary. What they suggest is that men kept the weight of their body on their toes and walked on their toes, because if you actually leaned back in these shoes, you'd fall back. So you have to be very carefully poised and walk in a certain sort of courtly way in order to use them.

Now, in the annals of useless fashions and sort of idiotic fashions is this glorious dress, which is a *robe à la Français*, a French dress, made not in France but in England in the middle of the 18th century. They're dresses that were worn in court in France, and in England, and in Spain, and in the Austro-Hungarian Empire, because in the middle of the 18th century, the court of Versailles, the French court, set the style standards for all of Europe. I mean, even the people in Saint Petersburg, in Russia, in distant Moscow, wore dresses like this because it was in fashion. This British dress is made of silk with metallic threads. It's silver thread. The difficulty with silver thread is, of course, it tarnishes. If you polish it too much, (a) it hurts the silk, and (b) it diminishes the thread. So one has to imagine this thread as being brilliantly polished and shiny when the dress was new and illuminating and moving as the person moved.

But when you look at these, there are two panniers, which are made of wood and whalebone, on the side, pushing the skirt out to the sides. The front is almost flat, and the fashion in this period of time was to have almost no bosom, so you're constrained by corsets up here, and you sort of come out, not in the front or the back, but on the sides. They're made for courtly appearances where you stand. It's impossible, essentially, to sit in this dress. There's no chair that would receive it. You can't walk through a door except going sideways. And so, therefore, people—courtiers or ladies in waiting— [would] line up and occupy sort of glorious space with their most expensive fabric, showing their importance and paying obeisance to somebody else. So the dress actually had a symbolic courtly function. It wasn't a kind of silly thing; it was something that had a deeply ingrained courtly purpose. One can study this dress in the original, look at the panniers, see how the whalebone was used, how the threads bring it together, where it's nipped and tucked, how it's created. And so, of course, costume designers, particularly for the opera and the theater, study dresses like this assiduously.

Well, if you were a man living in England in the 1830s, and you were like the "cat's meow," you would have worn this coat and these white breeches. Of course, what this coat and these white breeches do is that even if you're a kind of 5'4" average guy in sort of late Georgian London, in Regency London, you would look tall because your waist would be pulled up. The waist is very high. It's almost like the male equivalent of an empire dress. The cut of the coat is above the waist. The garment then flows above the faux waist, and the legs are lengthened and very long, and the trousers come down into the shoes, pull all the way down. There's this sense of lift, and elegance, and height that you have, not because you have it, but because the clothes give it to you. The relationship between the actual body and the apparent body, dressed by a superb London tailor, is very great indeed.

Now, in the middle of the 19th century—and, again, mostly generated from Paris fashion—there was this desire to have skirts that were like the Platonic form of a skirt. If a skirt could be as large as a skirt could possibly be, then it would be good. These skirts had these enormous contraptions underneath them. You wore a slip, and then you wore this enormous whalebone-and-wood contraption, and then you had sort of acres of fabric coming down from you, and a long train coming down the back, which meant, of course, that you could not wear this dress out of doors because it would get dirty. And even getting from the house into the carriage was an iffy thing to do and you had to go on other sorts of surfaces or else the whole bottom of the dress would be ruined or would be dirty. Here, you can see why women's shoes aren't such a big deal, because you can't see them.

The dress actually denies the lower part of the form, and the woman's body comes out of an apparent cloud of very fine, beautifully draped, and beautifully gathered fabric. This is a dress that's actually American. The collection of these enormous dresses, made in the middle of the 19th century, at the Met—they have English ones, they have French ones, they have Austrian ones, and they have American ones. I've chosen the American one because it has also a kind of military quality. The kind of braiding along the top and on the sides comes from military uniforms, which suggests that it may actually even have been made during or immediately after the Civil War, when one was thinking a good deal more about military ideas and sort of solidarity with the military if you were a wealthy woman in New York.

Now, this is one of the most fun dresses, if indeed, it's a dress, made in 1911 by Paul Poiret, the great, great, great French designer. Poiret was one of the early designers in France who had very close ties with the theater and who was very well aware of publicity, and even social and gossip publicity, as a way of gaining more business. In 1911, he gave an extraordinary party called the party of "The Thousand and Second Night." So you have 1,001 nights—we know the 1,001 nights, but this is the next night, "The Thousand and Second Night." What he did is he invited extraordinarily wealthy people, and then members of the *demimondaine*, sort of actresses, and beautiful women, and attractive young men for the aristocratic women, and he dressed everybody so that everybody who came to the party was dressed looking as if they came out of an Arabian Nights tale. This is one of the costumes from that party.

You can just imagine, in the years before the First World War, being in a ballroom in Paris, all decorated to look like Aladdin created it, with people coming in down staircases and in entrances dressed like this, with their slim bodies, and their marvelous sort of senses of human proportions, and their kind of theatricality. It's as if the entire party was in the theater. The sense of that meant that it was, of course, an instant sensation in the gossip columns. There were photographs published of it. There were posters of it, and Paul Poiret became famous as a result of parties like this, and the Met has one of the costumes.

Caroline Reboux was one of the great, great designers in the pantheon of French designers, and of course, Paris has been the capital of design in women's clothing since the middle of the 18th century. Some would argue that it still is today. Caroline Reboux made very simple and elegant clothes, and towards the end of her life—she died in 1927—she made a series of startlingly modern clothes, odd for a woman who was born in 1835 and was ancient by the time that she designed this beautiful silk cape. All of the seams are at a bias. All of the colors come from—she was very interested in the Old Testament and in what people wore in the Old Testament. She learned from biblical scholars about the actual meaning of the words in Aramaic and the various languages that compose the Old Testament, to give her a sense of the colors that people wore. She created modern costumes that were completely unprecedented in terms of costume design, with this sense of the antique, of fashion from the beginnings of Western time.

Now, of course, the most famous fashion designer of the first half of the 20th century is Coco Chanel, and the Met has great collections of Coco Chanel. I've chosen two costumes, (a) because I like Coco Chanel, and so she deserves two, and (b) because I love both of these costumes. This is a coat from 1927. The House of Chanel was incorporated in 1913, just two years after Paul Poiret's party, and it still exists today, as you know. This is an unbelievably simple evening coat made of silk, with a little bit of metal embroidery, that embroidery that you see around the base and at the neck. The scarf that goes around the neck is made of metal, and so it glints and shines. The silk is very fine, and it falls almost like a Grecian costume. There's a sense in which it isn't structured anymore. It's like Caroline Reboux, and it's from exactly the same year as Caroline Reboux, in that one sees fabric falling over the natural contours of the body. And, of course, if you have a coat like this, you have to have a body to go along with it.

Her most famous design, of course, is her business suit, and the idea of a woman having a business suit was an idea that comes from the most liberated of women designers and the first really successful woman fashion designer, Coco Chanel. This is a suit of 1938, which was, in fact, owned by the first great curatorial advisor to the Costume Institute when it came to the Met, the famous Diana Vreeland, who was one of the legends in fashion design, who was the editor of *Vogue* magazine, who was probably the great tastemaker of the middle and latter part of the 20th century, and who owned this suit in red because her friend Coco Chanel owned it in black. The two of them, being rivals in a certain way, friendly rivals, could not have the same suit in the same color. [Note] the nipped waist, the appropriateness of it, the high neck, the sort of architecture of it, the modesty of it, and the sense of being businesslike, that I'm not here to be an object of sexual desire; I'm here because I'm smart, and I'm going to get the best of you. That's projected very well in this suit of 1938.

Now, the shoe collection at the Met is huge, and there are thousands of fascinating shoes, but none of them [is] as cool as this. This is also 1938, the same year as the Chanel suit, and it's by Salvatore Ferragamo, the great leather designer, shoe designer, of Italy, and one of the great designers of the 20th century. It's a sandal which, of course, makes a short woman look enormously tall but doesn't make her look heavy because it's pillows of color. Your little gilded sandal from Classical time is supported on this kind of tutti-frutti layering of pillowed leather. It's all these wonderful colors of leather, all beautifully pillowed, and it's as if each of them is lighter than the next. There's nothing like it. I mean, there's no shoe like it that was made before. There's no shoe like it that was made after. Indeed, when you look at it, you sort of think it's from the late [19]60s in the times of Pink Floyd and the late Beatles rather than from 1938.

And then, the elephant dress, *"L'Eléphant Blanc,"* by Yves Saint Laurent when he was working for Dior—one of the most beautiful women's dresses ever made. It clings to your body underneath, and then these beautiful, beautiful layers of thin silk with metallic thread and glass beads of different sizes, which move and shimmer as you walk. Or Rudi Gernreich—the collection of 20th-century fashion is fantastic—the Austrian-born American designer who could have designed for the Jetsons. Here we are in 1967 with women's fashion, and if it's as if it's sort of architecture of the body, with the matching boots. You have three strips of beige and two strips of hot pink, with a good deal bared. The baring is done, of course, with plastic, so the dress is held together with fabric and plastic. Again, they look like nothing in the previous history of art.

The last costume I'll show is one of my favorites. It's by the really wonderful Spanish designer Miguel Adrover, who lived in New York and went back to Spain and sort of renounced fashion designing in 2002. Before he went back to Spain and the world of his birth, he made this ridiculous and charming and amusing dress, which is an old, store-bought cotton T-shirt that says "I love New York," onto which he put these miraculously complex, multilayered—with all of these little bits of chiffon. It's a sort of silk-blend chiffon, and the sleeves probably took the seamstress who made them weeks to make. They're put on like little sort of shoulder pads on this completely ordinary and banal T-shirt. It's as if it's a farewell to New York. It is putting together the two things that New York does so well, which is the high and the low, sort of street art and incredible refinement, merged seamlessly into this costume, which is, of course, appropriately in the Metropolitan Museum's collection.

Now, the Antonio Ratti Textile Center was established in 1995, and it represents a really great need on the part of the Met. You've seen, as we've gone into the various departments of the Met, that we've looked at textiles in lots of them. We've looked at carpets and textiles in the Islamic Department. We've looked at textiles in the Asian Department, in European Decorative Arts. We've seen bedcovers, and you see tapestries and all sorts of things. The problem with the textile collection at the Met is that no one was in charge of it. Every department that had textiles [kept their own] textiles, and none of the curators knew how to keep them, knew how to conserve them, knew how to deal with them. And so in order to do that for the whole museum, in 1995, the Met established the Antonio Ratti Textile Center, where all the textiles from all the departments are kept, cataloged, conserved, documented, photographed, and made whole again.

So the textiles all over the Met are now well cared for in one place. It's, again, like the prints and drawings study room and the photography study room—you have to make an appointment to go. But the collections are enormously rich and interesting. If you're interested in textiles themselves, rather than textiles transformed into costumes—and by textiles, I mean an entire variety of textiles. Anything made of any kind of plant substance would be in this department—any woven, any knitted, any blocked, any form of textile. What's riveting about the collection is that when you pull together and create effectively a new department of textiles, then the whole riches of the museum become clear. What had been scattered is now collected. What had been poorly cared for is well cared for. And so only at the end of its second century—of the second century of its operation, the 20th century—did the Met recognize that its holdings were so great that it needed to deal with them responsibly.

I'm going to give you a little tour. Some of this might, at first glance, be boring, but I hope to make it not so. This is a sheet of royal linen which was made in the middle of the 2nd millennium B.C., so it's 3,500 years old, approximately. It's a work of textile that is one of the most ancient pieces of surviving textile because, of course, textiles rot through time. It's very difficult to find ancient textiles except in very, very dry places, and of course, Egypt is one of them. This is a royal sheet which would have been a shroud for a body. It's of such fine linen—it's flax—it's so fine that it's like pashmina if you could lift it up. The curators in the Ratti Textile Center say that it would be impossible to make today, that it's not possible to make something of this fineness and refinement. Even though it is unadorned and simple, it is one of the most extraordinarily complex to make works of art in the entire museum, and it's something that, again, as I said, we could not make today.

Now, this is a mantle made in Peru in the 1st or 2nd century B.C. It's also really old, and Peruvian textiles, particularly those that are buried in the great deserts by the sea—which is the driest part of Peru—survive for millennia because there is essentially no moisture in the ground. They're buried, and because they're buried, no light comes upon them. This is a kind of textile which it's sort of hard to explain. You have to look at it really, really closely, and maybe if we could zoom in onto it in some way, you could see that it is both woven and crocheted. It's a kind of technology that uses a loom but also uses techniques of crocheting to bring these feline masks—when you look at it, you see this series of masks with eyes. You see tails and arms. The more you look at it, the more complex it is. Then it's very thin. You're looking actually through it when you look at it. It's as thin as the Egyptian cloth. Technologically, in order for it to be figured out, for its techniques to be figured out, the Ratti Textile Center had to use a computer to understand it. A human being, unaided, could not understand how this garment was made, what the pattern was that made it possible to, as it were, unravel and re-ravel again.

Now, they have very rare early textiles. It's fascinating to look at textiles that survive as long as sculptures, or paintings on panel, or bronze statues, or objects that are made of immutable material. This is a linen fragment from the 3rd or 4th century A.D. It's a Coptic fragment, which means that it was made in Upper Egypt or into Eritrea. It's a fragment that was produced probably for a funerary [purpose]. A lot of these objects are made to be wrapped around bodies and for funerary purposes. It's in perfect condition. The color looks like it looked when it was made, and the fact that it survived this long and this well is extraordinary. It represents either Luna— the figure has a moon shape on her, and she's either Luna or Diana, because Diana also has a moon shape. But because of the fact that Coptic art is Christian art, it is more likely that she is Luna because Luna was not a pagan goddess like Diana. [Note] her little, rosy cheeks; her wonderful hair; the sort of braided garland of flowers on the side.

This is a fragment of printed textile made in Persia. It's an Islamic textile from the 10th or 11th century, with these block prints of lions. The lions are printed on it, and it looks almost like modern-day ceramics. It looks like tiles. One of them is positive and one is negative, and one is positive and one is negative. It's probably also a funerary fabric, and it would have been wrapped around a body or associated with a body who needed to project a sense of power, the power of the lion. We've seen that all the way throughout the arts in the ancient Near East.

Now, this imperial textile, from 1330–1332, was made in China, and it has within in the names and portraits of two emperors of China, of Yuan China, the Yuan Dynasty, one of whom is the great-great-grandson of Genghis Khan, and the other of whom is his son. It's a very large woven textile. It's made completely of silk, but it has gilded paper woven in to represent clouds in gilded form. In the center is a Bodhisattva, or the Buddha Maitreya, the Buddha of the future, such as we've seen in many other things. If you think of that gilded altar, that gilded Chinese altar, which is a little bit earlier than this, it has the same sort of quality, that with the Maitreya in the center and the Mandorla around.

This is a *mandala*, and a *mandala* is the entire world arranged with concentric circles and squares, with various symbols of power and time. So it's a kind of cosmic diagram. There is no Chinese textile that survives in any collection in the world—not in China, not in Paris, not in London—that is of this quality and of this date, so this is a unique object. To get an appointment to see it, you practically have to have three Ph.D.'s in Chinese art history or be a high official. It's almost never shown, but it's beautifully photographed. If you think about it for a second, the reason that these textiles are almost never shown is that all of them are light sensitive. The longer they're exposed to light, the less long they'll live. That means that they have to be kept in darkness. They have to be kept in very low humidity, and that's why there's the Antonio Ratti Textile Center.

The last object I want to look at is a beautiful length of velvet which was woven in the late 15th century in Venice. It was woven by a series of craftsmen who'd learned their craft from the Ottoman

Empire, from the great weavers of Istanbul, who had learned their craft from the great weavers of Constantinople. It's one of the most glorious objects in the collection. What's wonderful about looking at it, studying it carefully, is that we could walk upstairs from there, go up to the European Paintings Gallery, and go and look at the wonderful Raphael *Madonna and Child* surrounded by saints, and see an almost identical piece of velvet with a slightly different pattern, woven in exactly the same time, painted by Raphael. That's only possible in a great museum.

Lecture Eighteen
American Art—1650–1865

Scope:

At a time when Americans felt culturally inferior to Europeans, The Metropolitan Museum of Art was among the earliest American art museums to both devote whole galleries and acquisition funds to American art and seek out gifts of entire collections of American art. Unlike American art collections in Boston and Philadelphia, The Metropolitan Museum of Art's collections have always sought to be national rather than regional in scope—they do not even give particular attention to the achievement of New York-based artists and artisans. The first of two lectures will survey the painting, sculpture, and decorative arts produced in America from the 17th century through the end of the Civil War in 1865. These works include iconic paintings like Emanuel Leutze's *Washington Crossing the Delaware* (1851) and Gilbert Stuart's 1795 portrait of George Washington, as well as masterpieces by artists like John Singleton Copley and Thomas Cole. The lecture also explores the museum's offering of superb examples by America's first internationally significant artists, the Hudson River School. These paintings will be placed in the context of "folk" or "self-taught" artists like Ralph Earl and Edward Hicks and will be treated in terms of the oscillation between London and Paris as artistic models for American production. The lecture also will consider the development of American interiors, furniture, and decorative arts during the same period.

Outline

I. The ideology of The Metropolitan Museum of Art was to inspire artists and create a condition to improve and make more international the American art movement that began in the 18th century.

   A. By the end of the 19th century there was a desire on the part of certain American collectors to look at the origins of American art.

   B. The Metropolitan Museum of Art was one of the first museums to go back and collect 17th- and 18th-century

American art and to form a portrait of American art that included painting, sculpture, furniture, ceramics, silver, and textiles.

C. I am going to give two lectures dealing with the museum's collection of American art.

   1. The first lecture will deal with the arts up to the Civil War.

   2. The second lecture will deal with the arts up to the 20th century and the development of the museum's Department of 20th Century Art [Department of Modern Art].

II. We are first going to look at a series of period rooms.

A. The greatest rooms produced in America were collected by the museum very early and put into the American Wing in the mid-1920s, which set the standard for all displays of American art in American institutions.

B. The Hart Room (1680) is a post-and-beam construction and contains works of furniture, including a bed, that were original to the room and part of an American idea of provincial English comfort. Had the room been European, the museum would never have collected it; the feeling on the part of the museum, however, was that Americans needed to understand where they came from and how they defined their styles.

C. The 18th-century Marmion Room from King George County, Virginia, is a cabinet in space that reminds us of the most sophisticated rooms in the European galleries produced in England and France.

D. In the Verplanck Room (1767), from a country house off the Hudson River, you can see that we are looking at a family with very English tastes. They are not hard-working American farmers but people of means like the provincial aristocracy in England.

E. The Metropolitan Museum of Art does not think of itself as being only about New York.

   1. The museum is very interested in Southern decorative arts, such as the Richmond Room (1810).

2. One sees in the room's French origins a combination of English and French Neoclassical taste—already, American rooms were at an international level.

III. The Metropolitan Museum of Art's collection of decorative arts is superb. Four objects give a sense of the range of material and illustrate the fact that the museum is not afraid to collect material that does not look sophisticated.

    A. A turned chair from 1640–1680 is technically simple but possesses a level of provinciality.

    B. A high chest of drawers ("highboy") from 1762–1775 has always been known as the "Madame de Pompadour highboy" due to the bust at the top that has always been thought to represent the official mistress of Louis XV. The object was made in Philadelphia before the American Revolution and tells you a lot about the wealth and sophistication of the American colonies.

    C. The museum's collection of silver is huge; some of it can be seen in the period rooms and some can be seen in other cases (such as a silver teapot designed by Paul Revere, Jr. in 1782, which looks as if it could have been made in London).

    D. The museum also has terrific collections of work by folk artists, including a sugar bowl made by Rudolph Christ (1789–1821) that is deeply inventive and tells us about taste and style outside of the metropolitan cities.

IV. The Metropolitan Museum of Art has a great collection of American paintings. Its collection is the broadest, and it is the least afraid of works of art that were collected and formed in Europe.

    A. American history paintings are not that common; we are more obsessed with describing our landscape and our people than we are with painting our history.

        1. The museum has the largest and most famous American history painting: Emanuel Leutze's *Washington Crossing the Delaware* (1851). The work has always been popular in America and endows George Washington with a sense of divinity.

        2. John Trumbull painted numerous history paintings, including *The Sortie Made by the Garrison of Gibraltar*

(1789), which uses figural poses from Roman sarcophagi and Christian paintings.

B. Matthew Pratt's *The American School* (1765) depicts the school of Benjamin West, the American painter who succeeded Sir Joshua Reynolds as the president of the Royal Academy in London. When this painting was made, there was no art school in America; artists went to Europe to learn how to make works of art.

C. One of the largest works of art in the museum is John Vanderlyn's *The Palace and Gardens of Versailles* (1818–1819), a giant panorama meant to educate Americans about the grandeur of Versailles.

D. The museum has wonderful examples of paintings of great American heroes.
   1. The museum bought Charles Willson Peale's 1779–1781 painting of George Washington from the president's descendents in 1897.
   2. There are more than 18 versions of Gilbert Stuart's portrait of George Washington (begun in 1795), but the museum is convinced that its version is one that was painted (at least in part) from life.
   3. *Daniel Crommelin Verplanck* (1771) was painted by John Singleton Copley, the great portrait painter of Boston.
   4. There is also a strand of American portraiture that deals with ordinary people, such as Ralph Earl's portrait of Elijah Boardman from 1789, which communicates the idea of the self-made man.

E. *Still Life: Balsam Apple and Vegetables* (c. 1820s) is one of James Peale's most charming still lifes. The painting is flat and the composition is uninteresting, yet it is one of the best American still lifes from the 1820s.

F. *The Falls of Niagara* (c. 1825) by Edward Hicks addresses the American idea of manifest destiny. Manifest destiny and its pictorial embodiment are expressed in three other paintings in the museum.
   1. Thomas Cole's *View from Mount Holyoke, Northampton, Massachusetts, after a Thunderstorm— The Oxbow* (1836) looks down into the Connecticut

Valley and sets a standard for American painting that was met by two other artists.

2. Frederic Edwin Church's *Heart of the Andes* (1859) depicts a place of such majesty and beauty that one wants to go there immediately; there is the sense that America, by painting the whole hemisphere, in some way owns it.

3. Albert Bierstadt's *The Rocky Mountains, Lander's Peak* (1863), shows us a mythic ideal of America before Europeans arrived.

Recommended Reading:

Caldwell, Roque, Johnson, and Luhrs. *American Paintings in The Metropolitan Museum of Art, Vol. 1.*

Gardner, and Feld. *American Paintings: Catalogue of the Collection of the Metropolitan Museum of Art I: Painters Born by 1815.*

Roque. *The United States of America (The Metropolitan Museum of Art Series).*

Questions to Consider:

1. Should folk art and art by self-taught artists be included in the museum's collection? Why or why not?

2. Who is your favorite pre-Civil War American artist that is represented in the museum's collection and why?

Lecture Eighteen—Transcript
American Art—1650–1865

When the Metropolitan Museum opened in its wonderful new building in Central Park in 1870, it was already deeply committed to the collecting and display of American art. There were men—all of [the members of] its board, of course, were men in 1870, as they were well into the 20th century. But on the board, unlike many other American museums, were amongst the most important American artists at the time. The idea of the museum was that it would be a global museum. It would be a museum that would reflect the artistic brilliance of the entire world, but it would do so largely for the benefit of American artists and artisans. The ideology of the Metropolitan Museum is that it was there to inspire artists and to create a kind of condition to improve, and make more international, the American art movement that had begun when we became a nation in the 18th century.

The idea that we would have works of art that could be seen by artists in art school, that could be seen by collectors—where artists themselves could come to the gallery and talk with their patrons, looking at other works of art—where there can be a kind of level set to which American art would rise because that level was there was a very important part of the Metropolitan Museum. It became increasingly important as the museum went forward. By the end of the 19th century, there was a kind of desire, an almost sort of provincial desire, on the part of certain American collectors to collect American, to look at the origins of American art. The Metropolitan was one of the first museums that went back and began to collect 17th- and 18th-century American art and to begin to form a whole portrait of the arts in our country. By arts, I do not just mean painting and sculpture. From the very earliest point, the Metropolitan Museum was interested in furniture, ceramics, silver, textiles—the whole range of arts and artifacts and decorative arts produced in America.

Now, I'm going to give two lectures which are going to deal with the arts in America as presented by the Metropolitan Museum. The first one is going to go up to that watershed point in our history, which is, of course, the Civil War, and the second will deal with the arts at the Met after the Civil War and up to the 20th century, when a new

©2008 The Teaching Company.

department takes on the task of showing American art, which is the Department of 20th-Century Art. You're going to see American arts in all their medias, from the beginning of American art to the Civil War, to the mid-1860s, and then a second lecture which is sort of coequal with the rise of the Metropolitan Museum itself, showing truly how international American art had become because of the instigation of institutions in the United States and in Europe specifically like the Metropolitan Museum.

What we're going to do first is to look at a series of period rooms. We've seen that the Met has always been interested in transporting environments so that people in America and in New York who go to the museum, who can't afford to travel to Europe, can't afford to go to the ancient Near East, can't afford to go to Egypt, will be able to see whole environments produced by the people, either ancient or modern, or Renaissance or Baroque, in those cultures. That was also true for America. The greatest rooms produced in America, or the most typical rooms produced in America, were collected by the Metropolitan Museum very early and put into an American wing which opened in the mid-1920s and which sort of set the standards for all display of American art in all American institutions. The collecting and display of American art at the Met has always been at the cutting edge, and you're going to see that it continues to be so.

The first work of art that we're going to see is the Hart Bedroom, which is a bedroom from Ipswich, Massachusetts, built sometime before 1674. The man bought the land in the late 1630s and died in 1674, and so the room was constructed in that period of time. It's a post-and-beam construction in the room, and it's a very low space with whitewashed walls, dark beams. One feels very protected in it, and of course, because it's a bedroom, it has a whole series of furniture, works of furniture which were original to the room and which are part of an idea of American sort of provincial English comfort. You have to remember when you look in this room, when you look at the cupboard from sometime in the 17th century, it was made in the Plymouth colonies, and it's a cupboard that looks as if it could have been made in a provincial city of England. We have to remember, of course, that Ipswich, Massachusetts, was a provincial city of England, though it was in the colonies.

One looks at the little cradle, and it, too—from the latter part of the 17th century, made in eastern Massachusetts—looks like a work of art that you could actually find hundreds of them if you traveled throughout the rural parts and the small cities of England in the 17th century; so, too, the ceramics. The blue and white ceramic chargers which one sees in this room were actually made in England and, of course, imported to the colonies quite easily. And [look at] the glorious bed, a wonderful 17th-century bed. You can feel, when it's cold in the winters in Ipswich, drawing the draperies back, getting into the bed, and being warm in this wonderful sort of red room-like space. The room is not really remarkable, and if the room had been an English room, or a French room, or a German room, or an Italian room of the same period of time, the Met would never have collected it. But it was an American room, and the feeling on the part of the Met was that we needed to understand exactly where we came from; how we, in this place, made our own world; and how we began to define, as we lived apart from England on the other side of the Atlantic, our own styles.

Now, the second room is from roughly a century later. It's from a plantation house in Tidewater called Marmion, and it was built by the Fitzhugh family. There's this marvelous room, which is an irregularly shaped room, and you can see already, when you look at it, we have very delicate pilasters with gilded Ionic capitals. You have little painted decorations of flowers and garlands. One has beautiful inlaid paneling and painted paneling. There are mirrors and paintings. The room is a whole kind of cabineted space that reminds us of the most sophisticated rooms that we saw downstairs in the European galleries produced in England and France. One can see that Virginia, with its plantation culture, was advanced in the 18th century. The people had traveled widely—the Fitzhugh family was very well traveled, in fact—and there wasn't such a great gulf between one side of the Atlantic and the other in the 1770s in Virginia.

Now, the third room is a room from a country house off the Hudson River, north of New York City, of the Verplanck family. You can tell instantly from the name that it's a Dutch name, and so the original Dutch colony, the families that came to the original Dutch colony that survived in the United States when it became English and when it became American, many of them were the wealthiest and most distinguished people. This is a beautiful room from their country house north of New York City. You can see that we're looking at a family with very English tastes in this case. It's a room [from] about the same time as the room in Tidewater but rather different because, of course, we're in a much colder climate. The room is smaller. The ceilings are low to protect the heat in the winter. One sees family portraits by distinguished artists, damask-covered furniture made by American craftsmen in the latest English manner, ceramics made obviously in Europe, some paintings above the fireplace which are mythological, which attest to the sort of level of taste and education of this family. Of course, we know, we can see immediately, that they have plenty of leisure time, and they have plenty of money because they play cards, they write letters, [and] they're literate. They're not these kind of hard-working American farmers and workers. They're people of means. They're people who are very much like the provincial aristocracy in England, who didn't have quite as much money to go into London all the time. But there's a certain level in this room that is very high.

Now, the fourth room that we're going to look at is another room in the South, and you can see quite easily that the Metropolitan Museum doesn't think of itself as being only about New York and only about the way that wealthy people lived in the city of New York and in its country houses. But it really takes on the entire nation as its place, and it's very interested—New York was very interested because it had deep ties with the South, being a port city—in Southern decorative arts. This is the Williams House, and this beautiful room [is] from 1815, built into the Williams House in Richmond, Virginia, a rather grand house in Richmond, Virginia.

You can see immediately that the Williams family was very sophisticated. The wallpaper that surrounds this room was made in Paris, and it represents the monuments of Paris. So if you were a young lady or a young man who was a son or daughter of the Williams family and you were in this room taking your tea and chatting with people, even if you had not yet been to Paris, you would learn about Sainte Clotilde, and Notre Dame, and the Arc de Triomphe, and the Louvre, and the major buildings of Paris, so that when you did go to Paris when you were 18 or 20, when it was appropriate for you to travel, you would actually already know your way around, and you would feel as if you were plugged in to this great city, even if you lived in Richmond, Virginia. The furniture in the room is designed by Duncan Phyfe from New York and another cabinetmaker whose name is Lannuier, which obviously tells us that he had French origins. So one sees a combination of English and French Neoclassical taste in this glorious, very sophisticated room, which by 1815, American rooms were already at an international level.

Now, the collection of decorative arts at the Met is superb, and I can only give you a little, tiny sort of hint of it by just showing you four objects. I'm going to show you two pieces of furniture and two objects of decorative art, one silver and one ceramic, to give you a sense of the range of the material and of the fact that the Met is not afraid to collect material that doesn't look sophisticated. This turned chair from the middle of the 17th century is a perfect exemplar of that idea because it's very technically simple. It was made by a cabinetmaker who obviously knew how to turn wood, and he turned wood to his heart's content, making every single element of this chair turned and turned in ways in which you can tell that his craftsmanship is very good because each of the four turned objects down below the arm [is] identical and the turning is exactly right. So he's a skilled turner, but there is a level of provinciality to this chair. If this chair had been a 17th-century chair in England, France, Germany, or Italy, or even Spain, it wouldn't be in the Met. But it's an American chair, and so we like it very much.

The second piece of furniture is a very sophisticated piece of furniture, made in Philadelphia between 1762 and 1775. It's a sort of high chest of drawers, or "highboy," produced by the absolutely finest of Philadelphia craftsman, though it's not signed, and so one doesn't know who the craftsman was. It has always been known, since it came to the Met in 1918, as the "Madame de Pompadour highboy" because there's a bust of a woman up at the top who has always been thought to be Madame de Pompadour and who looks rather like Madame de Pompadour, the official mistress of Louis XV. It's odd to think of a sort of proper family in Philadelphia having the official mistress of Louis XV on their highboy, and it might just as well, in their minds, have been a figure of hope or faith or something else, but it came to be known as the Pompadour [highboy]. You can see all of its detail, very elaborate brasses, probably which came from England, put onto this mahogany and tulipwood object, very, very sophisticated, beautifully made, beautifully carved, and at the level of London. This is an object made in Philadelphia before the

American Revolution, and it is at the same level of an object made by Chippendale in England. That tells you a lot about the wealth and the sophistication of the American colonies.

Now, the Met's collection of silver is huge, and you see some of it in the period rooms, and you see some of it in cases. They have all the great makers. This is a beautiful silver teapot from 1782 by Paul Revere. We all know about the midnight ride of Paul Revere, and in fact, you'll learn a little bit more about it a few lectures from now because there's a painting of it in the Met's collection. He was a silversmith, and this is one of his teapots from the 1780s—very simple, very refined at the same time, with extremely elegant detailing. The whole quality of it is perfect. The balance of it is very good. It looks very English. It looks as if it could have been made in London. It wouldn't have been exactly in high style in London—it's a little bit old-fashioned to be in London—but its level of craftsmanship is very high.

What's wonderful about the Met is that the Met also has terrific collections of works by itinerant artists, popular artists, and almost "folk" artists, if you will. This is a terrific sugar bowl made in the South in the Moravian community in North Carolina by a man named Rudolph Christ, who lived between 1750 and 1833. This is a sugar bowl from 1789–1821, sort of at the middle point of his life. It's an object that has none of the sophistication of Paul Revere, but it's an object that is deeply inventive, charming, and amusing and an object that tells about taste and style outside of the metropolitan cities and outside of the life of the haute bourgeoisie.

Now, to deal in the realm of paintings, the Met has a really great collection of American paintings. Their collection of American paintings is probably the best. I mean, the rivals are Boston and Philadelphia. Of course, if you're from Philadelphia, you think the Philadelphia collection is best, and if you're from Boston, you think the Boston collection is best. If you're from Washington, you think the collection between the National Museum of American Art and the National Gallery is the best. But I'm not from any of those places, and so I'm going to say that the Metropolitan Museum's collection is the best because it's the broadest—it has representations from all over the country—and it's the least afraid of works of art that were collected and formed in Europe, in the sense that works of art can have associations and origins in Europe and that many

American artists either went to Europe to be trained or came from Europe to the United States.

I'm going to talk about two works of art which are history paintings. American history paintings aren't that common. We are more obsessed with describing our landscape, and our peoples, and where we are, and what we look like, and our towns than we are with painting our history. Probably the largest and most famous American history painting, however, is at the Met, and you can see it here. It's by an artist named Emanuel Gottlieb Leutze, and it was painted not in the United States but in Germany. In fact, it's signed with the artist's name and signed with the name of the city in Germany where it was painted, so that even when you're looking at it in the Metropolitan Museum, you know that it was not painted in the United States. Of course, when you hear the name Emanuel Gottlieb Leutze, you don't think American; you think German. Of course, he was a man who was equally at home in both places.

This is an absolutely enormous painting. It's almost 20 feet long. The figures in it are life-size. It's one of the most famous works of art produced in America, and it's, of course, *Washington Crossing the Delaware*, and it was painted in 1851. The story of this painting is an interesting story because Emanuel Leutze painted the first version in 1849, and it was so popular that it was bought immediately by a German museum, which unfortunately was firebombed in World War II, and so the painting no longer exists. But he made a second version of the painting to be sent to America, and it's this version of the painting, [made] in 1851, and this version, of course, survives.

It came to the Metropolitan Museum late in the 19th century, and it's a work of art that, even when it was first shown in New York in the 1850s, was bought for over $10,000, which was like $500,000 in those times. It's a work of art that has always been popular in America. It was engraved. It was sent around the country on tour. It has a kind of position as "the painting" of our great leader George Washington in the most appalling of conditions, in the wintertime with a ragtag army, going across the Delaware with a sense of his incredible purpose. Of course, in 1851 when it was painted, that purpose had come true, so it was possible to endow this figure with a kind of almost divinity. It's almost as if this is the study for Mount Rushmore.

Now, the second history painting is by America's greatest history painter. His name was John Trumbull, and he painted a lot of history paintings of historical subjects, mostly battles. He went in for battles because institutions like to buy battles and generals like to buy representations of battles, and the idea that you can paint heroic men doing heroic things sold for him. His own collection of paintings went to Yale University, and it was the first—actually, the first university art museum was the John Trumbull gift to Yale University in the 19th century, early in the 19th century. But the Met has this wonderful picture, which was painted in 1789, the year of the French Revolution. It's called *The Sortie Made by the Garrison of Gibraltar*, and it's a scene of English history. Of course, it was painted not in the United States for the American market but in London for the English market.

One sees how American painters, the most ambitious of them, went to Europe, went to London, or France, or Germany, to make their fortunes, to work in the more sophisticated markets of those places. One sees this very sophisticated scene, with the general here. One sees the general. We're at Gibraltar. We can't quite see the Rock of Gibraltar because we're too near it. He has defeated an enemy. The enemy is dying down below. The figures are derived from Roman sarcophagi [and] from Christian paintings. A lot of his poses come from depositions of Christ and baptisms of Christ, of which he had many prints. What he does is to model his figural poses on great figures in earlier art and to create a new kind of world in so doing.

Now, this is a charming picture by an artist named Matthew Pratt, and it's called *The American School*. It's a picture that, really, I could have begun the lecture with because, of course, the American school here in 1765 isn't even in America; it's in London. It's the school of Benjamin West, the great American painter, who succeeded Sir Joshua Reynolds as the president of the Royal Academy, being the first American who was the president of the Royal Academy in London. But he taught, for his own pleasure, American artists at his home to be artists. Here, one sees Benjamin West in the center, rather grandly looking—he's criticizing a composition, a drawing made probably by this student, who also has a palette in his hand. We see younger students.

You can see immediately how art was a trade that you learned when you were young. You could start when you were 12, or 13, or even younger, and you worked in the place of a great man, and you learned first to draw from sculpture. Then you learned to draw from nature, to make compositions. Then you learned to paint—there's a painter over here—and then you were criticized by the great man, Benjamin West, who wanted to improve American arts. Of course, there wasn't even an art school in America when this painting was made, and so artists went to Europe to learn how to make works of art. You can learn about art school in the 18th century in London by standing in front of this marvelous painting.

Now, the next work of art I want to show you is one of the largest works of art in the Met, and it was made by one of my favorite artists, John Vanderlyn. It represents an entire panorama of Versailles. He went to Versailles in 1814. He had already won the grand prize in the Salon in 1804 and was the only American, the first American, artist to win the grand prize in the Paris Salon. So some American artists went to London, some American artists went to Germany, some American artists went to Paris. He painted this enormous panorama in the end of the teens, and it was set up in old City Hall Park, the park in New York before Central Park. There was no Central Park in 1821, when this painting was first shown in this building constructed specifically for it. It was for time travel. It was for Americans to go into it and learn about the grandeur of Versailles. You can go into this room, look at the painting for hours, and almost be in Versailles. If you're very careful, you can find in it the artist himself, who's pointing to the czar of Russia, who visited the gardens of Versailles on the same day in 1814 as he [Vanderlyn] did.

Now, of the paintings of the great heroes of America, the Met has wonderful examples. This is a Charles Willson Peale, the great Philadelphia painter, portrait of George Washington. Peale painted the first version of this painting, which is in the Pennsylvania Academy, in 1779. Washington's family liked it so much that they commissioned from Peale this version, which the Met literally bought at the end of the 19th century, in 1897, from the descendants of George Washington. One sees George Washington in his soldierly attire with all of his sort of—he's not going to fight, but he's presented as if he's a general. In back of him is Trenton, New Jersey, one of the places that he won a battle. Charles Willson Peale went to the sites of the battles and painted many versions of this picture.

Now, if we want to know really what Washington looks like, we have to look at this famous portrait by Gilbert Stuart, an artist who was American, trained in England, came back to the United States, and was one of the few artists who actually was allowed to paint Washington from life. There are more than 18 versions of this painting, some of them painted by Gilbert Stuart or his studio, and others, copies of those, to hang in state houses, and in governors' rooms, and whatever throughout the early years of the American Republic. But the Met is absolutely convinced that this is the version that was begun, painted at least in part, from life. So we have to imagine that we're actually looking into Washington's eyes as he comes to Gilbert Stuart's studio in New York in 1795.

Now, portraiture in America is fascinating. This little boy is a Verplanck. His name is Daniel Crommelin Verplanck, and [his portrait] was painted in 1771, at exactly the same time that you saw the room in their country house. Of course, it's the view of the Verplanck's country house out the window. One sees this wise little boy. What's interesting about this painting is it was not painted by a New York painter; it was painted by John Singleton Copley. John Singleton Copley was the great portrait painter of Boston, but the Verplancks were so rich and so grand that they wanted the greatest painter of portraits in America. They chose John Singleton Copley very wisely, and he came and painted this little boy with his little pet squirrel on a string. You see this beautiful view out to a sylvan landscape. He looks as if he's the lord of the manor even if he's only nine years old.

There's also a strand of American portraiture that deals with ordinary people. One of my favorite portraits in the Met is this one. It's by an artist who lived and worked mostly in Connecticut, named Ralph Earl. He sort of traveled around, painting people who wanted to be painted. This wonderful man is named Elijah Boardman, and the picture was painted in 1789. As we can see, Boardman is in his dry goods store in Connecticut. The painting is full-scale. The man is exactly the height that he was. You get to know him quite well. You get to know his library. When you see the painting enlarged, you see all of the bolts of fabric, through the door, in his store. We're now in his part of the house, and we can see him. He's beautifully dressed. The painting is quite naively painted—if it wasn't an American painting, it wouldn't be in the Met—but it's also charmingly painted and very honest. One learns a good deal about how it was to be a businessman in the end of the 18th century. This is an American painting, not a British colony. We're in 1789, so we're in the United States of America, and he's in one of the states. He's ambitious. We can see all of his books, and the painter gives us the titles. We can see Sir Thomas Moore's *Travels*. We can see the plays of Shakespeare. We can see *Paradise Lost* by Milton. We can see the *London Magazine* of 1786, just three years old, and we can see that he's very London-focused but very literate for a shopkeeper in Connecticut. The idea of the self-made, educated man, however naively painted, is communicated really brilliantly in this picture.

And this—Charles Willson Peale, you'll remember, painted Washington. Well, one of his sons—he had lots of sons, and this is James Peale. This is one of his most charming still lifes. When you see it in the Met, you see it over a dining room sideboard, charmingly. It's all this stuff from the garden—every kind of cabbage and new sort of plant that one could grow in this fertile country of America. Again, it's naively painted, very flat, and the composition, while interesting, isn't very original. There's not much of a sense of balance, and so if it was an English painting, it would probably be in storage. But it's an American painting, and it's one of the best American still lifes from the 1820s—it's from the early 1820s. You can look at it forever. Each crinkle and each leaf of the cabbage, all the shiny parts of the tomatoes, and this extraordinary balsam apple in the front, which is a fruit from Asia that was actually grown in Jefferson's garden and was a medicinal plant but which obviously was used here because it's so interesting visually.

Now, the American landscape is what I want to end the lecture with, whether naive—this is *The Falls of Niagara*, painted by Edward Hicks, who is one of our great "self-taught" artists, an artist who, towards the middle of his life, in 1825—he'd gone to Niagara Falls in 1819—he painted this wonderful picture with a text around it. The frame is by him, and he tells you what to think about the picture. It's all about Manifest Destiny, and about how America owns its own land, and about how we have the most beautiful and extraordinary landscape in the world, and that we have the right to it. And because we're here and our landscape is so great, we are a great people, and we can expand into the landscape. It's this phrase in American history, when we learn American history, called "Manifest Destiny."

If we are here, our destiny is manifest. We fill the landscape, and we represent the landscape, and the landscape becomes us and our symbol.

This concept of Manifest Destiny and its pictorial embodiment is so beautifully expressed in the Met in three great paintings that I want to end the lecture with those three great paintings. The earliest of them is by an American artist named Thomas Cole, who traveled extensively in Europe—actually throughout Europe—but who was really wedded to the American landscape. His masterpiece—of all of his great American landscapes, the greatest one—is the *View from Mount Holyoke*, painted in 1836. He's up on a hill. If you've ever been to that area, there's this marvelous mountain. He has climbed up the mountain. There's a blasted stump, so we know that lightning has struck at an earlier point. If you look very carefully, there's another artist painting the view.

We're looking down into the Connecticut Valley, and what we see is the famous oxbow of the Connecticut Valley, where it turns around this big broad river, which runs through a sort of fruited plain. You see little farms, and [you get] this sort of sense that the landscape is rich and fabulous and that a storm has passed through the landscape, clearing [it]; [note the] light coming in, the reflections on the water. One can look at this picture with all of its pictorial detail for hours. It was painted not so far from either New York or Boston, and yet the landscape looks incredibly wild, as it was in the 1830s. It set a standard for American painting that was extraordinary and a standard that was met by a whole series of other artists, and I just want to discuss two.

The second painting I want to discuss is by Frederic Church. Frederic Church had a huge house called Olana, up the Hudson River. He painted many landscapes in America, but he became so great and so famous that he began to travel widely all over the New World, painting its glories throughout its length and breadth. This is called the *Heart of the Andes*, and one can see that it was painted in South America. It was painted in 1859, a little bit later than the Thomas Cole, but here we are in the mountains of the Andes with this sense of incredible grandeur, of this huge waterfall, of fabulous flowers in the foreground. This painting is shown in one of the grandest frames ever conceived by man, with drapery and all sorts of swags and things around it. One can look at it almost with a magnifying glass. There are little figures, and insects and birds flying around, little villages and farms in the distance. One feels as if one is in a place of such majesty and beauty that you want to go there immediately. Again, there is the sense that America, by painting the whole hemisphere, both north and south, actually in some odd way owns it.

Now, the painting with which I want to end is a painting by Albert Bierstadt, an artist born and trained in Germany. He came to America in the 1850s and began to paint the Rocky Mountains. This is a great picture of 1863 called *The Rocky Mountains, Lander's Peak*. It's an enormous painting, like the Frederic Church before it, and it shows us the kind of mythic ideal of America before Europeans. One sees extraordinary mountains in the background. One sees the waterfall at Yellowstone, sort of imported down to Colorado for the occasion and turned into this little, puny thing to make the mountains look even taller; this wonderful, very reflective lake. And then in the foreground, a very large and peaceful camp of Native Americans with their two groups of tepees, their horses, playing their games, with a sense of their being at one with the landscape. The quality of this picture made one almost want to get rapidly on a train. Of course, this is very shortly before the arrival of the transcontinental railroad. You could go almost all the way across the country. One sees that American wish to control the continent and to be not so interested in Europe but to be interested in ways that we can define ourselves as even greater than Europeans.

Lecture Nineteen
American Art—1865–1900

Scope:

The Metropolitan Museum of Art had a huge impact on the production and reception of art in New York City. As a result, the museum's collections of American painting, sculpture, and decorative arts from the last three decades of the 19th century are greater than those from the previous three centuries. Although American artists continued to flock to London, Paris, Rome, and Munich for their artistic training, numerous independent art schools and professional art academies opened in the United States—from New York to Cincinnati and St. Louis to California. Artists like Whistler, Cassatt, and Sargent—who spent most of their professional lives in Europe—or artists such as Homer, Eakins, and Chase—who, while aware of European trends, worked in America—were of an unparalleled cosmopolitanism; their works are exhibited in major European capitals as well as throughout America. The art scene in late 19th-century America, when considered in terms of its decorative arts (by firms like the Tiffany Company and the Herter Brothers) and sculpture (by Augustus Saint-Gaudens and Daniel Chester French), rivaled that of any traditional European capital.

Outline

I. All of the works of art we looked at in the last lecture were made before the Civil War. In this lecture, I want to turn to the years after the Civil War.

   A. By the 1870s, Americans began to make up for lost time and take up cultural production.

   B. Eastman Johnson's *The Hatch Family* (1870–1871) embodies the success, materialism, calm, and multi-generational nature of a country that put the war behind it. One can see that the New York of this era was clearly the richest city in America.

   C. We are going to see, as we go through The Metropolitan Museum of Art, the embodiment of that money in works of decorative arts, sculpture, and painting.

II. American furniture of the 1870s, 1880s, and 1890s is extraordinary.

    A. Alexander Roux's cabinet, made around 1866, embodies a level of craftsmanship as high as any European cabinetmaker. It is a work of art invented for a new, optimistic American wealth that was deeply sophisticated and knew about Europe but did not need to copy a particular style or source.

    B. A library table from 1882 by the Herter Brothers was made for William H. Vanderbilt's Fifth Avenue mansion.

        1. The table depicts both hemispheres and illustrates Vanderbilt's global empire.

        2. One can visit the Department of European Sculpture and Decorative Arts and find equally vulgar and equally grand furniture but nothing that looks quite like this piece.

    C. Augustus Saint-Gaudens designed a fireplace for the entrance hall of Cornelius Vanderbilt's mansion (William H. Vanderbilt's son) between 1881 and 1883.

        1. The mosaic at the top contains an involved inscription in Latin, indicating that the family was well educated.

        2. The fireplace is about the power of money to impress; it also reflects an interfamily competition.

    D. The loggia from Louis Comfort Tiffany's Laurelton Hall (c. 1905) has references from all over the world; the loggia's design was taken from a palace near Agra in India.

III. American sculptors in the same period of time also were accomplished. I want to discuss works by two sculptors.

    A. The first sculptor is Augustus Saint-Gaudens, who designed the Vanderbilt fireplace.

        1. *Hiawatha* (modeled 1871–1872; carved 1874) was made in Rome, the fountainhead of all Western sculpture.

        2. The source of the sculpture is *The Song of Hiawatha*, the 1855 epic poem by Henry Wadsworth Longfellow.

        3. The object is deeply ambivalent in its relationship between the Indian and the white man; it raised questions about the true meaning of America because it acknowledged the fact that there were Native Americans before there were Europeans.

    4. Saint-Gaudens also sculpted *Diana* (1893–1894), the weather vane on top of what was to be Madison Square Garden. The museum owns a two-foot gilded cast of this figure, made in or after 1894.

  B. Saint-Gaudens's major rival was Daniel Chester French.

    1. He is known for *Alma Mater*, which stands outside Columbia University, and the statue of Lincoln in the Lincoln Memorial.

    2. *The Angel of Death and the Sculptor* from the *Milmore Memorial* (1889–1893; the museum's version, 1926) is a funerary monument that reminds one about the museum's mission to inspire artists.

IV. The paintings of this period in The Metropolitan Museum of Art comprise a definitive collection of American painting.

  A. *The Champion Single Sculls (Max Schmitt in a Single Scull)* from 1871 is by Thomas Eakins, the first American painter who could be shown alongside any European artist.

    1. Eakins studied with Gérôme, one of Paris's great Orientalist painters; thus, there is a transference of the highest level of French academic painting to Philadelphia in the early 1870s.

    2. Most of Eakins's paintings are in the Philadelphia Museum but this work is in The Metropolitan Museum of Art—illustrating that the museum wants to take on the nation with its collection.

  B. Mary Cassatt joined the Impressionists in the Impressionist exhibition of 1879.

    1. She did not disguise her gender, unlike other female artists who were afraid their paintings would not sell because they were women.

    2. *The Cup of Tea* (c. 1880–1881) was shown at the Impressionist exhibition of 1881.

    3. The painting's subject, Cassatt's sister Lydia, is a model for the wealthy, fashionable young American woman in Paris.

C. The single most controversial painting in The Metropolitan Museum of Art is John Singer Sargent's *Madame X (Madame Pierre Gautreau)* from 1883–1884.
1. Madame Pierre Gautreau was one of the most scandalous women in Paris; in the 1880s, her revealing dress was considered shocking.
2. When the painting was first shown, the shoulder strap of the dress was on her arm, implying that the dress could just tumble off.

D. James McNeill Whistler, like Sargent, spent almost no time in the United States, though he had American patrons.
1. *Arrangement in Flesh Colour and Black: Portrait of Theodore Duret* (1883) is one of his great portraits of New York and represents one of the most important French art critics.
2. The portrait has a quality of international élan that only Whistler could capture during this period of time.

E. *Arques-la-Bataille* (1885) by John Henry Twachtman is concerned with tones of color. Its aesthetic comes from Japanese paintings, screen paintings, and prints. The museum also owns a small-scale study painted at the site, as well as the larger picture painted in his Paris studio.

F. I want to show two paintings by the stars of the American Impressionist movement.
1. In Childe Hassam's *Celia Thaxter's Garden, Isles of Shoals, Maine* (1890), one can see the artist applying a European idea of art to the United States.
2. William Merritt Chase's *At the Seaside* (c. 1892), like Hassam's piece, was painted out of doors (instead of from a sketch) so that the natural light saturation affected the way he saw nature.

G. Winslow Homer's *The Gulf Stream* (1899) is an intensely painted seascape depicting the ocean as something not benign but terrifying.

Recommended Reading:

Luhrs, ed. *American Paintings in the Metropolitan Museum of Art.*

Salinger. *Masterpieces of American Painting in the Metropolitan Museum of Art.*

Questions to Consider:

1. How did the art produced in America from 1865 to 1900 rival European art traditions?

2. What role did New York City play in the development of American art from 1865 to 1900? What work of art in the museum sustains your conclusions?

Lecture Nineteen—Transcript
American Art—1865–1900

In the last lecture, we learned a good deal about the ways in which America as an artistic nation defined itself in opposition to, and in reference to, Europe—Germany, England, and France being the three most important countries. We also learned the ways that we actually embraced the landscape of our hemisphere and used it as a kind of dramatic set for our own collective dreams. All of the works of art that we looked at in the last lecture, however, were made before the Civil War and before the extraordinary national drama in which we turned really upon ourselves and [clashed over] our divisions and our problems for a period of five long years, which really ripped apart the country and created a kind of sense of American-ness that was very different after than before. In this lecture, I want to turn to the years after the Civil War.

By the 1870s, Americans began to make up for lost time and began to take on this kind of cultural production. They were incredibly rich. The war, like all wars, had created a kind of industrial machine in the United States that had revved up in ways that it wouldn't have had there not been a war—one of the few advantages of war. I want to begin the lecture in New York, in the living room of a great New York family called the Hatch family. The Hatch family lived at 39th and Park Avenue, very near where the Morgan Library is today and where Mr. Morgan was to build his great mansion a little bit after they [the Hatch family] lived there. One sees this family painted in their living room by the great American artist Eastman Johnson. It's an embodiment of the success, the materialism, the calm, the sort of multi-generationalness, the sense that we sort of put the war behind us.

One sees arranged in this glorious room a whole family. The room itself is fabulous. The draperies are beautifully done. The light fixture is absolutely new. There's a Hudson River painting to the left. There are three sculptures over the mantelpiece. There are custom-made bookcases fitted up for the family's library, so clearly we're in the library. There's an Aubusson carpet all around. There's a commissioned table in the center of the room. Then there is this copious family. We see Mr. Hatch here and Mrs. Hatch here. One sees a whole brood of children. I count 11, and maybe you all should go to the Met and see whether you agree or disagree with me. But in any case, a lot of children, ranging in age from a baby to an older boy, and the girl seems to be the oldest one in the family, all born to this lady, who is in mourning, like her mother, for her father. This is the father of Mr. Hatch, so one sees three generations, an enormous generation, all arranged reading, playing, chatting very informally but with a kind of command of their space.

One can see that the New York of 1870–71 was clearly the richest and clearly the largest city in America and that its financial markets were being run by men who, like today, made a good deal of money. We're going to see as we go through the Met, the residue, the embodiment of that money in works of decorative arts, sculpture, and painting.

Now, to begin with furniture, American furniture of the 1870s, [18]80s, and [18]90s is extraordinary. This is a cabinet made just after the Civil War, in 1866, by an American of French origin, a cabinetmaker named Alexander Roux. When you look at it in detail, you see it has many kinds of wood—rosewood, tulipwood, cherry, poplar, and pine. Sometimes he gilds; sometimes he makes wonderful cartouches of flowers and tendrils; other times he creates frames for ceramic plaques which were made particularly for the case. The case is very rich, beautifully finished, the highest level of craftsmanship, as high as any European cabinetmaker. It doesn't actually look like anything made in Europe. It's a work of art that was invented for a kind of new optimistic American wealth that was deeply sophisticated, knew about Europe, but didn't need exactly to copy anything, made new combinations from many sources. By this point in America, there were many illustrated magazines and books. The libraries were getting better. There was a sense in which you could be fully sophisticated without going back to Europe, and Alexander Roux was a cabinetmaker who was clearly an original cabinetmaker, who made his own contributions.

Now we're going to look at a table which is one of the most fun works of art to look at in the American Wing at the Met, and it's by the Herter Brothers, who were sort of the Rolls Royce of cabinetmakers in New York, the most expensive cabinetmakers in New York. This was a library table made for William H. Vanderbilt in his great mansion on Fifth Avenue in 1881–1882. It's an enormous piece of furniture. We can see it here on one end, and one sees the entire hemisphere, our hemisphere, with North and South America, beautifully done, with mother-of-pearl and inlay, a kind of garland around them, incredibly deeply carved rosewood. Rosewood is one of the hardest woods to carve, one of the most beautiful woods, and one of the most expensive to find large trees to make a table of this kind of scale.

If you ran around to the other side of the table, you would see the other hemisphere, so it's a global table. It's a table that shows that William H. Vanderbilt had access to the entire world, that his empire was global, that he thought globally. If that isn't enough, when you look at the top of the table, it's strewn with mother-of-pearl stars which form the constellations of the skies. It's as if on Fifth Avenue in New York, William Vanderbilt has control of the world, and that is expressed in a table, which again, looks very little like anything produced in London and very little like anything produced in France. You can run down to the galleries of European decorative arts and see equally vulgar and equally grand furniture but nothing that looks quite like this.

Now, if you were to walk up a few blocks on Fifth Avenue, you'd go to the mansion of his son, Cornelius Vanderbilt, and you'd see this extraordinary fireplace which was designed by a wonderful sculptor named Augustus Saint-Gaudens. It was a fireplace in the entrance hall of this vast mansion. There are two carved caryatids holding up the fireplace. One of them is love, and the other one is peace, so we have love and peace on either side. There is a mosaic on the top, with a very involved inscription in Latin to indicate that the family was well educated. And, of course, every educated American in the 19th century knew Latin.

The translation of the Latin text is as follows: "The house at its threshold gives evidence of the master's good will. Welcome to the guest who arrives; farewell and helpfulness to him who departs." Notice in this there's no mention of women; it is the "master" and "him." There's no "her," anyway, and no "mistress." So this is about the power of money and the power of money to impress. You hire the best and the most expensive sculptor to make a fireplace for you in your house on Fifth Avenue, right up the street from your dad's house. The sort of interfamily competition is extraordinary and expressed very well in the Met.

Now, a little bit later—in fact, quite a lot later—in 1905, the greatest American decorative artist of all times, Louis Comfort Tiffany, built his own house. It was a house called Laurelton Hall. It was in Cold Spring Harbor near the Hudson River, in the Hudson River Valley, north of New York. It had 84 rooms on eight levels. It was an extraordinary house, and it had sort of references from all over the world. This loggia is in the Met with the wonderful stained-glass windows by Tiffany, and the wonderful light fixtures by Tiffany, and the tiles by Tiffany, and the design by Tiffany. The design of this was taken from a palace near Agra, where the Taj Mahal is, in India, so one sees the global reach of Louis Comfort Tiffany. The house itself, when you look at it, was enormous and had many references to many places. So if William Vanderbilt had "the globe" built into his library, Louis Comfort Tiffany, with all the success of Tiffany's—and, of course, his family owned Tiffany's, and Tiffany's was as successful during his lifetime, if not more so, than it is today—could afford to build a house that was essentially a portrait of the world.

American sculptors in the same period of time were also extraordinarily accomplished, and I want to discuss works by two sculptors. The first one is Augustus Saint-Gaudens. I mentioned him because he designed the Vanderbilt fireplace in the 1880s on 59th and Fifth Avenue, the Cornelius Vanderbilt fireplace. But here is a work of art [from] a little bit earlier. This is [from] 1874, and it was made not in the United States but in Rome. Of course, if you want to be a great sculptor, you go to the fountainhead of sculpture, of all Western sculpture, which is Rome, and you get a piece of marble from Carrera, and you carve a subject with incredible skill, the skill which is as great as any artist at any time in history.

The subject in this case is Hiawatha, so one has an American artist in Rome carving an American Indian, a Chippewa chief named Hiawatha. Of course, his source is not reality but literature. It is *The Song of Hiawatha* by Longfellow, which he was reading—reading out loud, probably—as he made this object. He shows us an American Indian chief from lore, from American literature, as a kind of thoughtful, brooding man, rather than as a man of power. It's an object that is deeply ambivalent in its relationship between the Indian and the white person, and it shows him in completely white marble as this very exotic yet thoughtful man, a man who isn't a man of action but a man of contemplation. It sheds a whole new light in terms of sculpture on the Native American and America. When it was first shown in Rome, and then it went back to America, it raised all sorts of questions about the true meaning of America because it acknowledged the fact that there were Native Americans before there were Europeans.

Augustus Saint-Gaudens was also asked in 1893—he was commissioned—to do the weather vane on top of what was going to be Madison Square Garden. One sees Madison Square Garden this extraordinary building, with a sort of Sevilla-like tower by McKim, Mead & White. [Saint-Gaudens] responded [to the commission] with this extraordinary *Diana*. The *Diana*, when it was made, was so heavy that it didn't work, and he had to thin her down. It went through a whole sort of series of permutations. The Met owns a two-foot gilded cast of this Diana, who is the most lithe, elegant, and glorious figure, a figure that competes with any Diana painted or sculpted by any artist, one of the triumphs of American art but in European terms. [She is] a Classical goddess on top of a building that has to do with Spain, created by an American artist who wanted to be as good as any European, and surely, he succeeded.

The artist who was his major rival as a great sculptor at the end of the 19th century was Daniel Chester French. We can see Augustus Saint-Gaudens is a name that has French origins, and his father, though he was born in Dublin, was a French shoemaker and his mother was Irish. He moved to the United States when he was young. But Daniel Chester French was sheerly American. We all know him very well for having carved *Alma Mater* at Columbia, which you see here. Or if you go to the Lincoln Memorial in Washington, the great statue of Lincoln is by Daniel Chester French. He's part of our national history, but very few of us know his name. The Met has a number of great sculptures [by him], and I'm only going to show you one.

This is *The Angel of Death and the Sculptor from the Milmore Memorial*. The Milmore Memorial was made in memory of two brother sculptors, Martin and Joseph Milmore, who after their deaths, had a memorial in bronze made by Daniel Chester French, which is a sort of essay about sculpture. One sees the marble version commissioned by a group of museum trustees to come to the Metropolitan Museum. The original was done in 1889–1893, and the marble version was done much later. It's one of the great objects in the Met. One sees the young sculptor, very lithe and attractive. He's sculpting an Egyptian sculpture, sculpting a sphinx. So in the Met, one thinks back to what we saw in the entrance hall of the Met when we came in, and [we see] this wonderful angel who, with her flowers, and her wings, and her superb drapery, is reaching out to control his hand. It's as if some kind of divine spirit is affecting the chisel of the artist.

In the marble version, this is much more powerful than in the bronze version, which is in the cemetery, of course, because it was a funerary monument. When you see this in the Metropolitan Museum, and you think about American sculpture and how far American art had come since the Metropolitan, then you understand the meaning of the museum. The museum was to inspire artists and to give them a level, a technical level, which they had to attain. There is no doubt that Daniel Chester French attained it. An interesting side point is [that] his brother was the director of the Art Institute of Chicago, so it's a family who thought deeply about museums.

Now, let's go on a little sort of tour of the paintings of this period in the Met, and the collection is so great that this is a kind of once-over-lightly of really wonderful things. When you go to the Met and whenever you stand in front of this, you'll see 5 other, or 10 other, or 30 other works of art that you will want to look at with equal attention when you go to the collection because the collection is really virtually a definitive collection of American painting. The painting I begin with was painted not in New York but in Philadelphia. It's *The Champion Single Sculls*, and it's the friend of its artist, who was Thomas Eakins, who was in some people's opinion, including mine, the first great American painter, the first American painter who could be shown with any European artist, and who reaches a level that is truly international.

In this painting, which was painted in 1871—the same period, the same year almost, as the Hatch portrait with which the lecture began—one sees a man alone in the early morning, exercising. He's a champion, we are told. He has won the race, and he is exercising in the early morning. We see it's on the Schuylkill River, very near, actually, the Philadelphia Museum, which would be off to the left, though it wasn't built until the [19]20s, in the next century. One sees these earnest Americans who exercise in the morning. There's the railroad bridge in the background. There's a kind of crystal-clear light.

There is a sense of being unencumbered by the past, but it was painted by an artist who had just come back from Paris—and who had studied with one of the great Orientalist painters, named Gerome, in Paris—and had been Gerome's best student in the late 1860s. So there's a transference of the highest level of French academic painting to Philadelphia in the early 1870s. Eakins spent the rest of his life in Philadelphia, and this is probably, arguably, his single greatest painting. Whereas most of his paintings, the largest group of his paintings, are of course, in the Philadelphia Museum, this is in the Met. It means that—it shows us that the Met doesn't care where something comes from if it's American. It wants to take on the nation with its collection.

Now, we go to the first woman artist we've had in the entire class, and that is Mary Cassatt. Mary Cassatt was born in Pennsylvania to a very good family. Her brother was a great railroad entrepreneur. Her own family had sort of upper-middle income, and they followed her. She was trained at the Pennsylvania Academy, and she decided that in order to be really a great painter, she has to go to Europe, so her mother and father go with her. They go to Paris, and then they go to Spain, and then they come back to Paris. She meets Edgar Degas, the great Impressionist painter; and becomes really interested in Modernism; and becomes the second woman artist of real quality to join with the Impressionists when she joined them for the first time in the exhibition of 1879.

She was an artist who, with Monet, Renoir, Degas, Pissarro, Sisley, all of the great artists of the Impressionists, she was an equal to them, and she was a woman, and she was American. What's riveting is that she signed her paintings with her name, Mary Cassatt. She didn't disguise her gender, [as] many women artists did because they wanted to sell their paintings, and they were afraid if they put Mary or Gertrude or whatever their first name was that their paintings wouldn't sell because they were by women. Mary Cassatt was defiant in this. This is a wonderful painting called *The Cup of Tea*. It was painted in the early 1880s, and it was shown in the Impressionist Exhibition of 1881, which was one of the greatest Impressionist exhibitions, where it was seen with paintings by Degas, and Renoir, and Caillebotte, Pissarro, Monet. It was a painting that showed that even in the avant-garde, even in the most advanced artistic circles in the world, in Paris in the late 1870s and the early 1880s, an American woman made her mark.

This painting—it's actually rather controversial in an odd way that it's in the American Wing because, of course, she would have been much happier if it was hanging with the French painters that were her real colleagues and friends, but it's in the American Wing. It represents her sister Lydia drinking tea in a kind of—obviously, she's dressed all up in the latest Parisian fashion. She has her gloves on. We're in this kind of American circle. There were many Americans in Paris at this period of time, and they went to each other's houses, and they tried out their French, and they went to the museums and sights together. They lived rather well because you could live much better on the dollar in those days than you can now.

Lydia is a sort of model for the wealthy, fashionable, young American woman in Paris. Now, when this picture was shown in Paris in 1881, the French had no idea, really, that this was an American woman painting an American woman. It was simply a French painting. Cassatt, whose last name was actually spelled with one *t* at the end, added another *t* to the spelling of her name to make it seem more French. If she'd added a *te*, it would have been even more French. This frothy, wonderful painting is one of many major paintings by Cassatt in the Met, and you can look at others when you go to see it.

Now, the single most controversial painting in the Metropolitan Museum, and a painting that was controversial from the very minute that it was made, is John Singer Sargent's famous portrait *Madame X*. The portrait of Madame X was painted in Paris in 1883, finished in early 1884, and shown not at an Impressionist exhibition but at the Salon, at the official exhibition in France, where it was a *succès de scandale*. It was absolutely shocking to the French when it was shown for the first time. What's interesting about it is it was painted by an American artist who had almost, essentially, at this point in his life, never been to America. He was born in Florence. His parents were from the United States, obviously, but they could spend their money more easily and live better and more cheaply in Europe. So he grew up as a kind of itinerant all over Europe, learning to paint in Paris, living in London, being completely conversant in many

European languages. He spent a tiny period of his time—in fact, he traveled to America rather than was an American.

But this woman—her name is Madame Pierre Gautreau, and she was an American—she was born in New Orleans, and she was one of the most scandalous women in Paris. She was extraordinarily beautiful. She wore revealing dresses, as is clear, and she powdered her body with a kind of lavender-tinted powder that made her sort of glow in the lights of a great ball. One sees Madame Gautreau here with this dress, with the plunging décolleté, an enormous amount showing. It almost looks like a contemporary film star. Somebody could wear this dress to the Oscars and look perfectly normal, but in the 1880s, this dress was shocking.

What's more interesting about it, today, you can see that her strap goes up like this, just is a mirror image of this one. But when the painting was shown in the Salon, this strap was down here on her arm, showing that the dress could almost tumble off, and it was even more shocking. What was great about being shocking is that the painting made both her and Sargent instantly famous because, though it was in the catalog as *Madame*... or ***, and now *Madame X*, an anonymous woman, everybody knew this lady. What Sargent did was he knew French well enough and French society well enough that he knew how to shock and how to get publicity and, therefore, how to get more commissions. He died in 1926, the most famous American artist, with a show after his death at the Metropolitan Museum.

Now, the second of the formal portraits is by James Abbott McNeill Whistler. When you're in England, Whistler is considered to be an English painter, and when you're in the United States, Whistler is considered to be an American painter. Of course, Whistler was an American throughout his life, but like Sargent, spent almost no time in the United States, though he had American patrons. He was born in Saint Petersburg, Russia. His father worked for the railroad, worked for the czar and built railroads in Russia with his American expertise. Whistler was trained as an artist in Paris and lived mostly in London in his mature life but keeping an apartment in Paris.

This is a wonderful portrait, one of the great portraits of New York, and it represents one of the most important French art critics, whose name was Theodore Duret, who was one of the friends of the

Impressionists, a collector of Impressionism, one of the great art critics and art historians of his time, a bit of a dandy, as you can see. You can see how international this picture is because it was painted not in Paris, where Duret lived, but in London, where Whistler lived. So Duret makes a trip to the London studio on Tite Street, makes his pose in this glorious tuxedo with his hat. He's carrying the beautiful, sort of slightly frothy pink cape of a woman, an unseen woman, so we imagine him to be quite a successful rake. The portrait has a quality of international élan which is simply extraordinary and which only Whistler could capture at this period of time.

So, too, this—one of my favorite American landscapes, painted by John Henry Twachtman in 1885. It's a huge picture, a picture that is called in American art history a "tonal landscape" because it's not very concerned with color—the colors are all grayed—but it's concerned with tones of color. It has no figures. It's very large. It's very elegant. It looks almost Asian or Japanese, and its aesthetic comes from Japanese painting, screen painting, and Japanese prints. It was painted in a little village called Arques-la-Bataille, which is in the north of France near Dieppe. Again, we have an American in France painting, at the very highest level in the 1880s, a landscape of a kind of elegance and refinement and clarity of composition which is extraordinary. The Met also owns the small-scale study painted at the site, as well as the large picture painted in Paris in his studio.

Now, there were these people—a very interesting group of artists—called American Impressionists, and I just want to show you two paintings by the stars of that movement. This is by Childe Hassam, an artist who was born outside of Boston; trained in Boston; spent several years of his life in the late 1880s in Paris, where he learned the latest art trends; and came back to the United States. He's in Maine in the summer of 1890 visiting a friend named Celia Thaxter. He is in her kind of wild garden looking over Maine.

One sees that he has seen paintings by Monet and Pissarro, that his palette is very light and informal, that he paints with a kind of immediate application of paint very much like the Impressionists in France, and that there is a kind of optimistic ease and gentility about the painting which is remarkable, but the subject of it is American. It's the application of an idea of European art which is applied to the United States by an artist who was enormously sophisticated [and] went back and forth enough in his life that he was always sort of juiced up by the latest European painting. Of course, by the 1880s, there were major galleries of European art in New York. So if you worked in New York, you could go to the Duran-Ruel Gallery and see paintings by Monet and Renoir even as this picture was being painted in Maine in 1890 after Childe Hassam had returned from his first trip.

The second painting is by William Merritt Chase, who was an artist who painted a lot on Long Island at this placed called Shinnecock. This is a marvelous landscape which is called *At the Seaside*, painted about 1892. It's not very large because both of these pictures were painted out of doors—as the French say, *en plein air*—in front of the motif. What you do, rather than doing a little sketch in front of the motif, is you paint the whole painting in front of the motif, and you allow the light saturation and the brilliant light of a summer day to affect the way that you see all of nature. Here, one sees a group of women—mothers and children—on the beach at Shinnecock, and one can see that they have Asian umbrellas, umbrellas that come from Japan or were made in Europe or the United States to mimic Japanese umbrellas.

There is one European parasol in the front, this little white parasol in the front. They're wearing brilliant colors. This charming, little baby in pink is playing in the sand with her little pail of bright red. This sort of yellow, and red, and the blue of the sea with purples in it create a kind of chromatic dance on a summer day in Shinnecock, showing that Chase was every bit as good as Monet or Boudin in France and that he could do the same thing in the United States with an even added benefit of being more like the Japanese, with this Japanese influence more overt in his painting.

I want to end with a seascape which is one of the great paintings at the Met. It was painted by Winslow Homer, an artist who was a native American artist who went to England, went to Europe, for a while in his life but was essentially a pure American landscape painter. In 1898–99, he made a trip to the Bahamas, and he painted this picture called *The Gulf Stream* in 1899, a large landscape which is one of the most terrifying pictures of his career. It represents an Afro-Caribbean sailor who has been through a huge storm. His boat has been ravaged. He has lost his map, his mast, his sail, his navigating instruments. He's completely lost. He's in the middle of this vast storm, and he's surrounded by sharks whose fins come out of the water, and you can see blood all over the water. It's a painting of a kind of terrifying intensity, as the sea is not something benign but someplace terrifying. When he exhibited this picture in 1900, it so terrified the audience that it was suggested to him that he put in another boat so that we could think, as we looked at it, that this man would be rescued.

Lecture Twenty
20th-Century Art—Before World War II

Scope:

After the founding of the Museum of Modern Art in 1929, The Metropolitan Museum of Art collected mostly contemporary American art and waited for the works in the Museum of Modern Art to become sufficiently "old" enough to be transferred to its galleries (as stated in the Museum of Modern Art's charter). Because this rarely happened, The Metropolitan Museum of Art was forced to create its own Department of Contemporary Art in 1967, which was incorporated into the Department of 20th Century Art three years later; in 1987, the collection was given large galleries in the Lila Acheson Wallace Wing. The first of two lectures will deal with the superb holdings of painting, sculpture, and decorative arts from the first half of the century, including masterpieces by members of the European vanguard such as Picasso and Matisse, as well as major Americans like Charles Demuth and Georgia O'Keeffe. The lecture will also deal with the small but superb group of sculptures from the first half of the century as well as with the developing collection of early Modernist furniture and decorative arts. The culmination of the lecture will be the living room from Frank Lloyd Wright's Little House, which, though housed in the American Wing, is firmly a part of the museum's collection of 20th-century art.

Outline

I. The Metropolitan Museum of Art was always interested and active in dealing with contemporary art.

    A. The museum collected the work of living artists from the moment it was founded.

    B. Early in the 20th century, it received a fund specifically for buying American contemporary art.

    C. The museum was interested in the relationship between what people were making now and what people had made in the past.

D. In 1929, the Museum of Modern Art (along with the already-established Whitney Museum) took on responsibility for contemporary European and American art.

E. In 1946, the author Gertrude Stein willed her portrait made by Picasso to The Metropolitan Museum of Art because she did not want it to be seen only with 20th-century art.

F. With this and a collection gifted by Alfred Stieglitz, the museum decided to form the Department of 20th Century Art. The department does not differentiate from European and American artists because, in the view of the museum, they are of equal level and quality.

G. I am going to give two lectures on the Department of 20th Century Art, divided by the great war of the mid-20th century: World War II.

II. We are going to look in this lecture at works of art in the department made before World War II, starting with the work of Pablo Picasso.

A. *Harlequin* (1901) reflects many of the museum's drawings and prints that represent one of the characters of the *Commedia dell'arte*. If this painting was in the Museum of Modern Art instead of The Metropolitan Museum of Art, one would not think about the long history before it.

    1. The subject looks off to the left in a melancholic gesture; other works in the museum, whose subjects' heads are weighted down on their hands, clearly reflect this gesture.

    2. The picture asks questions of everything that had been done in old centuries by taking a stock figure and imbuing it with real concerns and tragic sadness.

B. Picasso's 1906 portrait of Gertrude Stein is one of the great portraits in the history of art.

    1. Stein has the quality of being self-absorbed and strong in a way that excludes the viewer.

    2. The painting was a confrontation of two of the most monumental egos of the 20th century.

    3. The influence of early Iberian sculpted heads, with their stylized facial features, is evident in Picasso's depiction of Stein.

4. Picasso was also influenced by Ingres's 1832 portrait of Louis François Bertin.

C. Later works by Picasso abound in the collection. There are certain pictures that fit in The Metropolitan Museum of Art better than they do at the Museum of Modern Art, such as *Girl Reading at a Table* (1934).

   1. The portrait has a sense of abstraction and compactness that reminds one of other representations of female muses in the museum's galleries.

   2. The picture has an Old Master quality, as if Picasso were remembering the art of the past.

   3. Florene Schoenborn, one of the great collectors of Modernist art, gave this piece to The Metropolitan Museum of Art instead of the Museum of Modern Art because she felt it reverberated throughout the centuries.

D. Henri Matisse was the great opposite of Picasso. He was the most important color painter in France after the Impressionists and Gauguin.

   1. He relaxes the lessons of Gauguin, making his paintings flatter and calmer.

   2. *Nasturtiums with the Painting "Dance"* (1912) is a painting about another Matisse painting from early 1909, *Dance (I)*, in the Museum of Modern Art.

   3. The second version of this painting is 1912's *Nasturtiums with "The Dance" (II)* in the Pushkin Museum in Moscow.

   4. These great works of art reverberate with other major works, just like Old Master paintings.

E. The most important Surrealist painter who took vision beyond the senses and painted what he dreamt or feared is Salvador Dalí. The quality of the bizarre in *The Accommodations of Desire* (1929) is seen in many points in the history of art.

F. One of the great things about going to the Department of 20th Century Art is that it makes one want to rush out and see pre-20th-century paintings that are in advance of these works.

III. The collection of 20th-century sculpture is equally important.

A. *Antigraceful* (1913; cast 1950–1951), by the Futurist sculptor Umberto Boccioni, is a portrait of the artist's mother.

    1. Futurists thought that all art before them had been obsessed with the past; they wanted to rearrange art and think about the future.

    2. The piece is a sort of four-dimensional object in which Boccioni sees his mother from various points of view; it looks like an African mask in motion.

B. Purity of form is reflected in *Bird in Space* (1923) by Constantin Brancusi.

    1. Cycladic sculptures were important to him.

    2. The museum's marble seated harp player and standing female figure are more typical of Cycladic art's absolute abstraction.

    3. *Bird in Space* is one of 18 bird forms in stone and bronze made throughout the 1920s; the forms are a representation not of a bird but of flight.

C. Gaston Lachaise's 1927 sculpture *Standing Woman (Elevation)* displays female proportions that one sees only in paintings by artists like Rubens and Titian. The notion of both the figure's enormous weight and its grace is something this sculpture conveys like no other sculpture in Western art.

IV. I want to turn to 20th-century paintings before World War II.

A. *The Figure 5 in Gold* (1928) by Charles Demuth is actually a portrait of William Carlos Williams. It is one of eight portraits which have no features of the individual but which accumulate qualities of that individual and embody them in paint.

B. Grant Wood's *The Midnight Ride of Paul Revere* (1931) comes from the Henry Wadsworth Longfellow poem, "The Midnight Ride of Paul Revere."

    1. The town is a generic American town and the rider is a generic rider, creating an American sense of identity.

    2. Wood thought more about early Italian painting than about contemporary art; thus, this work fits gloriously in the museum.

C. Georgia O'Keeffe's *Cow's Skull: Red, White, and Blue* (1931) is an image of America different from anything we have seen before.

D. Balthus's *The Mountain* (1936) reminds one of earlier depictions of the seasons by Millet and Bruegel; the artist's landscapes and figures have deep sources in the history of art.

V. I want to end with a look at the decorative arts during this period.

   A. A 1904 washstand by Charles Rennie Mackintosh is a modern piece, unrelated to the past and without ornamentation.

   B. Josef Hoffman's tea service from around 1910 is reduced to pure form.

   C. An armchair designed by Ludwig Mies van der Rohe in 1927 only has antecedents in the Bentwood furniture designed in Vienna and Paris in the 1890s and looks like nothing from the past.

   D. A room from Frank Lloyd Wright's Little House in Wayzata, Minnesota (1912–1914), makes one think of an ideal American place.

Recommended Reading:

Lieberman. *Painters in Paris: 1895–1950.*

Tinterow. *Modern Europe.*

Questions to Consider:

1. Why is the museum's collection of modern art so important?

2. Choose a work of modern art in the museum's collection and describe why it is important to you.

Lecture Twenty—Transcript
20th-Century Art—Before World War II

As we've seen in our lectures on American art, the Metropolitan Museum was always interested and active in dealing with contemporary art. When it was founded in 1870, it had artists on its board. It collected the work of living artists from the very moment that it started. Early in the 20th century, it actually received a fund specifically for buying American contemporary art. The idea of the museum as a repository of old art, which was the European idea of a museum, was from the very beginning of the Metropolitan Museum, not believed, not accepted as an idea. The museum was interested in the relationship between what people were making now and what people had made in the past and [in] making a kind of family museum in which the past and the present spoke to each other in an always shifting kind of dialogue.

As the Met grew, it began to establish more and more, and buy more and more, works of artists who were alive or just recently dead. It bought works that were sometimes made the year before, or even the year of, their purchase. As the 20th century went on, it [the Met] began to have more and more works of art from the 20th century. Now, what happens in New York, of course, is that in 1929, there's this creation of a new museum called the Museum of Modern Art. That museum took on the responsibility for contemporary European and American art. Already, there was a museum of American contemporary art, started by Gertrude Vanderbilt Whitney, that's now called the Whitney Museum, so the Met's mandate to collect contemporary art was not so great.

But what happened in 1946 was an extraordinary event which made the Met rethink its whole commitment to the 20th century, to the art of the century in which it was then living in 1946. And that [event was the death of] Gertrude Stein, the great American writer who was an expatriate for most of her life; who'd lived virtually all of her life in France and in Paris; and who'd made all these extraordinary trips to the United States, where she lectured in Amarillo, and San Francisco, and Chicago, and sort of shocked and amazed Americans, and was a kind of star of the avant-garde. When she died, in her will, the great Picasso portrait of her—one of the most important paintings of the 20th century—was willed to the Metropolitan Museum.

Now, why did she do that? She did it because she didn't want her works of art, her great portrait, to be seen only with 20th-century art. She thought that it was a great work of art, and she wanted it to be in the greatest museum of her own country, which was the Metropolitan Museum. She wanted it to be seen with works of Roman sculpture, and with Bronzino, and with Rembrandt, and with the works through the ages. And so the gift of this work of art was shocking to the Museum of Modern Art, which would have killed to have had it in 1946, and it galvanized the Met into thinking about the 20th century. The 20th-Century Department was created much later, but curators began gradually to think about the 20th century as a department of its own, and finally, after World War II, and after that gift, and after the gift of Miss O'Keeffe—Georgia O'Keeffe's husband, Stieglitz, died in 1949, and his collection, or a part of his collection—came to the Met.

Suddenly, the Met had all of these 20th-century things, both European and American. It decided to form a Department of 20th-Century Art and to put these collections, think about these collections, in a concerted way. What's interesting about the Department of 20th-Century Art is that there is no differentiation of Europe and America. Both European artists and American artists are in the 20th-Century Department because, in the view of the museum, they're of equal level and equal quality. I'm going to do two lectures on the 20th-Century Department, and they're going to be divided by the great war of the mid-20th century, like the great war of the mid-19th century which divides America, and that's, of course, World War II. We're going to look in this lecture at works of art in the Metropolitan Museum's 20th-Century Department made before World War II.

We're going to start with a Picasso made in 1901, just one year after the turn of the century, a work of art of extraordinary quality, which came from the Loeb collection and which was given to the Met in 1960 at the death of Mr. Loeb. One sees here a *Harlequin*. We've seen many characters from the *Commedia dell'arte*, that Italian group of popular comics. We've seen paintings by Tiepolo's son, by Watteau. If you go through the museum, you can actually see many paintings, and many drawings, and many prints—no sculpture that I know—that represent one of the characters of the *Commedia dell'arte*, so immediately when you see this painting in the Met, if it was in the Modern, you wouldn't think about that long history before it, but at the Met, you do.

Now, the harlequin is a clown and a sad clown. We see him here in 1901. He's obviously in a café in Paris because Picasso, the great Spanish artist, was already living in Paris. He moved to Paris in 1899, and he was becoming one of the major figures of the avant-garde. One sees this sad clown with a sort of white face. He's obviously made up. Picasso makes that clear by making his hands flesh-colored and his face white. So we see he's made up, and he's in character, but he's not on stage. He's kind of unwinding from his time on stage. He's looking off very purposely to the left in a gesture that has to do with melancholia. If you go through the galleries at the Met and you look at Dürer's print of *Melencolia,* and if you see single figures whose hands are on their heads, and whose heads are weighted down on their hands—there's a sense of the weight that they carry in their heads and the fact that their hands need to transfer that weight—you see that very clearly.

The flowers in the background seem to come out of Van Gogh, and there is a sense [of] Van Gogh, who died almost literally 10 years before this picture was painted. One sort of sees Picasso thinking about the sort of whole history of entertainment, of the sadness of the clown. He plays upon it. The harlequin is generally dressed in black and red, and here, he is in blue and black. Black and blue in French means the same thing as it does in English. It means a bruise or beaten black and blue. So the meaning of the colors shifts from the traditional meaning of the harlequin, and [his costume has] squares upon squares rather than diamonds within diamonds, the traditional costume. Of course, the clown is young, and in costume, and sad. We have no idea who he is or what he's thinking about. The picture seems to start a new century by asking questions of everything that had been done in old centuries, by taking a stock figure who had always been amusing—or even if sad, charmingly sad—and here one feels that this is a real person in a real café, with real concerns. We think about the suicide of Van Gogh. We have the sort of sense that the sadness is tragic sadness, not ordinary sadness.

Now, if we turn to the next work of art, it is, of course, the portrait by Picasso—of course, the very same artist and the great artist—of Gertrude Stein. This is a fabled portrait; I mean, one of the great portraits in the history of art. Of course, you see its accession number, 1947.106, because it didn't get to the Met—her will is 1946; she gives it in [19]46, but it doesn't get to the museum until [19]47, and so you don't accession something until 1947. Then you see this extraordinary woman. She's not looking at us; she's looking off to the side. She is very mannish. She has the sort of quality of being extremely self-absorbed and very strong and strong in a way that excludes the viewer. It's as if we don't exist. It's as if we're not necessary.

Of course, the stories of this portrait are legendary. Here's this arrogant, young, amazing artist and an equally arrogant, not-so-young American writer, both living in Paris, each thinking that they're going to use each other to get someplace. Gertrude Stein goes to sit for Picasso, and they sort of stare into each other's eyes. Gertrude Stein herself records that there were 90 sittings for the portrait, and that Picasso could never get it, and she didn't like it, and he didn't like it. It was a kind of confrontation of two monumental egos, two of the most monumental egos of the 20th century. And so Picasso, in frustration, goes off to his summer vacation in Spain and takes the portrait with him and, as he told her later, painted it from memory.

But, of course, what he'd seen and what he was thinking about in the meantime were early Iberian heads—heads of the ancient peoples of Iberia, which were being discovered at this period of time—and African sculpture. If you remember the lecture on African sculpture, and the sort of stylization of the nose and the eyes and the mouth, and the sense of masks, of the face being a mask, you can see very clearly that this is what Picasso was thinking about. He repainted, as he said to her, from memory, brought it back, and the famous story, probably apocryphal, is that she, and many people, said about the painting that it doesn't look like her. Picasso's famous apocryphal reply was, "It will."

Of course, now it is her; it is her in the Met. We think of [Stein] probably [as] the greatest American collector of European vanguard art in the first three decades of the 20th century, and she exists in the Met. The Met, therefore, because of this picture, had to form a collection that was worthy of it, and it did. One can see here—this is a portrait in the Louvre of *Monsieur Bertin*, the most famous Ingres portrait—one can see very clearly that Picasso knew this portrait quite well and that he sort of infected the portrait of Gertrude Stein with the greatest male portrait by Ingres, who was probably the greatest portrait painter of the 19th century, of the century preceding him [Picasso].

Now, later works by Picasso abound in the collection. The collection is not so great as the Picasso collection at the [Museum of Modern Art], but it has its own byways. And because it's in a general art museum, there are certain kinds of pictures that fit in it better than fit at the Museum of Modern Art. So you can go from the galleries of the 20th century, and go into the rest of the museum, and explore pictures that look like pictures of the 20th century. This is a 1934 Picasso called *Girl Reading at a Table*, but of course, it's not just a girl reading at a table; it's a muse whose head is adorned with flowers. It's night; there's this strange lamp and this wonderful plant on the side. She's involved in reading at the table. We see her body and her orange dress. There's a sense of abstraction and compactness about this portrait, and it's something that makes you go into the galleries and look at other representations of muses, of female muses, whether they be by Manet, whether they be by Corot, whether they be by Rembrandt.

The picture, which is dark for a Picasso—and which has a kind of Old Master quality; it's as if he's remembering art of the past—makes perfect sense in the Metropolitan Museum rather than the Museum of Modern Art. [I]t was given by Florene Schoenborn, one of the great collectors of Modernist art, in honor of William Lieberman, who was one of the most important curators of the 20th-Century Department. Florene Schoenborn knew, from her apartment on Fifth Avenue, just what was in the Met and just what was in [The Museum of Modern Art], and so the Modernist pictures, the pictures that didn't have reverberations through the centuries, went to [The Museum of Modern Art], and the pictures that did have reverberations throughout the centuries, like this one, went to the Met.

Now, the great opposite of Picasso was, of course, Matisse, the colorist whose family was—he came from a textile family, an upper-middle-class family, very well-educated, very thoughtful man. He was supposed to become a lawyer, like many artists, and he gradually became an artist. He worked with Rouault in Paris; he had lunch with Pissarro in the early years of the 20th century. He becomes an artist who becomes the most important color painter in France after the Impressionists and Gauguin. He takes a lot of the lessons of Gauguin, but he relaxes Gauguin. He makes the painting flatter, calmer. He makes the energies different than those sort of compacted pictures of Gauguin. One sees here a painting that came to the Metropolitan Museum from the bequest of Scofield Thayer, a great avant-gardist, in 1982. Scofield Thayer was the publisher of *The Dial*, the literary magazine in London that published Pound and Joyce and Yeats and all the great Modernists and was himself one of the great Modernists.

This beautiful painting, called *Nasturtiums with the Painting "Dance"* from 1912, came to the Met in 1982. What's riveting about it is that in it, he [Matisse] is painting a painting. It's a painting about painting. In his studio, he has been working on the painting *La Danse*, and of course, the painting *La Danse* is in the Museum of Modern Art. Here, we see the whole painting of *La Danse*. And so one can go down Fifth Avenue to 53rd Street and turn right, and go into the Museum of Modern Art, and see the big painting, which is in the background in the painting in the Metropolitan Museum. In the Metropolitan Museum, it becomes a painting about painting, and that's another theme in the Met. You can go through the Met and see hundreds of paintings with other paintings in them.

Now, the most important Surrealist painter, the painter who sort of took vision beyond the senses and didn't paint what he saw but what he dreamt or what he feared, is Salvador Dali, the Spanish painter Salvador Dali. The Met has one of the most important paintings by Salvador Dali, from 1929, but it's absolutely tiny. It's 8 ¾ by 13 ¾ inches, this big. It compresses onto one surface all of his neuroses and desires; it's called *The Accommodations of Desire*, painted in 1929. We see his wife, Gala, whose back he adored, and his hands— they're obviously Dali's hands—caress her back. We see these pebbles, which they saw in a walk on the beach that they took in Spain. They looked at these rocks on the beach, and each of them seemed to erupt with a lion who has a whole face, or is red, or is faceless, or has only a mouth, or which bursts open with ants pouring out of them. The quality of the neurotic, of the sort of strange and bizarre, is also a whole strand in the history of art. It's not just a strand of Surrealism, but we see it in many points in the history of art. One of the great things about going to the 20th-Century

Department is it makes you want to rush out and see pre-20th-century paintings that are in advance of these things.

Now, the sculpture is equally important to the paintings. Again, you look at works of art differently in the Met than you do at [The Museum of Modern Art]. This is by Umberto Boccioni, the great Futurist sculptor. It is a portrait of his mom. Boccioni was a mama's boy, and he was a Futurist. The Futurists themselves thought that all art before them had thought about nothing but the past, and had been trying to deal with the past, and memorialize the past, and be greater than the past. They wanted to rearrange art and think about the future, think about how things could look in the future. They were like Futurama in the World's Fair. It's the sense of forward looking rather than backward looking, competing with dreams rather than competing with the accomplishments of the past.

So he [Boccioni] makes Mom, and he makes her in plaster in 1913. Of course, though he has plenty of money, he's working too quickly and he's too busy with things to actually get it cast into bronze, and he's killed in the First World War in 1916. These objects weren't cast until the 1950s. So the Met has this bronze sculpture of his mother, which looks like she's sort of morphing into another dimension. It's a kind of four-dimensional object in which he has seen her from various points of view, and thought about her, and thought about his dreams and memories of her, and made her come from the 19th century, when she was born, into the 20th century in this sort of bizarre way. It's as if this is an African mask in motion. It's as if somehow she has become part of a new tribe. It's a work of art of incredible quality, which came to the Met from the great Surrealist collector from Detroit, Lydia Winston Malbin, in 1989.

Now, if one thinks about purity of form—and we've talked about purity of form in several cultural contexts in the Met—one lands in the 20th century on the great Romanian sculptor who worked most of his life in France, Constantin Brancusi, who was Brâncuşi in Romanian. This is *A Bird in Space* from 1923, which came also from Florene Schoenborn after her death in 1995. It's a pure form. One of the cultures that was most important to the Romanian sculptor Brancusi when he learned to remake sculpture—when he was trying to take sculpture back to the essence, to the very beginning—is, of course, the sculpture of the earliest peoples of the Mediterranean, who were Cycladic peoples.

We've seen already the great harp player in the first lecture after the introductory lecture, the lecture on Greco-Roman art, with its pure surfaces of marble and its sort of sense that forms can be abstracted to an extraordinary degree. We can look at another object in the Met's collection, the standing female figure, more typical of Cycladic art, in which there's the sense of absolute abstraction, in which every element of the human body is made abstract. And then we return to this bird form, and it's one of 18 bird forms in stone and in bronze made throughout the [19]20s by Brancusi, which is not really a representation of a bird but a representation of flight itself.

The last of the sculptures I'm going to be looking at now is by a French-born sculptor named Gaston Lachaise, who fell in love with a Canadian woman in France, and he followed her to the United States. Her name was Isabel Nagle, and she was 10 years older than he was. He was born in 1882, and she was born 10 years earlier in 1872. She had this sort of glorious—she was a full-figured gal with very beautiful legs, and he adored her. She was already married, and he didn't care. He follows her back to the United States. He was obsessed with her. Finally, she leaves her husband, and finally, they get married, and she becomes his muse. In 1912, he began to do a plaster of her, which was of a kind of proportion of a woman that we really only see in paintings by artists like Rubens and Titian.

We very rarely see women like this in sculpture, and we almost never see them with all of their weight and all of their elegance resting on the balls of their feet. The notion of her being [both] enormously heavy and light and graceful at the same time is something that this sculpture conveys like no other sculpture in Western art. He worked on it in plaster between 1912 and 1918, when he finally achieved the sort of perfection of form he wanted, but he didn't have enough money to cast it into bronze, and so Scofield Thayer—the guy who gave the Matisse—gave him the money to cast it into bronze in 1927. The Met has this cast made during his lifetime—cast by Gaston Lachaise—of this extraordinary woman. When you see her, you feel good about weight. You feel good about people. You feel good about yourself. You feel that this kind of relationship between motion and stasis, between lightness and weight, is perfectly equilibrated in Gaston Lachaise's object.

Now, I want to turn to paintings, and I'm going to turn to a wonderful painting, one of my favorite paintings in the Met, which is

The Figure 5 in Gold, painted in 1928 by the American artist Charles Demuth. Charles Demuth was part of a New York-based group of artists who exhibited with the great photographer Stieglitz, whom we've talked about in earlier lectures. Stieglitz was married to Georgia O'Keeffe, and when O'Keeffe died, she gave this painting, her favorite Demuth, to the Met. *The Figure 5 in Gold* is actually, if you can believe it, a portrait, and it's a portrait of William Carlos Willliams, the poet. It's one of eight portraits which have no features of the individual but which accumulate qualities of that individual and embody them in paint.

In fact, William Carlos Williams, whose initials appear at the bottom of the painting, right in the center—and the initials of the artist, CD, over here—had written poetry already about a fire engine that he'd seen when he was a child with the number 5 on it. That image in William Carlos Williams's poetry was so powerful to Demuth that he made a portrait of him. William, of course, is *Bill*, and you'll look and you'll find *Carlos* if you look carefully. You'll see all of these little clues to the nature and identity of a man, and you will never see his eyes; you'll never see his hair; you'll never see his nose; you'll never see his face, but it is William Carlos Williams.

Or this: Grant Wood's masterful *The Midnight Ride of Paul Revere*, which was painted in 1931 and which was bought by that fund, the Hearn Fund, to buy contemporary art. It was bought in 1950, and it was no longer contemporary because it was already 19 years old, but it was definitely bought. Here, one sees Paul Revere tootling along the road, and of course, this comes from another poem, by Longfellow, "The Midnight Ride of Paul Revere": "Listen my children, and you shall hear of the midnight ride of Paul Revere."

When you read the poem—and when I was preparing the lecture, I read the entire poem, which I hadn't done since I was a child—what you learn is that this painting isn't taken exactly from the poem because none of the clues that are in the poem to the towns that he rode through as he was saying, "The British are coming, the British are coming" are this town. This town becomes a generic American town, and the rider becomes a rider that is going through America, creating a sort of sense of its own national identity, in a painting with a bird's eye view, with an artist who thought much more about early Italian painting and so-called primitive Italian painting, like many that we've seen in this course, than about contemporary art. And so this painting, too, fits gloriously into the Met.

Or [we see] O'Keeffe's masterpiece from 1931. She was 44 years old when she went to New Mexico. She didn't go with Stieglitz; she went on her own. She went in 1929. She adored it. She went back virtually every year for the rest of her life; she died there. She was the longest-living of the great women American artists. This is one of the iconic masterpieces of her career, painted not in New Mexico but in her studio on Lake George in upstate New York, where she summered sometimes with Stieglitz. She brought back the bleached bones from New Mexico of a great horned cow. She puts them in front of a sort of fabric, which seems to part for it, which she makes into a kind of rhythmic rhyme for the rhythms of the skull itself. [We see] this great black cross or stick, which it seems to be bolted on, and then these brilliant red stripes on the side. This is an image of America, but it's an image of America that is very different than anything that we've seen before, something that sticks in our minds and makes us think.

Or this is a great work of art, which is the largest painting by a major Franco-Polish artist, who was called Balthus. He called himself Balthus, and his real name was Klossowski de Rola, Balthus Klossowski de Rola. His father was a Polish art historian, and his mother was French. He was born in France. He was a great eccentric. He married aristocrats. He lived in a castle. He was a kind of anti-20th-century artist. This, his largest painting, which was bought by the Met in 1982, was to be one of four paintings that represent the four seasons. That immediately clues us in to the Millet autumn picture of the four seasons that we saw when we did the 19th-century European lecture or to the great painting by Bruegel of the summer, which represents all of the harvest seasons in the summer and relates to the painting in Vienna.

This is also summer. It's a picture called *Summer*, but it's a summer picture filled with kinds of anxieties that are only felt in the 20th century. We have various couples in it; a woman, a young woman, stretching; a young man, tired; a woman sleeping inexplicably by herself; another young man having an identity crisis in the corner; a couple on the side seeming as if they're about to leap to their deaths in the great cliff-like landscape. It's a picture that makes you think, why are they there, and what are they doing, and where did the figures come from? Of course, Balthus knew the history of art cold; he knew the Louvre cold. His landscapes and figures all have deep sources in the history of art, and this painting reverberates throughout the Metropolitan Museum for that reason.

I want to end with the decorative arts, which are so extraordinarily well represented at the Met. There are major works by most of the great architects and great designers of ceramics, and silver, and furniture. You can see chairs by Mies van der Rohe, wash stands by Charles Rennie Mackintosh, and tea sets by Josef Hoffmann. But the one work of art that is undoubtedly the masterpiece—the most important work of art from the first half of the 20th century in the decorative arts—is a period room. For that reason it's not in the 20th Century department but in the American Wing. It is worth going to simply to stand in it. It is the living room of the Little house in Wayzata, Minnesota. Wayzata is a suburb of Minneapolis, and the Littles were a family of some means who commissioned Frank Lloyd Wright in 1912 at the height of his fame to do a rather large house for them. When the parents died and the children didn't want the house the Met was able to acquire the furnishings, the windows, the stained glass, the light fixtures, the rugs, everything from this room, all of which was designed by Frank Lloyd Wright in 1912 as a total work of art.

It's a room which is deeply American. Frank Lloyd Wright was born in Wisconsin. He was middle-aged practically before he went to Europe. He had a sense that if America was going to be great, it had to invent its own forms, and had to find those form in the earth. The style he created was called "the prairie style": long horizontal lines; a sense of being attached to nature; these huge walls of glass on both sides that look out to rather fierce winters in Wayzata as well as beautiful hot summers. [There is] a wonderful hearth, the furniture was designed by him, the windows were designed by him, the lamps were designed by him. As you can see the family couldn't be [art collectors], but it could have a sense in its American-ness of European roots. That sense is made very clear by the *Nike of Samothrace*, the cast of which is on the little writing desk in the back. There is no finer prairie-style room outside of the Midwest than the Little house living room in the Metropolitan Museum. It reminds us when we visit the great city of New York that its not just New York that's great, but America that's great.

Lecture Twenty-One
20th-Century Art—After World War II

Scope:

In 1969, The Metropolitan Museum of Art's "New York Painting and Sculpture: 1940–1970" exhibition marked the first time in which a great art museum took down its crown jewels of painting to display contemporary art. After the exhibition, The Metropolitan Museum of Art's holdings increased extraordinarily. The museum's collections from the second half of the 20th century are particularly strong in the work of the so-called New York School of abstract painters, who came to dominate world art in the 1940s. The museum owns major works by members of this informal group, including Jackson Pollock, Mark Rothko, and Willem de Kooning. Since the 1960s, The Metropolitan Museum of Art has been committed to exhibitions of recent art; thus, the collection contains major holdings in other regional trends in the history of art (such as Pop art, Op art, and Postmodern art). Over time, The Metropolitan Museum of Art's collection has become more eclectic and more publicly accessible than the canonical collection of post-World War II art at the Museum of Modern Art.

Outline

I. In 1969, The Metropolitan Museum of Art held an exhibition titled "New York Painting and Sculpture: 1940–1970."

   A. The exhibit was curated by Henry Geldzahler, the curator of the Department of 20th-Century Art.

   B. He took down all the European paintings in the galleries and replaced them with works by artists who painted in New York, most of whom were still alive.

   C. The exhibition marked the first time in which a great art museum had taken down its crown jewels to put up contemporary art.

   D. The point of the exhibition was that New York City was now the art capital of the world. After 1969, the holdings of The Metropolitan Museum of Art increased extraordinarily as the world after World War II became as important as the ancient world.

II. We are now going to be dealing with the collection of art in the Department of 20th-Century Art made after World War II.

    A. Some of the most powerful works of art made in the late 1940s were made by European artists who had lived through the war.

    B. Alberto Giacometti was a Swiss artist who worked in France. *Three Men Walking (II)*, made in 1949, is a sculpture that raises questions being asked by the most profound writers and philosophers after the war (e.g., Jean-Paul Sartre and Samuel Beckett). The three skeletal figures reflect the combinative power of despair and hope that one felt so strongly after World War II.

    C. The German artist Max Beckmann lived out the war in Amsterdam. During that time, he began to make a series of triptychs, one of which is *Beginning* (1949).

        1. We see a series of deeply disturbed childhood memories affected by psychoanalysis and all the pressures upon modern life that both world wars placed upon Beckmann.

        2. Beckman is the subject of the triptych, and there is an attempt at a heroic escape from this flawed childhood and an attempt to tell viewers about the problems of living after World War II.

    D. When one looks at *Three Men Walking (II)* and *Beginning*, one is reminded of the African and Oceanic art galleries and the galleries of early Christian art, respectively. One thinks about religion and modernity when looking at these supremely difficult works of art.

III. We are now going to look at a sequence of major masterpieces of American postwar painting made by artists who worked in New York.

    A. Clyfford Still's *1947-8-W-No.1 (PH-114)*, made in 1947, is a canvas that has been attacked with paint by an artist interested in the battles of colors (in this case, the battle between black and white). There is the sense that one is watching a drama with as much emotional intensity as any work but without a particular subject.

B. Many artists who became major members of the avant-garde in New York in the late 1940s and early 1950s were immigrants.

    1. Willem de Kooning was Dutch and became a major force in American painting by the late 1930s.

    2. *Attic* (1949) has a double meaning: the attic of a house and Attic in the sense of being from the Mediterranean.

    3. What de Kooning was interested in was the pictorial representation of energy, which can be seen in both The Portonaccio Sarcophagus and Poussin's *The Abduction of the Sabine Women.*

C. Jackson Pollock's *Autumn Rhythm (Number 30)* from 1950 is another work of art about sheer pictorial energy.

    1. Pollock did not paint on an easel but dripped paint onto a canvas on the floor; he did this so often and with such skill that he became a great master of calligraphic painting.

    2. The Metropolitan Museum of Art has huge holdings of calligraphic painting.

D. Mark Rothko was one of the great colorists who reinvented color painting. *No. 13 (White, Red on Yellow)*, made in 1958, was given to the museum by his estate in recognition of the great 1969 exhibition.

    1. The piece is much more complicated that one first thinks.

    2. The work is so reduced that it washes away centuries of old color painting.

E. If Rothko's paintings are about subtlety, Ellsworth Kelly's paintings are hard and strong. *Blue Green Red* (1962–1963) looks as if it was made by a machine, even though it was painstakingly made by hand.

F. Roy Lichtenstein's *Stepping Out* (1978) illustrates the lack of constraints on artistic freedoms.

    1. The female figure is a Cubist play on Marilyn Monroe, and the male figure reflects figures in works by the French painter Fernand Léger (such as 1944's *The Three Musicians*).

2. One sees the interplay between New York and France and between 1940s art and 1970s art.

G. There is no modern artist more about New York City than Andy Warhol, who observed the city as only an outsider can.

    1. He understood the importance of photography and the power of the image.

    2. In *Self-Portrait* (1986), he wears a wig and prints camouflage on the back of the image (referencing another artistic product that has to do with war).

H. James Rosenquist's *House of Fire* (1981) is a Surrealist painting of different consumer goods. The work is about advertising and is painted with an airbrush, as if Rosenquist were painting a billboard.

I. In 1969, The Metropolitan Museum of Art held an exhibition called "Harlem On My Mind," curated by sociologist Allon Schoener.

    1. The exhibit stressed the importance of one of the most thriving urban aesthetic laboratories in the world.

    2. Romare Bearden's *The Block* (1971) is a series of six panels that re-creates the urban life of Harlem.

J. Red Grooms's *Chance Encounter at 3 A.M.* (1984) reflects how important New York City is for the arts.

Recommended Reading:

Lieberman, Messinger, Rewald, and Sims. *20th Century Art Painting 1945–85: Selections from the Collection of the Metropolitan Museum of Art.*

Miller. *Modern Design in the Metropolitan Museum of Art, 1890–1990.*

Questions to Consider:

1. Describe some works in the museum that belong to the New York School. What makes them part of that school?

2. Who is your favorite post-World War II artist represented at the museum and what appeals to you most about his or her stylistic approach?

Lecture Twenty-One—Transcript
20th-Century Art—After World War II

I'll never forget that in 1969, when I was a junior at Yale, I made a trip to New York, and there was this extraordinary exhibition which had been reviewed all over the country. It was called, "New York Painting, 1940 to 1970." It seemed odd to me that the exhibition was in 1969 but the exhibition ended in 1970, but that's academic. It was at the Metropolitan Museum. It was curated by this young man, the curator of the new department, only two years old—the Department of 20th-Century Art at the Met, and his name was Henry Geldzahler. He was only 33 years old. I was only 20, and it was an exhibition that took on the subject of painting in New York essentially since the war. There were a few paintings done during World War II, but most of them were done after the war. What he had done was something extraordinary. He had taken down all of the European paintings. Remember those four lectures on European paintings. They were all gone. All the galleries were not deep red, gold, plum, brandy, and green. They were white, and they were replaced—all the Van Eyck's, Rubens's, Raphael's, Watteau's, and David's were replaced by works by artists who painted in New York and had painted in New York. Most of them were still alive, and it was the first time I think probably in human history in which a great art museum, a museum like the Louvre, the Hermitage, or the Kunsthistorisches Museum, had taken down their crown jewels and put up contemporary art.

The point of the exhibition was that New York now was the art capital of the world—that its painting was the most serious, the most important, the most internationally interesting, the most bracing painting being done anywhere—that Paris, of course, was a has-been, that Europe was a has-been, and where it was, where it was happening, was New York. Now, Geldzahler was a showman. He was a man who realized that a big gesture could make a big difference, and a big difference indeed it made, because after 1969, the holdings of the Metropolitan Museum in New York–school painting increased extraordinarily in the sense that the world after World War II was as important in the museum as the Old World or as the ancient world. That was made all the clearer by this exhibition.

What I want to do is to sort of share a little of the excitement of that exhibition and another exhibition from the same year that I'll tell you about a little bit later and show you the effect of temporary exhibitions and curatorial chutzpah on the way that a whole institution works. We're going to be dealing now with the collection of art in the 20th-Century Department made after World War II. Now, the earliest works that we're going to be looking at are European, and I want to make it very clear that the collection of the Metropolitan Museum is both European and American in the 20th-Century Department and that some of the most powerful works of art made in the late [19]40s were made by European artists who had lived through the war, who had thought about [and] had experienced the horrors of the war like American GIs, but unlike the American population as a whole except through films, and newsreels, and whatever.

I'm going to turn first to a sculpture by Alberto Giacometti, who was a Swiss artist who worked in France. Of course, when the war came, not being a fool, he went back to Switzerland and lived out the war in Geneva, but he was deeply affected by the war and the whole sense that the war had changed the way that people interacted with each other and the whole idea of a human person. What is an individual? What have we been reduced to by the war? The Met has this marvelous sculpture called *Three Men Walking*, made in 1949—the year I was born, so therefore, I am attracted to things made in 1949. This is a sculpture of three identically scaled men who are almost skeletal. They are thin. There is very little left of them. It's almost as if they've been desiccated by the war. It's almost as if they survived furnaces—that they walked out still alive from the horrors of the war. They are at once together and alone. We imagine them walking down a street or walking in a square. Their feet, their enormous feet, are attached to the bronze base underneath them. It's almost as if they can't move. It's almost as if they're stuck in the earth, but they're obviously walking. This is after the war, and they're walking. They're very close to each other, and we want to know: Will they touch? Will they get by each other? Who will run into whom? What is the meaning of these three figures? Are they men or women? What gender are they? The sculpture raises all sorts of questions, which were questions that were asked by the most profound writers and philosophers after the war, many of whom were friends of Alberto Giacometti.

In fact, Giacometti had a great exhibition in New York in the late 1940s, and the catalog of the exhibition, the essay for the catalog of the exhibition, was written by Jean Paul Sartre of *Being and Nothingness*, a philosopher who rethought philosophy after World War II, just as Giacometti rethought sculpture after World War II. Another of his greatest friends was the great Irish playwright Samuel Beckett, and you can imagine Beckett writing a play about these three desiccated figures who are stuck to the earth and who can't communicate with each other. Such is the sort of combinative power of despair mixed with a little bit of hope that one felt so strongly after World War II.

Now, the second object I want to discuss was also finished in 1949—not made completely in 1949—and it's made by the great German artist Max Beckman. Max Beckman was already elderly in the war. He was born in 1884, and he was so traumatized, being a German, during the war that he spent the war in Amsterdam. He lived out the war in Amsterdam, and during that period of time, he began to make a series of triptychs. Of course, triptychs are not modern at all. We've looked at altarpieces, triptychs, diptychs, and works of art that were made to be worshipped. They are works of art that have a kind of reverberance throughout the history of art and are very important for the history of art. This is a triptych that was begun in Amsterdam in the mid-[19]40s. He [Beckman] came to the United States—he came actually to Saint Louis—under the patronage of the May family and finished this triptych in the United States in 1949. It's a triptych called *Beginning*. It's the eighth of his 10 triptychs. It's monumental, and it's all about his own childhood.

On the left, one sees him as a sort of little boy wearing a crown and a cape and looking at the window. One sees an organ grinder and a whole series of figures out of this window that seems like a cross—seems like something that is portending a terrible future. On the right, one sees a whole series of little boys in a classroom with a globe, and a bust of an important person, and a picture on the wall. The little boys are all supposed to behave, and they're being told what to do by a teacher in a way that seems also portentous and grave. In the center, one has the little boy, and one presumes the little boy is Beckman himself, riding a hobbyhorse or a rocking horse with a kind of military gusto, with his sword, his pink suit, his cape in the side. There is this sense that he is riding into the distance. But, of course, he is on a hobbyhorse, and he is riding nowhere. There is a clown-like authority figure in the door [and] a woman down below, who is, of course, much too old for him to desire but is obviously a desirable woman. We are looking at a kind of series of memories of childhood that are deeply disturbed, that are affected by psychoanalysis, affected by the war, affected by all of the pressures upon modern life that both the First and the Second World Wars had placed upon Beckman himself and in which he places—he sort of excoriates those forces in his life by painting them as triptychs. He is the subject of the triptych, and there is a kind of attempt at a heroic escape from this flawed childhood and an attempt to tell all of us who are viewers about the problems of being a person after World War II.

Now, these two works are not fun, and each of them has an enormous depth of time. When you look at each of them in the Metropolitan Museum—again, you long to go into the galleries and look at other thin sculptures. You want to go into the African galleries and the galleries of Oceanic art when you look at the Giacometti, and you want to go into the galleries of early Christian art and religious art when you look at the Beckman. You're thinking about religion and modernity when you look at these supremely difficult works of art.

Now, works of art of that type were not in Geldzahler's exhibition because they weren't made in New York. One of them was made in Amsterdam and Saint Louis, and the other one was made in Paris. But we're now going to look at a sequence of major masterpieces of American postwar painting made by artists who did work in New York.

This is a painting by Clyfford Still. It's an enormous painting, very tall. It dominates you. You would have to be an NBA player to be taller than it. It's a work of art that seems to rise up above you. It was painted in 1947–1948, and Clyfford Still is a fascinating artist. He was born in the Dakotas, so therefore, he is not a New Yorker. Like many people from the provinces who gravitate to New York, he clearly didn't feel at home where he was born. He needed to express himself someplace else, and this work of art called *W Number 1, PH-114*, which means photograph 114, is a work of art that is really about nothing except the enterprise of painting on a canvas. It has no subject. Its subject is not even a geometric. It's not like Mondrian.

It's not like any great artist who had worked to clarify painting by reducing it to rectangles, squares, and diamonds. It is a canvas that has been attacked with paint by an artist who is interested in the battle of colors, in this case, the battle of black and white, with white coming in at the edges [and] infiltrating the black. The black infiltrates the white. There is no sense of what is a figure and what is the ground. Sometimes the black wins. Sometimes the white wins. Sometimes the white is a shape. Sometime the black is a shape, and then the black is itself infected with all sorts of forms. You see lots of little touches of red and blue, a little bit of white here, dark red down at the base, and there is a sense that you're watching a kind of battle or drama that is occurring which has as much emotional intensity as any work of art ever made but which has no subject. So it's a work of art that has an enormous reverberance throughout the history of art but no clear precedents. What it is trying to do many works of art have already succeeded in doing, but it's doing it in a wholly new way.

Now, many of the artists who became major members of the avant-garde in New York in the late [19]40s and early [19]50s were not Americans. They were immigrants, and we are, of course, a nation of immigrants. We've seen in the last lecture and in the lecture about American artists how much the Atlantic Ocean is a kind of semi-permeable membrane in which we keep going back and forth each way between Europe and America.

We have here an artist named Willem de Kooning who was Dutch. He was born in Rotterdam in 1904. He comes to the United States in the [19]30s. He becomes a sort of major force in American painting by the late [19]30s. He is deeply attached to New York. He becomes a New Yorker as only an immigrant can, and in 1949, he paints this painting called *Attic*. *Attic* in this sense has a double sense. It's both the attic of a house, and it's Attic in the sense of being "of the Mediterranean." So it's Attic, [meaning] "Greek," and attic in the house—these double senses. We see this kind of concatenation of forms, and here, there [are] figure and ground. But figure and ground seem to be ceaselessly battling each other on one surface. The color white predominates; there are lines which move through the painting and which define forms that look like heads, and spears, and various and sundry other things. We can't quite make out anything, and just when we think we have a figure, we don't have a figure. It disappears into paint, and the black lines and the white forms merge with each other in a kind of ineluctable energy source. The act of looking at this picture is deeply satisfying pictorially but not deeply satisfying if you want it to represent something. Of course, what de Kooning was interested in was the pictorial representation of energy itself, and he looked to lots of works of art in the past.

One of the great things about this being at the Met is that one of his major sources was Roman sarcophagi, and we looked at the Badminton Sarcophagus. This is a sarcophagus, which is still in Italy, of a battle between the Romans and the barbarians, and you sort of squint or it's out of focus, this work of art. The same sorts of chaotic pictorial energies become clear when you look at it. Or, if you go to the European Paintings gallery and see the great Poussin, *The Abduction of the Sabine Women* from the early 1630s, and you just sort of forget about the townscape, and the sky, and the foreground and go right into the figures, all of whom are intertwined in each other in an extraordinary way. It becomes clear that the major sources for this glorious painting by De Kooning [were] pictures, representations, of battles, whether ancient, or whether Renaissance, or whether Baroque. What he has done, and you understand this so strongly when you're at the Met, is to take all of this energy from art history, to throw out the references, and to reinvent it in modern form.

Now, the next work of art is by Jackson Pollock, who was born in Wyoming, a little bit like Clyfford Still, from the middle of nowhere—my family is from Wyoming, so I know it's the middle of nowhere—creates works of art, and this is one of his greatest paintings, *Autumn Rhythm* from 1950, which came to the Met in 1957, just a year after Pollock himself died in an automobile accident in 1956. And one can see another work of art that is about sheer pictorial energy. What Pollock did was to paint not on an easel, not with the work of art being vertical and him painting on it as if it's a window upon a world or a mirror of the world in back of him, but on the floor as if it's a kind of dance diagram, and around, and around, and around the great canvas he would go, hurling paint with a kind of balletic force. He did it so often and with such skill that he became a great master of calligraphic painting.

The Met has huge holdings of calligraphic painting, Chinese, Japanese, and of course, one can look at the calligraphic ceramics by the Maya. You can go throughout the museum, and the glorious thing about looking at contemporary art, modern art, at the Met is that all of the rhythms of the past live in these great works of art. This is *Autumn Rhythm*, and again, we think of seasons and seasonal time, and what was he experiencing in the autumn of the year in which this work of art was painted, 1950? How do those rhythms affect our view of it, and how do they reverberate with the history of art? How does the word *rhythm*, which of course, has more to do with music than anything else, tell us what to think about this work of art, which becomes in a way a kind of jazz dance, a kind of record of a performance of an artist.

Now, Mark Rothko was one of the great colorists, and Mark Rothko was born in Russia, came to the United States, was an artist who sort of reinvented color painting. The Met has color painting for millennia. We have color painting back with the ancient Romans. One can look at the way in which human beings have dealt with color throughout the centuries, and this work of art, which is called *White, Red on Yellow*, from 1958, was given to the Metropolitan Museum by the estate of Mark Rothko more or less in recognition of that great 1969 exhibition. One sees two strong lozenges, the top one which is white, but it's a white that is very much infected with gray and other colors. So it becomes a kind of pillow of color, and its edges are slightly blurred and irregular. One has a sense that it's the size that it is because it wanted to be that size, and below it is an enormous and much stronger rectangle of a very brilliant red-orange, or an orange that's so strong that it holds the bottom of the picture. Then, when we look at it really carefully, we see that there's another rectangle in the middle, which is a yellow rectangle, floating on the yellow background, that is almost invisible. When you notice it, you realize that you're looking at a work of art that is much more complicated and that has gone through a much longer thought process than you at first thought. Mark Rothko essentially made paintings about the softness and glory of color, about the way in which colors can interact with each other in a figure/ground way and a figure/figure way in a kind of sense that is unprecedented in Western art. Though there are many great colorists and the Met has major examples by all the great colorists from Titian onward, this is a kind of color painting that is so pure, so reduced, so clear that it seems to wash away the centuries. It's as if you don't need all of that old color painting, but in another sense, he learned [from the history

©2008 The Teaching Company.

of art], being a man who lived in New York [and] who went to the Met as well as to the Modern. This painting fits in the Met because his paintings were first seen in the Met [in] a grand public exhibition, and of course, his children and his estate were grateful for that reason.

Now, here's a color painting that is slightly different. Ellsworth Kelly is an American artist, a deeply American artist, but spent the years after World War II in France and learned about art and civilization in Paris in the late [19]40s and early [19]50s before coming back to the United States. This is *Blue Green Red* of 1962–1963. If Rothko's paintings are sort of all about subtlety, the paintings of Ellsworth Kelly are hard and strong. This is a painting that is on canvas, but you almost can't find the canvas. There's no texture of the canvas because the paint is applied so strongly and in such a flat way that it's almost as if it has been painted by a machine. He is to color painting what Ingres was to painting in the 19th century—something precise and definitive, as if there is no other way this painting could be. Mark Rothko—you can feel that he's shifting and changing each of the rectangles of color and thinking about them in a kind of process. With Ellsworth Kelly, when you look at this painting, painted in [19]62–1963, it seems inevitable. It seems as if somebody invented it in their mind, and it was made by a machine, even though it was painstakingly made by hand, just like all of those illusionist paintings with all of the little, tiny figures and the superb portrait that we saw of Ingres earlier on. There is no evidence of the artist except the artist's mind.

Then, to look at pop art, which was also celebrated in Geldzahler's great exhibition, this is Roy Lichtenstein's *Stepping Out* of 1978, and it's a wonderful work of art because the wonderful thing about Americans is that we can quote anything. We're free. There are no constraints upon our freedoms, and when you look at this work of art, you see this sort of strange guy with his girlfriend. Of course, the girlfriend is a kind of Cubist play on Marilyn Monroe, with the big lips, and the eye, and the blonde hair, but done à la Picasso. Her boyfriend is this sort of dorky, working-class guy in the back, and if you go up the street to the Guggenheim Museum, you'll see the same guy in several guises by Fernand Léger, the great French Modernist painter. So there is a kind of interplay between New York and France and between art made in the [19]40s by a French artist and art made in the [19]70s by an American artist.

Now, there is no more important modern artist, no modern artist who is more about New York in a way, than Andy Warhol. Andy Warhol was born in Pittsburgh. He was born into a very devout family. He became a kind of commercial artist early in his career, and moved to New York, and did ads, sort of shoe ads and various and sundry things that have to do with the commercial world. His works of art were so skillful and so smart; he observed the city as only an outsider can do. Of course, Pittsburgh was once the richest city in America, and of course, the Fricks, and the Mellons, and the Carnegies, all of the rich people, left and came to New York. So Pittsburgh was a provincial place when he [Warhol] was born in 1928. When he came to New York, it was "the big city," and it's only outsiders who really can see something as it is because they're not involved. They're like anthropologists of the city. He would walk down the street and see things, and the whole city became his oyster. He began to understand the importance of photography and the importance of the image because, of course, when you see billboards, and ads, and windows all of the time, what you see is the image. Here, he has made an image of himself wearing a wig, and he has printed on the back of that image camouflage, which was, of course, developed by artists, mostly French artists, in World War I. So it's a very clever play: This is me. This is me fake in a wig, and it's me fake as camouflage. So it's not really me, and I'm making a reference to another artistic product, which has to do with war, which was developed by artists. So it's a work of art that you think is simple, but it's not. The Met has this marvelous example of Andy Warhol.

Now, James Rosenquist is one of the sort of second-tier, one would say, of pop artists, artists who sort of deal with the streets, and deal with what one sees, and deal with ads. And the longer I live, the more I realize that he is a major master, and he is an artist who, in 100 years, will be thought of as one of the great artists of the late 20th century. This is a painting from 1981 called *House of Fire*. It's absolutely enormous. It's more than 16 feet long and 6 feet high, and it has got this sort of phalanx of lipsticks coming at you from one side; an upside-down shopping bag, beautifully painted, with its baguette, and its basil, and its bananas, and all of its stuff—I guess they're all *b*'s—coming out of it, almost as if to spill on the ground;

[and] an enormous vat from an iron factory or a metal factory of molten steel or molten something, coming in a window that is covered with Venetian blinds. So you have this kind of Surrealist putting together of different things, but they're all consumerist goods. They're all about making things. They're all about advertising, and in fact, the painting is mostly painted with an airbrush as if he's painting a billboard. It has the proportions of a billboard.

Now, in 1969, the Met did another exhibition called "Harlem On My Mind," which was equally great as "New York Painting, 1940 to 1970." It was curated by an extraordinary man named Allon Schoener, who was a sociologist, not an art historian. Its point to New Yorkers is that you don't get yourself. You don't understand that up north on the north side of this park, of Central Park, is one of the most thriving urban aesthetic laboratories in the world, which is Harlem. An African-American artist named Romare Bearden went to that exhibition in 1969, and he began to make his masterpiece, which is called *The Block*, which was finished in 1971 and which is in the Met. *The Block* is Lennox Avenue between 132nd and 133rd Street. It's a series of panels, six panels, each of which is 4 feet high and 3 feet long. So it's 18 feet long and 4 feet tall, and it shows you everything that happens on that block—the figures, the life. When it was first shown, in 1971, it had recordings of sounds from the block, and it sort of re-created in an urban form the life of Harlem. It was because Romare Bearden went to an exhibition at the Met that he made this object, which is now in the Met [and] came to the Met in 1978, fewer than 10 years after the exhibition. You need to stand in front of this work of art because it's one of the greatest American works of art. It has nothing to do with all of the theories of abstraction that you have seen before.

Now, another American artist who was sort of interested in American mythology is an artist named Red Grooms, and Red Grooms made this wonderful painting in 1984. It's called *Chance Encounter at 3 A.M.* In 1983, he read an article in *The New Yorker* about the fact that Willem de Kooning and Mark Rothko had each met each other—because they didn't know each other—in the late [19]30s, and they had taken a walk at 3 am—their hard travails as artists—and they sat down in Washington Square Park with the great Stanford White Arch and the statue of Garibaldi. They sat next to each other in their paint-splattered clothes, and they started talking and met each other. It was this chance encounter at 3 am that Red Grooms turns into a painting, an enormous painting, which really tells us how important New York is for the arts. When you can see two artists who don't know each other; who come from different countries, one from Russia and Lithuania, the other from Rotterdam in the Netherlands; they are working in their studios. They come together in New York. They come to the park at midnight because they're exhausted. They sit down exhausted, looking out at the night, and they meet each other. Then, something electric and magical that could only happen in a city happens, and that is what happens at the Met: Mark Rothko and Willem de Kooning could meet each other in Washington Square Park in the 1930s; be painted in the 1980s by another artist, Red Grooms; [and] paintings by all three men are in the Met. All three men have gone often to the Met, and it makes you understand how a great museum can change the lives not only of ordinary people who walk into it but of artists who make the most original and important creations of our culture.

Lecture Twenty-Two
The Robert Lehman Collection—1400–1800

Scope:

When the great financier Robert Lehman died in 1969, he left his entire collection of works of art (built by himself and his father, Philip Lehman) to The Metropolitan Museum of Art on the condition that it be shown on its own as a "museum with the museum." When the Lehman Wing opened in 1975, there was considerable controversy in the press about the donor's right to control "from the grave"; the collection, however, is so rich, varied, and important that it is more or less like having the Frick Collection at home at The Metropolitan Museum of Art. The Robert Lehman Collection is so diverse that its catalogue comprises more than 40 hefty volumes covering all media of European and decorative art from 1300–1950. The first of two lectures will deal with the collection's major masterpieces of Old Master painting, mostly purchased early in the century by Philip Lehman but with judicious additions made by Robert. Included will be paintings by Botticelli, Petrus Christus, El Greco, Rembrandt, and Canaletto, along with a select group of works from the graphic and decorative arts; the aim of discussing these and other works will be to link them with their counterparts in the regular galleries of The Metropolitan Museum of Art.

Outline

I. Robert Lehman (1891–1969) was an American financial titan who spent his life forming a collection large and important enough to have formed its own museum.

   A. Lehman was devoted to The Metropolitan Museum of Art and had been a trustee for years.

   B. He had been an enemy of the fate of J. P. Morgan's collection, which was split among the museum's various departments.

   C. Lehman decided to give his entire collection to The Metropolitan Museum of Art on the condition that it be kept together and shown more or less in its entirety in rooms largely based upon his family's townhouse on 54th Street in New York City.

    D. The Lehman Wing is in the back of the building facing Central Park.

    E. After his graduation from Yale, Lehman became the curator of his father's collection of Old Master pictures; by the time Lehman was 40 years old, he was one of the best art historians and connoisseurs in the world.

II. I am going to take you on a tour of the Old Master paintings and drawings in the Lehman Collection.

    A. The Lehman Collection has many works by great artists with other works in the museum.

    B. The Robert Lehman Foundation has prepared a definitive multi-volume catalog of the Lehman Collection.

    C. There is a kind of intimacy that develops between a scholar and works of art in the Lehman Collection, which operates as an entity of its own.

III. The Lehman Collection has many good works from the early Italian Renaissance because Lehman went to Yale (which has one of the greatest collections of Italian gold-ground painting) and collected with a very discerning and knowledgeable eye.

    A. Bernardo Daddi's *The Assumption of the Virgin* (c. 1340) is a fragment of an altarpiece hung low on the wall so one can study the extraordinary brushwork and execution that, in the original altarpiece, would have been too high up to see closely.

    B. There are a large number of panels by the Osservanza Master (which probably came from one big altarpiece) representing Saint Anthony Abbot at various points in his life. The Lehman Collection has *Saint Anthony the Abbot in the Wilderness* (c. 1435).

        1. The work almost looks like a Surrealist painting.

        2. The Lehmans bought this painting because there were two other panels from the same altarpiece at Yale, including Sano di Pietro's *Saint Anthony Abbot Tormented by Demons* (c. 1435).

C. Giovanni di Paolo's *The Creation of the World and the Expulsion from Paradise* (1445) is part of a fantastic altarpiece, another fragment of which the museum has in its regular collection is *Paradise*.

D. Sandro Botticelli's *The Annunciation* (c. 1485) is a predella panel: one of the narrative panels that runs underneath the devotional image for a large altarpiece.

    1. In this work, Botticelli masters one-point perspective.

    2. The work rhymes with a painting of the same subject that Lehman knew during his time at Yale: Neroccio de' Landi's *Annunciation* (c. 1475–1480).

    3. Looking at Leonardo da Vinci's *Annunciation* (c. 1473–1475) done around the same time as the Botticelli painting, one can see how incrementally painting in Florence developed in the 1470s, 1480s, and 1490s.

E. The Lehman Collection has another Annunciation painting by Hans Memling, a northern artist: *The Annunciation* (1480–1489).

    1. There is a sense of domestic closure in this work different from Botticelli's painting.

    2. The oil paint results in a chromatic brilliance not found in Botticelli's egg-based tempera; Memling's understanding of perspective, however, is not as advanced as Botticelli's.

F. *A Goldsmith in His Shop, Possibly Saint Eligius* (1449) by Petrus Christus tells us a good deal about contemporary life in the 15th century, as the saint is shown in the history of the painter. This image was the most important prototype for Quentin Metsys's *The Moneylender and His Wife* (1514).

IV. Great artists abound in the Lehman Collection. The richness of The Metropolitan Museum of Art is so vast that one has to unfortunately focus on a few works.

A. In El Greco's *Saint Jerome as Cardinal* (c. 1610–1614), one feels as if one is looking at an actual human being. El Greco is not making up a saint from his imagination but working from a model.

B. There is a glorious portrait by Rembrandt of a rather strange man: *Portrait of Gérard de Lairesse* (1665).

1. Rembrandt gives the subject a certain amount of gravitas beyond his years; we can see the artist is painting his own sense of mortality as he looks at this curly-headed young man.

2. In the museum's upstairs galleries, one can see Rembrandt's self-portrait from 1660 and imagine what it must have been like for the elderly Rembrandt to confront the young Lairesse.

C. The museum owns a painting by Lairesse: *Apollo and Aurora* (1671). Here, Lairesse goes beyond Rembrandt and thinks more about Italian Classical art and the art of Poussin.

D. *Condesa de Altamira and Her Daughter, María Augustina* (1787–1788) is a full-scale portrait by Francisco de Goya y Lucientes.

1. There is nothing else of luxury in the work, so one focuses only upon the subject and her relationship with her daughter.

2. The work is a mix between a portrait and a representation of the Virgin and Christ Child.

3. The subject was the mother of Don Manuel Osorio Manrique de Zuñiga, whose depiction by Goya can be found in the museum's European galleries.

V. Now let us take a look at the drawings in the Robert Lehman Collection.

A. The collection has one of Dürer's great self-portrait drawings (*Self-portrait, Study of a Hand and a Pillow*), done almost exactly at the same time as *Self-Portrait with Sea-Holly* (1493) [also called *Self-Portrait or Portrait of the Artist Holding a Thistle*]. The drawing has a wonderful verso, *Six Pillows*, which represents a set of pillows and reminds one of the wonderful plumped pillows in northern paintings of the late 15th and early 16th centuries, such as Rogier van der Weyden's *The Annunciation* (c. 1435).

B. Rembrandt van Rijn's sketch (c. 1635) after da Vinci's *The Last Supper* (1498) shows one great artist getting as close as he possibly can to another. He abandoned the subject—one of the few great subjects in the history of Christian art that Rembrandt did not paint.

C. The Robert Lehman Collection has an important group of 18th-century Venetian drawings.

    1. Canaletto's *Warwick Castle: The East Front* (1752) is so carefully done that it served the artist as a preparatory drawing for his sequence of paintings about this castle, one of which is *Warwick Castle, East Front from the Courtyard* (1752).

    2. Domenico Tiepolo's *The Burial of Punchinello* (c. 1800) is part of a sequence of drawings about a character from the *Commedia dell'arte* that makes us remember his painting *A Dance in the Country* (c. 1755), which features a similar character.

VI. There are marvelous decorative arts in the Lehman Collection.

    A. One can look at faience, earthenware, jewelry, Renaissance furniture, and picture frames.

    B. Bernaert van Orley and Pieter de Pannemaker's *The Last Supper* (1520–1530) is an extraordinary tapestry that represents the Last Supper as held around a square table instead of a long presentational table as in Rembrandt's drawing a century later. The artist based his tapestry on *The Last Supper* (1510) from Dürer's sequence of prints called *The Large Passion*.

Recommended Reading:

Hindman, D'Ancona, Palladino, and Saffiotti. *The Robert Lehman Collection at the Metropolitan Museum of Art.*

Szabó. *The Robert Lehman Collection: A Guide.*

Questions to Consider:

1. Why was Robert Lehman so important to the history of the museum?

2. Choose a painting from the Lehman Collection created between 1400 and 1800 and describe why it is important to you.

Lecture Twenty-Two—Transcript
The Robert Lehman Collection—1400–1800

On August 9, 1969, the great American financial titan Robert Lehman died at his home on Long Island. He'd spent his life forming a collection, adding to that already distinguished collection formed by his father, the financial titan Philip Lehman of, of course, Lehman Brothers. His life had been actually as much devoted to art as to the creation of the great firm which bears the family name, and it was the art collection that really consumed him in the latter years of his life. He had to think about, in those years, what he was to do with the collection. It was a collection large enough and important enough that it could have formed a whole museum on its own, like that formed by Henry Clay Frick a little bit further down Fifth Avenue.

But Robert Lehman was completely devoted to the Metropolitan Museum; he'd been a trustee for years. He'd been involved with it really since his childhood, with his parents, going to the museum, seeing the museum. His father had become a trustee, and he was so involved with the Met that he couldn't bear his collection being anywhere else. But he had been such an enemy of what had happened to the collection of J. P. Morgan, another financial titan of America. His collection, at his death in 1913, was given to the Met—or a good deal of it was given to the Met—and it was, of course, split amongst the various departments of the museum so that there was no sense when you came out of the door of the Metropolitan Museum that you knew really about the contribution of J. P. Morgan to the Metropolitan Museum.

And so what Robert Lehman decided to do is to have it both ways: to give his collection, his entire collection—probably the largest and most important single gift of art to the Met in its history—to the Metropolitan Museum on the condition that it be kept together and shown more or less in its entirety—responsibly, because a lot of the works are drawings, and so they can't be shown all the time—in rooms which were largely based upon the rooms of the family's house on 54th Street in New York. And so one has the sense, when you go to the Lehman Wing at the Met, that you're walking through a luxurious townhouse in New York, but you're in the Metropolitan Museum. And if you look at the map of the Metropolitan Museum, there's this sort of strange thing that looks like *Battlestar Galactica*, sort of heading off the back of the Met into Central Park, and that is the Lehman Wing, utterly discrete from the rest. You go through doors to get to it. You go into a different building when you get to it, and you go through a series of rooms, and you see these smaller rooms on the side around this vast two-story courtyard which are replicas—rather free replicas but replicas—of the rooms in the Lehman townhouse on 54th Street. In those rooms, one finds arrayed an extraordinary collection of works of art.

Now, who was Robert Lehman? Robert Lehman was born in 1891. He was born into a family of extraordinary wealth and privilege. He was educated at Hotchkiss first, and then he matriculated to Yale in 1909. He graduated from Yale in 1913, the same year as the Armory Show, and was, therefore, just thrown into the art world of early-20th-century America. After his graduation, he essentially became the curator of his father's very large and very important collection of Old Master paintings and spent most of the 1920s, his 30s, writing a definitive scholarly catalog of his father's collection of Old Master pictures. So by the time that he was 40, he was one of the best art historians, one of the best connoisseurs, in the city of New York; and in fact, in America; in fact, in the world. His languages were good. He was completely fluent in French, wonderfully well educated. He could read German and Italian with ease, and he had a kind of sense of fluency that comes from a lot of money, incredible intelligence, hard work, and perseverance.

I'm going to take you now on a little tour of the Old Master paintings and drawings at the Lehman Collection. And as you would suspect, the Lehman Collection has many works by great artists that are the same artists with works in the Metropolitan Museum itself, so there are these wonderful rhymes as you go through the Lehman Collection. When you see a work by Rembrandt, for example, you remember back to the two galleries of works by Rembrandt and his studio in the Metropolitan's own European Paintings collection. When you see a great tapestry, you think of the tapestries that you saw in the European Decorative Arts galleries, and the same kind of thing goes on and on. There's a sense in which the Lehman Collection has its own integrity and it's separate from the Met, but it has extensive rhyming with the Met. And as you go through the galleries, you think back to works of art, important works of art, that you've already seen in the galleries.

Now, for me to talk about these collections is a very important thing because the Metropolitan Museum, through the Robert Lehman Foundation, has prepared, or is preparing—is practically finished preparing—a definitive multivolume catalog of the Lehman Collection. Now, I was privileged to work on two of those volumes, both, of course, involved with modern art, the art of the next lecture. But it has meant that I've spent a lot of time in the Lehman Collection. And when you go into the offices, and get to know the staff, and go into the storage room, and go through the boxes of drawings repeatedly, there's a kind of sense of intimacy that develops between a scholar and works of art in the Lehman Collection which is very different from operating with the Metropolitan Museum itself because it's a little entity on its own. It has the quality of going to someone's home, a rather grand home albeit, where you see major works of art in a kind of hushed, private way.

Now, we're going to begin with the early Italian Renaissance, and the reason that we're doing that is that the collection is very, very good in the early Italian Renaissance. And the reason that it is, is that Robert Lehman went to Yale, and Yale has a great collection, one of the greatest collections in the world, of Italian gold-ground painting, which it acquired in the 19th century from a man named James Jackson Jarves. And so as an undergraduate at Yale, Robert Lehman saw superb works of art, which are early Christian art, and he collected with a very discerning and knowledgeable eye, helping his father in the 1920s and himself collecting later on in this area because he was a connoisseur in this area. One of the greatest panels is a Bernardo Daddi panel, and Daddi is from the generation of artists after Giotto. You'll remember we saw the great Giotto panel in the Metropolitan's European Paintings Department, and this is the next generation of artists.

We see Daddi working on a gold ground. This is a painting from the late 1330s, or about 1340, as the Met says now. One sees here the central subject; it's the *Assumption of the Virgin*, and one sees the Virgin in her own sort of shape going into heaven. Part of her girdle is going down, and we can see from this that the painting is a fragment. I talked to you about that before, that paintings were oftentimes cut and reframed so one painting could be two paintings and could be sold, therefore, to two collectors, and that's what happened to this Bernardo Daddi.

[We see] superb modeling and detailing on the angels in their [garments, which are] green on the top, pink in the middle, and blue on the bottom; wonderful sort of baguette-shaped clouds underneath the Virgin, who is ascending into heaven above. This is a fragment but a perfectly preserved fragment. And because it's a fragment and it's hung low on the wall, one can look at something that in the original altarpiece would have been so high—would have been the pinnacle of a very large panel and would have been very high—so we wouldn't have been able to study Daddi's extraordinary brushwork and sort of style of execution.

Now, one of my favorite artists in the whole history of art has no name, and he's called the Osservanza Master. There are a large number of panels by the Osservanza Master, which probably came from one big altarpiece, representing St. Anthony Abbot at various points in his life. The Lehman Collection has one of them, and we see *Saint Anthony the Abbot in the Wilderness*. This is from about 1435, and here he is, and there are these wonderful tiny animals. The trees are all without their leaves. There's this wonderful sort of curvature of the sky in the top, the two birds across, the superb little pink geometric chapel. It almost looks like a Surrealist painting, and it's a painting that was bought by the Lehmans because there were two other panels from this same altarpiece at Yale.

I show you one of them, and this is [*Saint*] *Anthony Abbot Tormented by Demons*. Which as you can see Yale attributes to an artist they call Sano di Pietro, which is the same artist as the Osservanza Master, but each museum has its own scholars with their own way of doing things, and these are from the same altarpiece. One can see that this time, the little church is gray rather than pink. The trees have sprouted their leaves because it's another season, and [we feel] the kind of charm and delight of this picture. These would have been panels at the lower part of an altarpiece, telling the life, scene by scene, of St. Anthony Abbot. He would have been large-scale up above, with an assumption of the Virgin, or with Christ, or with a major sort of subject of devotion above it. But these tiny little panels, which are now scattered in museums throughout the world—in Paris, in Berlin, in New York, in Washington, and New Haven—should sometimes be brought together so one can learn the identity of one of the most mysterious and beautiful artists in the history of art.

Now, this is a glorious panel, a panel that is so full of life and so original that when we look at it, we're stunned. This represents the creation and the expulsion of Adam and Eve from paradise; you see two scenes in the same panel. This is the entire world. Here's God the Father bringing down the world, and the world is a fascinating thing: this sort of series of concentric circles of the atmosphere, ending in the stars and constellations—you can see the little symbols for the constellations around the side—which seems to be whirling towards the angel Lucifer, who is throwing Adam and Eve out of paradise on the right. This is part of a fantastic altarpiece, [and] the Met, in its normal collection, already has another panel from the same altarpiece. This altarpiece was sort of, again, dismembered, and it's marvelous that the Met has two fragments, one in the Lehman Collection and one in the regular museum that was bought by funds from the Rogers Fund in 1906.

Now, we saw that incredible, long decorative panel painting by Botticelli in the first lecture, the lecture on the Renaissance at the Met, and this is an even greater work by Botticelli, though a tiny painting. It's a predella panel, and a predella panel is one of the narrative panels, again, that runs underneath the devotional image for a large altarpiece. This is a panel, a rather early panel, in the life of Botticelli; it was painted in about 1485. And, here, we see the angel Gabriel, and here, we see the Virgin in her own beautifully constructed space. And one sees that this is a work of art with exactly correct one-point perspective, that he had mastered one-point perspective.

But what's fascinating about this is it has a rhyme with a painting of the same subject, at Yale again, which Robert Lehman knew in his undergraduate years, which also shows perspective, and the angel Gabriel on the same side, and the Virgin on the other, by an artist named Neroccio de' Landi. It's a little, tiny bit earlier; it's about 10 years earlier. But what one can see when one makes a comparison is that these figures in this very correct, perspectively correct, scene are very flat. And when you look at the Botticelli, the figures are fully volumed. They occupy the space that has been created by the one-point perspective, and one can see already that Botticelli is a much more advanced artist than Neroccio. We have to sort of fast forward to an early work by Leonardo, done in the workshop of Verrocchio, his teacher, about the same time as the painting by Botticelli in the Lehman Collection. And one can see just how incrementally painting changed and developed in Florence in the 1470s, [14]80s, and [14]90s. And when you look at this tiny panel in its case, by Botticelli, in the Lehman Collection, it carries an enormous amount of significance.

Now, the Lehman Collection also has another *Annunciation* by a northern artist, by Hans Memling, whose work, of course, we will encounter, and did encounter, upstairs in the European Paintings gallery. This is a painting [from] almost exactly the same time as the Botticelli, the tiny Botticelli. It's much larger a picture, but what it does is it crams the whole scene into an interior room. Rather than that kind of relaxed and rather tranquil horizontal spread with an enormous amount of space behind it which we saw in the Botticelli, here, one sees all—there's Gabriel; there's the Virgin; there are these two angels. They're all sort of crammed in this bedroom of a northern Renaissance house. And there's a sense of sort of domestic closure in this work of art, which means that it's completely different. It's, of course, as you'll remember, painted in oil, whereas the Botticelli is painted in tempera, in egg-based tempera. There's a kind of chromatic brilliance as a result of that in the Memling, and there is an understanding of pictorial space and perspective but not quite so advanced as that of Botticelli.

Now, it's sort of not an accident that one of the greatest paintings about money-lending and banking in the entire history of art was owned by the Lehmans, and it was bought by Philip Lehman and cataloged by Robert Lehman. It's by Petrus Christus, and you'll remember the little wonderful portrait of the Carthusian lay brother on the red background with his beard that we saw in the galleries upstairs. Here, one sees St. Eligius; St. Eligius is the patron saint of goldsmiths. He's a goldsmith; he's in his shop. We have the customers; his scales and weighing of things; a wonderful convex mirror on the right side, showing us the town in which he is, the town of Bruges in which he is. All of his tools are arranged around us, and it's a painting of incredible quality and interest because it actually tells us a good deal about contemporary life in the 15th century in the north, because St. Eligius is not shown in his own history; he's shown at the time of the painter, at the time of Petrus

Christus. What's important is that this image is the most important prototype of the most famous painting about moneylenders and money-lending, by Quentin Metsys, at the Louvre, painted in 1514, considerably later in the next century, and which I discussed at some length in my Teaching Company course about the Louvre.

Now, great artists abound in the Lehman Collection, and there are such extraordinary examples that I feel terrible about showing only a few of them, but that's the case of this entire class. The richnesses of the Met are so vast that one has to focus on a few things. One of my favorite saints in the Catholic pantheon and one of my favorite paintings of that saint—the saint is St. Jerome, and this painting is, of course, by the great Cypriot artist who came through Italy to Spain and is now [considered] one of the great Spanish artists, named El Greco, called El Greco, "the Greek" in Spanish. Around 1610 to 1614, he painted this portrait of St. Jerome, and we really feel, when we're looking at this painting, as if we're looking at an actual human being. And clearly, there was a model, a particular man with particular features, a particular beard, these long and huge ears, and those sunken eyes.

And one knows that what El Greco is doing is not sort of making up a saint out of his imagination; he has found a model. He has found an old Spaniard who looks like he wants this saint to be, and painted him, and he's, of course, dressed—and this is towards the end of St. Jerome's life. And St. Jerome, we all know, the most famous paintings of him show him in his cave, beating himself and translating the Bible into Latin. His most important contribution to the early church was the unification of the Bible, linguistic unification of the Bible, into Latin. Much of what was read in the Catholic Church in the Latin Bible came from St. Jerome. We see him here with that book. It's not a printed book because, of course, St. Jerome didn't live in the time of printing. It's a manuscript, a double-column manuscript, of his own work, of his own attempt to bring the Gospels and bring the Bible, both testaments of the Bible, into the world of his time, the Latin world of his time. He now turns into a sort of great Spanish saint.

Now, let's go to Rembrandt because there's a glorious portrait by Rembrandt of a rather strange man. His name is Gerard de Lairesse, and Gerard de Lairesse was not French; he was born in Liège. Obviously, his ancestry was French. He was rather young when he went into Rembrandt's studio about 1665. Rembrandt was quite old, in fact, only had four more years to live when he painted this portrait. But Gerard de Lairesse was a sort of young man who wanted to learn from the greatest living artist. He was already a painter. He'd gone into Rembrandt's studio. He was wealthy enough to be able to commission from Rembrandt a portrait. We see this rather curious-looking guy, and it seems—the biographies of Lairesse said that he was born with congenital syphilis, which is why he had this sort of slightly stunted face and funny little nose, that funny little pug nose, which you see here. Rembrandt gives him a certain amount of gravitas beyond his years, and we can see that Rembrandt, in a certain way, is painting his own sense of mortality as he's looking at this curly-headed young man with his books. And, of course, Lairesse went on to write quite a lot in his lifetime.

And we can then run upstairs, thinking about Rembrandt looking at the young Lairesse in his studio in 1665, and you go up to the galleries in the Met, and you see Rembrandt's great 1660 self-portrait, painted five years earlier. [Here], Rembrandt is not looking at Lairesse but [at] himself in the mirror and sort of conjuring himself out of this dark, deep, browny-black background with his rich velvet hat, which almost sort of disappears into its blackness, and the face coming out of it. And one can then imagine, if you face these two paintings to each other, what it must have been like, the confrontation between the elderly Rembrandt and the young Lairesse in 1665.

And then, the Met being the Met, of course, owns a painting by Lairesse, and we can see what happened to Lairesse. I mean this painting is so the opposite of Rembrandt, and Lairesse went on to live until 1711 and wrote two important books in the early years of the 18th century, one about drawing and one about the history of painting. And each of these books is about how Rembrandt got it wrong, essentially. And so what happens to Lairesse is that he goes, in his own mind, beyond Rembrandt, thinking about Roman, Italian, and Classical art and admiring the art of Poussin more than the art of Rembrandt. How Rembrandt would have shuddered if he'd seen this painting.

Now, let's go to Goya. This is a wonderful painting by Goya. It represents the *Condesa de Altamira and Her Daughter, Maria Augustina*. It's a full-scale portrait. It's very large, and it has this wonderful commanding quality, but it's also very fragile; [note] her sort of frizzed hair, her incredible pallor of skin, [and] this tiny, little baby in her hands. This painting was painted in the late 1780s, 1787 or 1788. There's an inscription on the bottom which tells us who she is and her pedigree. She's sitting alone in the middle of this sort of wonderful, very stylish sofa, but there's nothing else around. It's almost like a photographer's studio in the 1860s where you shove a piece of furniture in front of a backdrop and put the person in.

There are no paintings; there's no carpet on the floor; there's nothing else of luxury, and so we focus only upon her and her relationship with her daughter. And it has the kind of quality of a mixture between a portrait and a representation of the Virgin and Child. We sense both things going on in Goya's mind. And what makes this painting all the more important at the Met is that she was the mother of our young figure Don Manuel Osorio Manrique de Zuñiga, whom we've already seen in the European galleries at the Met—the same family. So he is the little brother of that baby, and his mother is in the other painting. We've analyzed this as this extraordinary portrait of youth and innocence in the face of death, by probably the greatest portrait painter, undoubtedly the greatest portrait painter, of the late 18th century in Spain and one of the greatest portrait painters in the world; so again, [we note] the relationship between the Met and that.

Now, let's look at drawings. Robert Lehman loved drawings, and he has one of the great Dürer self-portrait drawings. Here, one sees the young Dürer with his hand and a pillow. It's done at almost exactly the same time as the *Self-Portrait with Sea Holly* of 1493 in the Louvre, which I talked about in the Louvre class. We have this young artist sort of looking at himself. He's only 22 years old when he makes it and beginning to think about how he makes and how he works things. And the drawing also has a wonderful verso—paper was expensive, and so you drew on both sides—which represents just a set of pillows which are kind of tossed around and wonderfully expressive. There's one on the recto and six on the verso, and they remind us of all of the wonderful plumped pillows in paintings, in northern paintings, of the late 15th and early 16th centuries. And I show you this one, by Rogier van der Weyden, which is in the Louvre in Paris, which has got a very similar group of pillows. And clearly, what he [Dürer] was doing was thinking about, studying, something that he was going to use in a future painting.

Or [we see] an extraordinary drawing by Rembrandt van Rijn, and this drawing is an early drawing from the 1630s when Rembrandt was sort of beginning his career, again, moving to Amsterdam and becoming a major artist in Amsterdam. And what is he looking at? This is the Last Supper, clearly. But what's he looking at when he looks at this? What he's looking at and what he's thinking about when he makes this drawing with Christ in the center, and the great canopy, and the arrangement of the apostles on the side is Leonardo da Vinci.

Of course, he never went to Italy—he never went outside of Milan to see *The Last Supper*, which was probably in better condition then than it is now. But he did have access to an engraving after the painting, and it shows one great artist, Rembrandt, getting as close as he could possibly get to another great artist, namely, Leonardo da Vinci. As close as he could get was this engraving, and so he made the drawing in the Lehman Collection and another drawing—this one very rapidly done, in the British Museum—of the Last Supper. And what he learned from doing these drawings is that *The Last Supper* had already been done by Leonardo and that he didn't need to do it, so he never painted the Last Supper. This is as close as he got to the work of this great Renaissance genius, and it led him to abandon the subject, one of the few great subjects in the history of Christian art that Rembrandt himself didn't paint.

Now, as one goes on, there is a really important collection of Venetian 18th-century drawings. And you'll remember when I gave my lecture on the 18th-century collections at the Metropolitan Museum in the European Paintings Department, we devoted a lot of time to the artists of Venice. Well, there is a definitive group of drawings in the Lehman Collection, [representing] all of the same artists who did the paintings in the Met. This is actually one of the greatest ones. This is one of the most important drawings by Canaletto. Remember I told you that Canaletto, though a Venetian and though spending most of his life in Venice, made one long trip to England, where most of his patrons lived, and went to visit several of the patrons at their country houses.

This is the east front of Warwick Castle, northwest of London, one of the great medieval castles in England. What he did is he went to the castle, stayed there with his patron, did several very elaborate drawings, of which this is one, a large pen-and-brown-ink drawing with a little bit of gray wash to give form and shading to this vast castle. It's very detailed, so you can read all the crenellations, and all the little windows, and where it's beginning to fall down, and where it has been restored. You can see the lords and ladies, and the servants, and people in the foreground of the drawing. It's so carefully done that it served him as a kind of preparatory drawing for his great painting of it. [Canaletto made] a sequence of great paintings of this castle, of which this is one. This is in the Birmingham Museum and Art Gallery in England, which is rather close to Warwick Castle. So one can see an artist using a drawing to create a painting, which he then sells for a fortune to the man who owns the house. The Robert Lehman Collection owns this drawing, which is one of the most important Canaletto drawings in America and which is a drawing that records in detail an extraordinary trip that he made to England.

You'll remember also when we were in the paintings galleries at the Met that we saw a wonderful painting by Giandomenico Tiepolo, the son of the great fresco painter who painted wonderful views of the Campagna and the *Commedia dell'arte*. The Lehman Collection has a drawing called *The Burial of Punchinello*. This was done about 1800, only four years before the death of Giandomenico, and it's part of a sequence of drawings of the life of this character in the *Commedia dell'arte*. And, of course, Punchinello never lived, and so when you do his life, you're creating a kind of fictional life of a clown or a clown-like *Commedia dell'arte* character who was simply a costumed human being. And what Giandomenico does is to give him a life, and this is his burial. He's being buried as a man; his hat is off. All of his fellow Punchinellos, all of them who are still alive, are with him, and they're putting him into the ground. It's a work of art that is both touching and funny at the same time, and it makes us remember the extraordinary painting from almost 50 years earlier, 45 years earlier, done by Giandomenico, upstairs in the gallery. We can see our Punchinello very much alive in the middle of that painting.

Now, I want to end with the work of decorative arts. There are marvelous decorative arts in the Lehman Collection, but I have time for only one of them. You can look at wonderful faience and earthenware; you can look at jewelry; you can look at Renaissance furniture. There's a very great collection of picture frames. But this is an extraordinary tapestry by Bernaert van Orley, made between

1520 and 1530, and it's *The Last Supper*. It's in wonderful state; all of its colors have survived. It has silver gilt thread, and so it's shot through with this extraordinary brilliance. One can see that it does represent the Last Supper, a Last Supper that's very different, that's very much more around a square table than that long presentational *Last Supper* of Leonardo, as drawn by Rembrandt in that drawing, which is about a century later than this.

What's interesting: It's by a great artist, but a great artist always has to have a source because who was at the Last Supper? They're all dead. Nobody knows what the room looked like, and so you have to invent a Last Supper. Bernaert van Orley decided—he looked through printed Last Suppers and decided that his favorite one was by Dürer, and he used this Last Supper from Dürer's sequence of prints called *The Large Passion*. He changed the setting utterly but kept the figures, and the table, and the sort of sense of compaction of the Last Supper; moved it into a kind of pavilion with a huge out-of-doors view; and created something which improved upon the Dürer and made the Dürer seem much more luxurious because, of course, a tapestry is much more expensive than a little print. It would have appealed to a very wealthy client, and it would have been in an extraordinary palace or house where the luxury of the scene represented had to be in accord with the house itself.

Now, you've seen throughout the course of this lecture that the Lehman Collection links in very powerful ways, over and over and over again, to the Metropolitan Museum's own collection. Though it is at the Metropolitan Museum, it's not in the Metropolitan Museum, and it makes going to the Metropolitan Museum all the more wonderful because you can rush to the Lehman Collection, wander around, choose your subject, your favorite thing, and then go back out into the Met and find the ways that that work of art rhymes with works of art in the permanent collection.

Lecture Twenty-Three
The Robert Lehman Collection—1800–1960

Scope:

The second of two lectures on The Metropolitan Museum of Art's Robert Lehman Collection will deal with the large and varied works of 19th- and 20th-century painting collected by Robert Lehman himself. Lehman was greatly affected by New York City's 1913 Armory Show, which exhibited more than 1,250 works of art by modern artists. As a result of the show, Lehman devoted his life to stressing the importance of modern art in the wake of Old Master paintings and drawings. This group of works encompasses both painting and the graphic arts and, like the works in the previous lecture, complements in every way the museum's permanent collections. This lecture will focus on particular masterpieces by Ingres, Matisse, Monet, Renoir, and Seurat. It will be complemented by a short discussion of some of the collection's masterful drawings by those same artists and others, such as Degas and von Menzel.

Outline

I. In the spring of 1913 (when Robert Lehman graduated from Yale), New York City held the first, largest, and most important exhibition devoted to modern art in the city: the Armory Show.

    A. The show exhibited more than 1,250 works of art by 300 European and American modern artists, including Brancusi, Matisse, Duchamp, Monet, Gauguin, and van Gogh.

    B. The show clearly had an effect on Lehman, who was blown away by what he saw.

    C. As a result of visits to the Armory Show, Lehman devoted the rest of his life to grafting modern art onto the tree of Old Master paintings and drawings.

    D. In this lecture, we are going to see more of Robert Lehman's collection than the collection of his father, Philip.

II. We are going to head right on into major works of modern art in the Robert Lehman Collection.

A. The collection has one of the most important portraits in Ingres's entire career: *Princesse de Broglie* (1851–1853). The subject looks at us with an acceptance of our gaze, as if she were accustomed to being looked at. One can go into the museum's shop and find reproductions of almost everything in this painting.

B. Jean-Baptiste Camille Corot's *Diana and Actaeon* (1836) reflects the way in which the French landscape was brought into the Salon.

    1. The Greco-Roman subjects are set in a sylvan landscape; one of the interesting things about Corot's subject pictures is that the subjects are subjugated to the landscape.

    2. The balance between setting and figure is one of Corot's most important contributions to the history of art.

C. Robert Lehman's father, Philip, was interested in Barbizon School paintings of the Forest of Fontainebleau that were fashionable in late 19th-century New York City.

III. Both Philip and Robert Lehman were open to Impressionism and Postimpressionism, which make up an important part of the collection.

A. Claude Monet's *Landscape at Zaandam* (1871–1872) is one of the great Monets in The Metropolitan Museum of Art. The museum has almost 30 paintings from Monet throughout his career.

B. One of the greatest late Impressionist pictures in the United States is *Two Young Girls at the Piano* (1892), Pierre-Auguste Renoir's first official success.

    1. Renoir became the greatest figure painting of the Impressionists alongside his friend, Edgar Degas.

    2. While Degas's figures are rooted in the Classical tradition, Renoir's figures are rooted in the tradition of Rubens, Watteau, and Boucher.

    3. There are three versions of this composition; The Metropolitan Museum of Art's version is in the best condition and is the most perfectly preserved.

C. At the Armory Show, Lehman was introduced to the painting of Henri Matisse. He realized that Matisse was important in the history of art with the creation of a new kind of color painting, Fauvism.

1. Fauvist paintings were so vulgar and unrelated to the way we see that they were described as painted by people without culture and civilization (*fauve* means "beast" in French).

2. Despite its size, *Olive Trees at Collioure* (1906) represents a significant moment in the history of color painting.

D. Matisse's friend, André Derain, painted *Houses of Parliament at Night* (1905–1906).

1. Derain takes lessons from Matisse's depictions of Collioure and applies them to London to create a chromatic symphony that makes it clear he had already seen Monet's 1903–1904 picture of the same subject, *The Houses of Parliament (Effect of Fog)*.

2. Monet's paintings of the Houses of Parliament are not as colorful as Derain's Fauvist picture; they push London toward a symphony of blues and greens.

E. Lehman also loved Pierre Bonnard, who was a member of the group of artists called *Les Nabis* ("The Prophets").

1. These artists were interested in seeing within their own daily lives a chromatic world so intense that the ordinariness of life is made extraordinary.

2. *Before Dinner* (1924) is so chromatically extraordinary that the emotion comes from the interrelationships among colors.

F. Balthus's *Nude Before a Mirror* (1955) represents a young woman who was the artist's muse.

1. The subject's pose and manner are so Classical that we know Balthus was familiar with the poses of Egyptian art.

2. In the museum's Egyptian galleries, one can find a similar hieratic pose in a work like the statue of an offering bearer from around 1985 B.C.

IV. The Lehman Collection's works on paper are extraordinary.

A. Ingres's *Study for "Raphael and the Fornarina"* (c. 1814) was made in preparation for an 1814 painting that is in the

Fogg Art Museum. One sees in Raphael's *Madonna della Seggiola ("Madonna of the Chair")* from around 1516 that the Lehman drawing is much more like the head in this painting than in the study for *Raphael and the Fornarina*.

B. Jean-François Millet's *Women Carrying Fagots* (c. 1858) made on blue-grey paper possesses a bone-chilling quality.

C. Degas's study of a ballet dancer (c. 1873) was made on hot pink paper that has faded over time.

    1. The ballerinas rearranging their clothing on the back of the drawing recall Degas's *A Woman Ironing* (1873).

    2. The drawing also has another rhyme in Degas's *Two Dancers* (1873).

D. There are three wonderful drawings in the Lehman Collection by Adolph von Menzel, the greatest German artist of the second half of the 19th century. *Studies of a Young Woman* (1870 or 1879) is a sheet of two heads, one against the light and one facing the light.

E. The Lehman Collection has six drawings by Renoir. *Young Girl in a Blue Dress* (c. 1890) is a fresh and fantastic watercolor that makes one realize he was as great a draftsman as his friend and rival, Cézanne.

F. The subject of Georges Seurat's *Study for "Les Poseuses"* (1886) looks at the viewer hieratically, as if she were an ancient Greek kouros or a work of Egyptian sculpture.

G. In Odilon Redon's *Pegasus and Bellerophon* (c. 1888), the mythical horse seems more human than its rider and looks at the viewer with a wisdom reflected in works of Greco-Roman antiquity.

H. The lecture ends with Felix Vallotton's *Street Scene in Paris* (1895) because of all the places in which Robert Lehman felt at home, it was Paris.

Recommended Reading:

Brettell, Forster-Hahn, Robinson, and Tomlinson. *The Robert Lehman Collection at the Metropolitan Museum of Art, Volume IX: Nineteenth- and Twentieth-Century European Drawings.*

Hindman, D'Ancona, Palladino, and Saffiotti. *The Robert Lehman Collection at the Metropolitan Museum of Art.*

Questions to Consider:

1. What impact did the donation of the Lehman Collection have on the museum and its stature?

2. Choose a painting from the Lehman Collection created between 1800 and 1960 and describe why it is important to you.

Lecture Twenty-Three—Transcript
The Robert Lehman Collection—1800–1960

In 1913, in the spring of 1913, Robert Lehman graduated from Yale, [as] you'll remember from the last lecture, and I return to that because also in 1913 was the first, and largest, and most important exhibition devoted to modern art held in New York. It's the famous Armory Show, and it was held in the Park Avenue Armory because it was the only building large enough to house an exhibition with more than 1,250 works of art by 300 European and American modern artists. It had Brancusi; it had Matisse; it had Duchamp; it had Monet; it had Gauguin; it had Van Gogh—in such abundance that no one in the United States had yet seen anything like it. Here, one sees a view of one of the rooms constructed for the exhibition in the Park Avenue Armory.

Now, Robert Lehman was an only child, and so he went home quite a lot to see his parents. It wasn't bad digs on 54th Street in a great mansion townhouse filled with works of art, and he saw, clearly, probably more than once, this exhibition, which so shocked New Yorkers. We don't know what he thought about it because he didn't write about it, but it clearly had an affect upon him because, unlike his father, who was already too old to be open to this radical art, Robert Lehman was exactly the right age, the right level of education, the right level of sophistication to be blown away by what he saw. As a result of these visits to the Armory Show between February 17th and its close on March 15th of 1913, when he was not yet 22 years old, the young Robert Lehman devoted the rest of his life, until his death in 1969, to grafting modern art onto the sturdy tree of European Old Master paintings and drawings, which had been the purview of his father. What we're going to see in this lecture is much more the collection of Robert Lehman than the collection of his father, curated by and published [not] by Robert Lehman, but his father, Philip Lehman.

We're going to head right on into major works of art, and the first one is one of the most important paintings, one of the most important portraits, in the entire career of Jean-Auguste-Dominique Ingres. We saw already a great male portrait from early in Ingres' career, in 1810, up in the European galleries in the Metropolitan Museum, and we've seen the contrast between the linear Classicism of Ingres and his archrival Delacroix who was a Romantic artist fascinated with color. Now, we turn to this Ingres portrait, painted between 1851 and 1853 in Paris, of the *Princess de Broglie*. First of all, the first thing that you think of when you look at his portrait is, wow, Ingres was an incredible colorist. Well, he wasn't really an incredible colorist. It's more that she had an incredible turquoise dress than he was an incredible colorist, but the way in which he used that color, the way in which he used it—and, of course, he was involved as much as she was in the choice of the dress—is extraordinary. This painting conventionally hangs at the long end of the whole axis of the Met, when you walk around the staircase, when you walk through that great church hall, and then you go through a sequence of galleries, and you see this brilliant turquoise blue that sort of draws you inexorably to it. It is the Princess de Broglie.

Now, who was the Princess de Broglie? She was one of a group of major aristocrats in Paris. She was a very young woman. She had recently married. She was already a bit sickly between 1851 and 1853 when this portrait was made, and in fact, she was to die of tuberculosis in 1860, just seven years after the painting was completed. Her husband, the Prince de Broglie, was so consumed with grief that he kept the portrait shrouded in his house throughout his lifetime and would pull off the drapery of it and look lovingly into her eyes. She was a famous beauty, and you can see why with that sort of milky complexion, perfectly regular features, wonderful composure, and a kind of mythic calm. She was famous for being a good conversationalist but not a brilliant one. But [think of her] entering the room, and there would be a hush over the room when she entered, (a) because her clothes were so great, (b) because she had such wonderful looks, and (c) because she had this kind of floating calm for which she was famous. We see her here. She is leaning on a yellow damask chair filled with her evening clothes, indicating that she has either just come back from the opera or the ballet, or is about to go out. You see her gold-embroidered shawl, her gloves, and her wonderful black velvet evening coat arranged on the chair. The dress itself is glorious, and one would love to go to the Costume Institute and see it downstairs. She looks at us with a kind of acceptance of our gaze. It's as if she's accustomed to being looked at, and she knows how to receive our gaze with a kind of, again, calm and, in a certain sense, passivity. It's a portrait which is unbelievably a *tour de force*, and when you look at it, [you see] all of

©2008 The Teaching Company.

the little folds in the satin and the marvelous crinkly details of the sleeves. You can get very involved in her jewelry. If you go into the shop at the Met, you can find reproductions of practically everything in the painting so that you could actually look like her if you want to, if you can afford the dress. One sees this level of detail that is extraordinary but which all gives way to a kind of general quality of the image. He knows when enough is enough, and of course, there is so much detail in this part of the painting and almost none around her in this kind of gray-blue background with a little gilding of the wall, her coat of arms here in the corner to establish her pedigree as an aristocrat—a painting of absolutely extraordinary quality.

Now, we go back a few years to a painting that has to do with the landscape in France and with the way in which the French landscape was brought into the Salon. It's by the earliest truly great landscape painter in France in the 19th century, whose name was Jean-Baptiste-Camille Corot. We've already seen Corot in the 1830s in the forest of Fontainebleau painting the trees as they looked and the rocks as they looked in a marvelous little study on paper, an oil study on paper mounted on canvas, which is in the European Paintings galleries. Here, one sees an enormous painting of 1836, the same decade of the study from life, which was sent to the Salon, to the official Salon exhibition. It's huge, and it represents *Diana and Actaeon*. So it has a subject from mythology, from Greco-Roman mythology, and it sets that subject in a beautifully sort of sylvan, wonderfully observed landscape, which is not a backdrop. This is one of the interesting things about Corot's subject pictures is that the subjects are, if you will, subjugated to the landscape. The figures are small. They fit in landscapes that [tell us that] he has looked at this tree in another location, and this group of trees, and the sort of particular characteristics of these trees in the background. He has looked at cliffs and rocks in the forest of Fontainebleau and constructed this particular group of rocks.

This is a subject in which we see Diana here, with her handmaidens around her, one of whom is coming in from the hunt with a dog— this idea of women huntresses, a sort of band of women hunting. Diana is, of course, about ready to bathe in the forest, and if we have really good eyes, you see over here the figure of Actaeon. And Actaeon sees Diana, and Diana, of course, refuses to be seen and doesn't want to be seen. What she does, as we learn from many,

many, many paintings and, of course, from mythology itself, is that she transforms him into a stag, who is then killed by his own dogs. So he becomes the victim of his hunting and the victim of his prurience. One sees him in the background, very small; you have to look for him. Already he is beginning to sprout the horns of the stag that he will become, and he will be consumed by the hounds that are around him. So the scene has a lot of Classical lore, but it's set in a really wonderfully observed and perfectly particular landscape setting which is as strong in the picture as are the figures. This balance between setting and figure, which Corot achieves in the 1830s, is one of his most important contributions to the history of art. This is one of his greatest Salon paintings. It's in, of course, the Lehman Collection, and there is nothing like it in the Met. There are many works by Corot in the Metropolitan's European Paintings gallery but nothing of this scale and quality.

Now, Philip Lehman, Robert's father, was very interested in Barbizon School paintings, paintings of the forest of Fontainebleau of mid-century artists, and they were very fashionable in New York in the late 19th century. He had a group of pictures of that type, which I'm not going to talk about. I'm going to talk about the taste of his son, Robert Lehman, and Robert Lehman was open to Impressionism and Postimpressionism and formed this fantastic collection.

Here, one sees a painting by Claude Monet, which is one of the great Monets amongst the many Monets in the Metropolitan Museum. The Metropolitan Museum has almost 30 paintings by Monet from throughout his career, major masterpieces of every decade, the 1860s, [18]70s, [18]80s, [18]90s, and into the 20th century before Monet's death at the age of 86 in 1926. This is a relatively early picture, painted when he was 31 years old. He had left France [during] the Franco-Prussian War and the Commune. He had stayed in England, and he made a little trip to Holland to visit Holland for the first time and see the wonderful canals and the windmills, to go to the Rijksmuseum in Amsterdam, and just sort of make a tour of the country that had invented Realist landscape painting.

Here, he is in Zaandam, and Zaandam was a little town where there were many hotels because the canals are wide and the weather is good. Monet rented a little boat from the hotel where he was staying with his wife and son, and went out into the canal in 1871, and painted the houses of rich Dutch people. They were probably second homes. Their first homes were in the city, and their second homes are on the canal relatively near the sea. There's a pleasure boat in the center and these marvelous colors—this sort of pistachio green, this wonderful grayed pink, the brilliance of the color of this willow tree in the background, a beautiful blue sky which is reflected in almost its entirety in the canal itself. And this [is a] world in which substance is very little and reflection and light [are] a good deal and in which everything is sort of evanescent and moving. We, as the viewer, are floating. We're not on land. We're in the water in a boat. So we're floating, and [we get] this sense of sort of change and everything shifting. In a few minutes, it will all be different, and when the clouds come in, when the sun changes, or when the boat turns, the world, too, will change.

Now, one of the greatest late Impressionist pictures in America is this Renoir. Robert Lehman loved Renoir, and he bought an absolutely iconic picture. This is a picture called [Two] *Young Girls at the Piano*. It was painted in 1892, and it's a painting that has a real reverberance in Renoir's career because it represents Renoir's first official success. In 1891, Renoir was commissioned by the Musée du Luxembourg, which was the museum of contemporary art in that period of time in Paris, the official, the government museum of contemporary art. He was commissioned to paint a picture for the museum, and he chose to do this composition—the composition of two girls, one blonde and one brunette, playing the piano. It's this very upper-class piano with a still life of flowers and a ceramic vase, a kind of interior genre scene. You see in back of the curtains a luxurious house with a painting on the wall and a soft sofa on the side; in the foreground, another luxurious chair with music that has been neglected or thrown off by the girls as, in the brilliant light of the day in the afternoon, they're singing and playing together. [They have an] enraptured quality—the sense that they're fully engaged in the music, one turning the pages, and the other playing the piano and also helping with the pages. They're both so consumed with the music that they're unaware of being seen. Renoir was a master figure painter. He had become the greatest figure painter of the Impressionists with his friend Degas. Whereas Degas' figures are very, very much more rooted in the Classical tradition, and much more angular, and much more linear in their confines, he [Renoir] is rooted in the tradition of Rubens and Watteau and Boucher and was fascinated with 18th-century French art. You can see the softness of these forms as one looks at this picture. Now, the painting for Luxembourg was such a success that his great dealer, Durand-Ruel, commissioned him to do a replica of it, a sort of free replica of it, which is this picture. Then, his greatest patron, Caillebotte, commissioned another. So there are three versions of this composition, of which the Met's is in the best condition and the most perfectly preserved. It is worth the trip to New York to see this painting.

Now, it was at the Armory Show that Robert Lehman was introduced to the painting of Henri Matisse, and he realized that Henri Matisse was really important in the history of art in 1905 and 1906, when he essentially created a new kind of color painting, which we know today as *fauve* painting. *Fauve* means "beast" in French, and the idea of it is that these paintings are so vulgar and so unrelated to the way we actually see that they were painted by beasts. They were painted by people without minds and without culture and civilization. It was these years, 1905 and 1906, when this painting was developed by Derain and Matisse in the south of France with a series of other painters, notably Signac, older painters with them, that he knew, Robert Lehman knew, was the most important time.

This is a small painting, only 17 by a little more than 21 inches in size. It was painted in the south of France in the summer of 1906, and it represents just trees outside of Collioure, which is a town on the Mediterranean in the south of France in the Riviera. He's not painting the sea, and he's not painting anything particularly interesting in itself. We just see these two trees that are kind of battling it out in the foreground. What we see is a whole series of colors that when we think about what this landscape must have actually looked like—I mean, the grass was green, and the mountains in the background were probably sort of blue and green, and the trees have brown bark—and then when we look at actually what we're seeing, we see all of these lavenders, oranges, purples, brilliant red-oranges, and colors that were probably not actually there in nature but are there in the picture. [W]hat he's doing is creating a kind of chromatic world which is almost savagely intense, in which one takes something rather benign, two trees on a lawn in front of mountains, and turns them into a kind of incredible dance of color and line. They seem almost to be battling with each other in a kind of conversation of lines, with these colors having a marvelous time. This little picture has a sort of wallop to it when you go down the wall, in spite of its size. It's this moment in the history of color painting which is of supreme significance, and it's before the painting of *The Dance* that we saw in the 20th-century collection.

Now, André Derain, Matisse's friend, was with him in Collioure, but afterwards, he decided to go off to London. He went off to London, and we all know London is the city that is gray, and foggy, and colorless, and drab. So he goes to London later in 1905–06. He is in London, and he is painting the Houses of Parliament. He makes the Houses of Parliament bright blue. He creates this world in which the Thames, the sort of sludgy Thames, is full of lilacs, pale lemon yellows, and kind of celadon blues, colors that we associate with Chinese ceramics of the Ming Period more than with the water of the Thames. He makes the building into a sort of brilliant, bristling blue world which invades the clouds, equally blue and with wonderful greens in them and little areas of pink. It's sort of a big picture, and one sees that Derain is going to London and taking the lessons from Collioure, from the south of France, and applying them to this gray city and creating a kind of chromatic symphony in blues with other colors that makes it clear to us that he had already seen Monet's paintings of the same subject. Monet goes in 1903 to London and paints a whole series of pictures of the Houses of Parliament which are much more like foggy London. They are not so shot through with so many colors as the *fauve* picture by Derian, but they push London toward the blue and this sort of symphony of blue and greeny-blues. One sees how this works in the history of French art.

Now, Robert Lehman also loved [Pierre] Bonnard, and Bonnard is a painter who, with his friend [Édouard] Vuillard, was a member of a group of artists called *Les Nabis*, "The Prophets." *Nabi* is the Hebrew word for "prophet," and they were interested in seeing within their own daily lives a kind of chromatic world, a world of color, which is so intense and so vibrant that the ordinariness of our lives is intensified and made extraordinary to us by our re-observation of it. This is a large picture from the mid-1920s, from 1924, which is called *Before Dinner*. One sees Bonnard's wife, Marthe, [and] a visitor, a wonderful sort of yellow-haired visitor, and we sort of wonder about the relationship between Marthe and the yellow-haired visitor in her chair. We see the two places set for dinner and wonder sort of where Bonnard is in all of this. We see that the painting was painted at night because in the upper right-hand corner is the light that sheds all of its light upon the table. And we see the shadow of the table. You begin to kind of go through this symphony of color that is almost like a Monet water lily wallpaper. In the background, you notice this wonderful little dog that's coming into the room from behind the chair, and you begin to become involved in a reading of a picture, the subject of which is utterly banal. It's completely banal, and it has nothing to do with anything enlightened. There's no mythology. You're not going to learn anything or feel better about yourself as a result of looking at the picture, but chromatically, it's so extraordinary that the emotion from the picture, the sense of the picture conveying something important, comes sheerly from color and from the interrelationships amongst color. This is one of the great masterpieces of color painting in New York.

The last painting I want to show you is by Balthus, and we saw Balthus's great painting of *Summer* with its sort of mysterious couples and a great cliff-like landscape in the Department of 20th-Century Art. This is an extraordinary painting from 1955 which represents a young woman who lived with Balthus and was sort of his muse. All through her sort of early teen years, she posed in the nude for Balthus, and many people have thought many things about that. I'm not going to go there, but one sees her here in the nude in front of a fireplace, looking into a mirror, arranging her hair in a kind of manner which is so Classical, so still, so perfect that, again, we know that Balthus knew the history of art. This is a picture that was painted before he goes to be the director of the French Academy in Rome, a job for which he was supremely well qualified because he knew so well the Louvre and the history of art. [We can see] that whenever he painted even his muse, his sort of nubile, teenage muse unaware of being seen in front of the mirror, he is thinking, of course, about Egyptian art and about the poses of Egyptian art. Of course, the Egyptian art that he knew was in the Louvre, but it's very easy to go from the Lehman Collection into the Egyptian wing [of the Met] and find a work of art like this, a wooden sculpture from almost 2,000 years before Christ, which has the very same hieratic pose. She is, of course, not arranging her hair but carrying something, so one arm [is] at her side and the other arm [held] at her top, with this kind of incredible clarity of composition that has its roots in Egyptian art.

Now, the Lehman works on paper are extraordinary, and I'm going to take you on a little romp through some of my favorite ones. This is a beautiful drawing by Ingres, and Robert Lehman loved Ingres. This is a drawing done about 1814 in Rome. It's probably his wife, Ingres' wife, as the model, and she's got her head a little bit inclined. She's wearing very little, except she's wearing something. She's not nude; she has a kind of drapery around her so that it's not an erotic drawing necessarily. This is a drawing that was made in preparation for a painting which is now in the Fogg Museum, which is a representation of *Raphael and the Fornarina*, who was Raphael's beautiful mistress, with whom he was deeply in love, who was his principal muse, and who was his model for this painting. This is a great Raphael Madonna, the "*Madonna of the Chair*," which is now in the Pitti Palace in Florence. One sees, in fact, that the Lehman drawing is much more like the head in the Raphael painting than it is like the head in the eventual Fogg study in which he brings her more upright. She looks at us in a way—there is a sort of transformation, and so one can see that he has made this drawing as he's studying Raphael's relationship with his muse. This is Ingres' relationship with his muse, his new wife, and the two are in parallel, both in preparation for a painting, which I've said already, of 1814, which is in the Fogg Museum.

Lehman also loved drawings by mid-century artists, and though he had one Millet drawing that proved to be a forgery, a fantastic drawing—that's absolutely right—and like all great collectors he occasionally made mistakes, but when the cream rose to the top, it was the best of cream. This is a wonderful drawing which is the best of cream, by Jean-François Millet, of a really simple subject, young peasant women carrying fagots from the forest to get them through the winter. They are sort of bowed under the weights of them. There is a sense of their inevitability, of the timeliness of this sheet, and it's a wonderful charcoal heightened with whitewash and charcoal on the border on a very deep blue-gray paper. It's the sense of the blue-gray of the paper that gives a kind of chill, a bone-chilling quality to this beautiful drawing.

There's a marvelous drawing by Degas in the collection which is one of my favorite drawings, and it shows a dancer with this wonderful squiggly, little line coming out of her shoe. She is sort of resting in between poses. This is not a balletic pose. This is an "I'm tired" pose, and "I'm stretching a little bit before the next round." It's on this wonderful paper that at one time was hot pink. It was really pink, and it was a coated paper, which has, of course, faded to a kind of pale pink through time. It has two sides; this is the back of the drawing, representing probably ballerinas fixing their tutus or rearranging their clothing but which relates very closely to a painting in the Met of the same year of an ironer, a woman ironing, which came from the Havemeyer collection. One can see how Degas investigates poses which are similar across different types of models and learns lessons at every point in time. The Lehman drawing has a rhyme in this beautiful painting from the Havemeyer collection in the Metropolitan Museum. It also has another rhyme in another drawing, also on this hot pink paper which is faded, also from the Havemeyer collection, which is in the Department of Drawings and Prints at the Met. Again, [we note] the links of what's in the Lehman with what's in the rest of the museum.

There are three wonderful drawings in the Lehman collection by the German artist Adolph Menzel, who was the greatest German artist of the second half of the 19th century. You've noticed that I've said almost nothing about German art, and that's not because I don't know anything about it and it's not because I don't like it. It's because there's almost none of it in America and certainly almost none of it at the Met. These three drawings by Menzel, along with some drawings by Menzel in the Drawings and Prints Department, are the only works by one of the greatest artists in the history of art because Americans, and the Met in particular, have always had a kind of prejudice against German art. So we have very little of it in our greatest museum.

This is a powerful sheet, undoubtedly from a sketchbook, of two heads of one woman, one against the light and one with light shining on it. This is *contre-jour*, "against the day," and this is with the light. She is wonderfully beautiful. He draws her eye, this thing, twice to sort of get it and get the relationship between the eyebrow, the sparkling eye, and her hair at the top. It's really rapidly done, and he loved it so much that he puts his initials, AM in '79, in the lower left-hand corner. Menzel made thousands of drawings, and there's hardly a bad one. He was one of the greatest draftsmen in the history of art, and one is grateful to Robert Lehman for having bought three drawings and given them to the Met.

Now, he [Lehman] loved Renoir, and we don't think of Renoir as a draftsman. We think of Renoir as a painter, but there six wonderful drawings by Renoir in the Lehman Collection, of which this is one of my favorites. It's done in the middle of the 1880s, and it represents his new wife, Aline Charigot Renoir (they were married by now), sitting with her wonderful round face and a new blue dress with her scarf in front of a mirror or a window. It's a kind of fresh and fantastic watercolor, the quality of which makes you realize that Renoir was just as great a draftsman as his great friend and archrival Cézanne.

This is a wonderful Seurat drawing, which is exactly the same date as the Renoir drawing but represents a paid model posed chastely, absolutely frontally, placed right in the middle of the paper, in his studio. This is a little stove to heat the studio in the corner with its jaunty, little legs. There's a work of art pinned to the studio wall behind her, and she looks at you hieratically as if, again, she is an ancient Greek *kouros* or a work of Egyptian sculpture transformed into a young woman in a painter's studio in 1886 in Paris. Now, there are no lines in this drawing. It's black chalk, which is carefully pushed on a surface of a very heavily textured paper. Sometimes, it's dragged lightly over the sheet, and it just sits on the ridges of the paper. Sometimes, he digs it in and the pressure is greater, breaking down the ridges of the paper to create these deep blacks of her hair, of her eyes, of the sides of her breasts, and of course, of this long strip of molding on the bottom—a masterful drawing.

This is from two years later by Odilon Redon, the great sort of Symbolist, we would call him, artist from Bordeaux, and it represents not something that one sees but something that one imagines. This is Bellepheron, and Bellepheron was the only human whom Pegasus would allow to ride him. One sees the great winged horse of antiquity and of lore, and we see the great winged horse in the corner of a kind of landscape that's just shot full of light. It's as if light is pouring forth from the upper left corner, and [we see] this horse, and the blackness of his wings, and this tiny man, Bellepheron, who seems to be grooming Pegasus. In the drawing, the horse seems almost more human than the human figure, and he looks at us with a kind of wisdom of the ages that only Greco-Roman antiquity could bring to Odilon Redon.

I want to end with a wonderful drawing by Félix Vallotton, which was made in 1895 in Paris, and it shows Paris on a windy day, with women running around; and their skirts, dresses, and capes being buffeted in the wind; a little Hansom cab here; a military group in the upper left-hand corner; a worker on the street; a kind of melee of people on the streets. I want to end with it because of all places in which Robert Lehman felt at home, it was Paris. His French was impeccable. He knew the city intimately, and he would have known exactly where this drawing was. It would have given him such pleasure as he looked at it in his New York townhouse, remembering his annual trips to Paris.

Lecture Twenty-Four
The People of the Museum

Scope:

Though The Metropolitan Museum of Art may be a veritable encyclopedia of art history, the museum—like all great museums—is only as strong and resilient as the curators who run it and the donors who provide it with magnificent works of art. As a conclusion to this course, we will look at the people behind the museum's success. We will consider the impact of the museum's many curators, from its first, Luigi Palma di Cesnola (1832–1904), to its most recent, Philippe de Montebello (b. 1936). While the museum's curators have defined the mission and goals of The Metropolitan Museum of Art, the museum's donors and benefactors—including historical giants like J. P. Morgan (1837–1913) and John D. Rockefeller (1839–1937)—have provided it with a bounty of rare and exciting works of art. The Metropolitan Museum of Art is an institution made by individuals, some of whom were successful financially and others who were successful in terms of their art expertise. Bringing together these two worlds creates an extraordinary museum; understanding their impact creates an equally extraordinary museum experience.

Outline

I. Throughout our journey through The Metropolitan Museum of Art, we have been into every single department. You now have a sense of the whole range of the collections at this extraordinary art museum.

    A. I want to give you a sense of the other people at the museum whose tastes are a bit forgotten because their works are scattered throughout the museum.

    B. The contents of The Metropolitan Museum of Art come, by and large, from donations by those who believe in the institution and its mission; oftentimes, visitors to the museum do not think about these donors.

II. The Metropolitan Museum of Art's directors manage the staff, hire people, control the museum, work for the trustees, and define the principles and future goals of the museum.

A. The museum has been fortunate to have a series of directors who have stayed for a long time, fostering a sense of trust in the institution.

B. The first director of the museum was Luigi Palma di Cesnola (1832–1904).

    1. He became a passionate archaeologist in Cyprus and formed a huge collection of art.

    2. In 1879, when the Louvre considered purchasing his collection, The Metropolitan Museum of Art immediately brought the collection to the United States and made di Cesnola the first director of the museum.

    3. He convinced the museum's trustees that they could collect original antiquities, not just plaster casts of works that were in European museums and at archeological sites.

C. Thomas Hoving (b. 1931) was director of the museum during the period when it attained its vast size.

    1. Everything he did was associated with publicity, and he put The Metropolitan Museum of Art on the map.

    2. One of his most famous acquisitions is Velazquez's *Juan de Pareja (born about 1610, died 1670)*; the acquisition of this painting in 1971 brought people to the galleries of European paintings.

D. Philippe de Montebello (b. 1936) has been the museum's director for the last 30 years.

    1. He has improved the quality of both the museum and its galleries (including the new gallery for Greek and Roman art) and has made a series of extraordinary acquisitions.

    2. One of these acquisitions is Duccio's *Madonna and Child*, which added to the superb group of early Italian panel paintings in the museum.

III. The Metropolitan Museum of Art's donors are an incredible group of people composed of many extraordinary individuals.

A. J. P. Morgan (1837–1913) was one of the greatest donors in the history of the museum; he was a trustee from 1903 until his death in 1913.

1. He gave a lot to the museum, including Raphael's *Madonna and Child Enthroned with Saints*.
2. His gift of period rooms, including the bedroom from the Sagredo Palace in Venice, changed the institution.

B. William Kissam Vanderbilt (1849–1920) gave numerous works to the museum, including Boucher's *The Toilet of Venus*, Sir Joshua Reynolds's *Captain George K. H. Coussmaker (1759–1801)*, and Sir Thomas Gainsborough's *Mrs. Grace Dalrymple Elliott (1754?–1823)*.

C. Henry Osborne Havemeyer (1847–1907) and his second wife, Louisine Elder Havemeyer (1855–1929), bequeathed an extraordinary collection to the museum that included *Whose Sleeves?* (Tagasode) from the late 16th century; Hokusai's prints (including *The Great Wave at Kanagawa*); Rembrandt's *Portrait of a Woman* (1632); El Greco's *View of Toledo*; Ingres's *Joseph-Antoine Moltedo (born 1775)*; Manet's *Mademoiselle V... in the Costume of an Espada*; Cézanne's *Mont Sainte-Victoire and the Viaduct of the Arc River Valley* (1882–1885); and Degas's *The Dancing Class* (probably 1871).

D. John D. Rockefeller (1839–1937) gave in more strategic ways. He had the economic power and foresight to make important pieces such as the Mesopotamian relief panels possible for the museum.

E. Jules Semon Bache (1861–1944) gave Petrus Christus's Portrait of a Carthusian.

F. Nelson Rockefeller (1908–1979) owned the Museum of Primitive Art, which became The Metropolitan Museum of Art's Department of African, Oceanic, and Ancient American Art; the museum would be poor without his belief in these kinds of art, including the mid-19th-century shield from the Solomon Islands, the Edo pendant mask, and the Mayan mirror bearer.

G. Jayne Wrightsman gave Vermeer's *Study of a Young Woman* (probably 1665–1667) to the museum in memory of Theodore Rousseau, Jr., who was the curator of European paintings. Other gifts of hers include *Rubens, His Wife Helena Fourment (1614-1673), and Their Son Peter Paul (born 1637)* by Rubens; *Allegory of the Planets and*

Continents by Giambattista Tiepolo; *A Dance in the Country* by Giovanni Domenico Tiepolo; and *Piazza San Marco* by Canaletto.

IV. The Metropolitan Museum of Art is an institution made by individuals, some of whom were successful financially, others who were successful in terms of their art expertise. Bringing together these two worlds creates an extraordinary museum.

V. All art is human; it is made by people for people. There are extraordinary lessons to be learned from works of art when you go to a museum, and this is what I hope has become clear to you as a result of these lectures.

    A. We have talked about the relationship between mothers and children throughout the history of art as seen in works like Berlinghiero's *Madonna and Child* and *Yashoda and Krishna*.

    B. We can look at babies in the history of art, such as the Olmec baby figure and Andrea della Robbia's *Virgin and Child*.

    C. We can see numerous repetitions of infants and little children—including the marble *stele* of a little girl or John Singleton Copley's *Daniel Crommelin Verplanck*—or young men who have made it in the world: Ralph Earl's *Elijah Boardman* or Bronzino's *Portrait of a Young Man*.

    D. We can see images of aging throughout the history of art in every culture, such as Rembrandt's *Self-Portrait* or the pre-Columbian seated figure. There is the sense that one can investigate the human understanding of the life cycle simply by going to a museum.

    E. One can go through the museum's various departments and find works of art that speak about the power of the sea or the abundance of the land, such as Ogata Korin's *Rough Waves* (1704–1709) or van Ruysdael's *Wheat Fields* (c. 1670).

    F. The museum offers a great place to gain both tolerance for and knowledge of world religion through objects like the altarpiece dedicated to Buddha Maitreya, Raphael's *Madonna and Child Enthroned with Saints*, or the mihrab from Isfahan.

G. The Metropolitan Museum of Art is literally inexhaustible—for that reason one should visit it throughout one's life.

Recommended Reading:

Frelinghuysen and Cooney. *Splendid Legacy: The Havemeyer Collection.*

Moffett. *Impressionist and Post-Impressionist Paintings in the Metropolitan Museum of Art.*

Weitzenhoffer. *Havemeyers: Impressionism Comes to America.*

Questions to Consider:

1. Why are gifts and bequests so important to the development of a museum like The Metropolitan Museum of Art?

2. Describe how select works discussed throughout the course illustrate various stages of the human life cycle.

Lecture Twenty-Four—Transcript
The People of the Museum

We're about to come to the end of a long and wonderful journey. We've been into every single department of the Metropolitan Museum, whether it's open to the public or not. You have a sense of the whole range of the collections of this extraordinary American art museum. And in the last two lectures, you've come to have a sense of the taste of one man, Robert Lehman, who gave the collection formed by him and his father, Philip Lehman, to the Metropolitan as an entirety, to be shown in its own wing. What he wanted to do in that gift is not to be forgotten, and he wanted to have his taste not to be forgotten. And what I want to do at the beginning of the concluding lecture is to give you a sense of the other people at the Metropolitan Museum whose tastes are a little bit forgotten because their works are scattered throughout the museum.

The Metropolitan Museum, unlike great government museums in other nations, the contents of which come from rulers and from military conquests, the contents of the Metropolitan Museum come, by and large, from donations. [These] donations [come] from men and women who believe in the institution and its mission, who have grown up going to its galleries, attending its trustee meetings, thinking that it is an important place, forming a collection with the help of curators and the directors with the idea of the museum in mind, and eventually allowing the museum to receive gifts from them, both during their lifetimes and at their deaths.

Oftentimes, normal visitors to museums don't actually think about these donors. But those of us who are in the profession—and I was a museum director and a museum curator for many years of my life—there's a saying that most normal people, when you go into a gallery and you read a label, you read it from the top down. You want to know who the artist is, and what the title is, and when it was made. And those of us in the profession either know or pretend to know all that stuff already, and so we read the label from the bottom up. We're interested in knowing who gave it and when because we're interested in the stories of the formation of the great American art institutions, which are stories about donors and stories about donors who are directed in their collecting and in their giving by the extraordinary staffs that have been assembled in American art museums.

Now, I'm going to talk about two kinds of people in this lecture. The first type of person I'm going to talk about are directors, directors who control the staff, hire people, control the museum, work for the trustees, and have a kind of mission to define the principles, and the future, and the goals of the museum. The Metropolitan Museum has been very fortunate in having a whole series of directors who have been director for a very long time. There's a sort of sense of longevity and of trust in the institution that comes from directors that serve a long time. The first director is no exception to that, and of course, what's interesting about him is that he was neither a New Yorker nor an American. His name was Luigi Palma di Cesnola, and we know, of course, from that, that he wasn't American; he was Italian.

He was a fascinating man. He was involved in the military. He fought in the Civil War even though he was Italian. He was later made a general in the American army as a result of his service in the Civil War. He became a passionate archaeologist in Cyprus. He formed a huge collection of art in Cyprus. That collection was fought over by museums throughout the world, and in fact, it was reported to the trustees of the Metropolitan Museum in the 1870s that the Louvre was considering buying his collection of Cypriotic art. And so they immediately got the collection to the United States, made him the director of the museum, and he became the first director of the Metropolitan Museum in 1879. And today, when you go into the galleries of Cypriotic art—there are three galleries of Cypriotic art—all of that art came from this man who convinced the trustees that they could collect original antiquities, not just plaster casts of works that were in European museums and archaeological sites. So we have to take our hats off to Luigi Palma di Cesnola.

Now, the second director I want to talk about—I'm skipping quite a lot—is Thomas Hoving. Thomas Hoving was the director of the museum during a long period of time in which it really attained its vast size. Remember in the first lecture, I talked about its constriction in the buildings built in the 19th and early 20th centuries and how it was not really until the postwar period where it filled out to its huge form and became a kind of behemoth in the park and New York. And the man who oversaw that expansion was Thomas Hoving. He was an extraordinary showman. He hired brilliant curators. He did great exhibitions. Everything that he did was associated with publicity, and the Met was put on the map by Thomas Hoving. It had been a very polite, even rather sleepy, museum before, and Thomas Hoving was the sort of P.T. Barnum, with a Ph.D., of museums. He created a sense in which everybody had to go to the Met. It didn't matter whether you lived in Los Angeles or Queens, you wanted to go to the Met because you read about it in the newspapers, because you heard about it on television, and because it became extraordinary and exciting.

He did something here. This is one of his most famous acquisitions, the great *Juan de Pareja* by Velázquez, which came to the Metropolitan Museum in 1971. The Met bought it secretly, and Wildenstein's, the dealer in New York, was the bidder, and nobody knew that the Met was buying it. It was a world-record price, and it made the front page of *The New York Times* when it was bought, not just because it was a great painting, but because Hoving had such an extraordinary sense of flair. And what happened is that the European Paintings galleries had become rather sleepy and tired, and the acquisition of this painting made everybody—all New Yorkers, and all tourists, and everybody—go into those galleries after the painting was bought in 1971.

Since 1977, Philippe de Montebello has been the director of the Metropolitan Museum, and you can tell by his name that he's not a native-born American either; he's French. He's from French origin, and in fact, *Montebello* suggests Italian origins before that, and so he is distinctly European. He speaks with this wonderful sort of, one would say, Maurice Chevalier accent, but by now, it's a Philippe de Montebello accent, and it's his own accent. He has presided over the sort of improvement of the big Met that Hoving created. He has made it higher quality, worked at it, improved each of the galleries, done the great new galleries for Greek and Roman art, and made a series of extraordinary acquisitions—very smart, very well selected, very much with his extremely able curators in mind, and I just show you one of them.

It tells you a lot about Philippe de Montebello that this is the acquisition I show you. It's a painting by Duccio, who was one of the great, great painters at the beginning of the Italian Renaissance. It's a painting which is about this big. It's tiny, and it's a painting that is completely by Duccio. It's of remarkable state and quality, and it's a work of art which added to the superb group of early Italian panel paintings in the museum, both in the Lehman Collection and in the Metropolitan Museum's own collection. The Metropolitan Museum paid $45 million for this little painting. It's something that tells you a lot about Philippe de Montebello because it was bought by a man who is a scholar-director, a man who actually wanted to fill a crucial gap in an already excellent collection, rather than to grab the headlines in *The New York Times*.

Now, let's look at some donors. They're an incredible group of people, and I could give a whole course on the donors to the Metropolitan Museum, but I'm going to race through a few of the more extraordinary of them. Of course, J. P. Morgan, John Pierpont Morgan, was one of the greatest donors in the history of the Met. He was a trustee of the Met from 1903 until his death in 1913. He was an extraordinarily great collector. He also founded the Morgan Library. A lot of his collection also went to the Wadsworth Atheneum in the town of his birth, Hartford, Connecticut. Of course, he wasn't a New Yorker, and we have to remember that the museum is not the New York Museum of Art; it's the Metropolitan Museum of Art, meaning it's a museum of many cities, of all cities. And so people from all over America have come to New York, have made New York their home, and have given their things to the Met.

Morgan gave a lot to the Met, [including] probably the greatest painting by Raphael, who was one of the three great artists of the Italian High Renaissance with Leonardo and Michelangelo. This painting is at the Met, and it came to the Met through John Pierpont Morgan. But even more extraordinary in terms of a change of the institution is his gift of period rooms. He was very interested in Americans traveling and virtual travel, and this is the glorious bedroom from the Sagredo Palace in Venice from 1718. I've already talked about all of these things. You see this bedroom, and it's a room that takes you someplace, and Morgan believed in that and gave his works of art, his money, and his sort of persuasive powers to the Met for that reason.

Now, the Vanderbilts were a family—not a New York family but a family who made New York their home. The number of Vanderbilt houses that line Fifth Avenue [is] extraordinary. I've talked already about two pieces of Vanderbilt furniture, a great fireplace and a library table, from other Vanderbilt homes. I'm talking now about William Kissam Vanderbilt, who lived between 1849 and 1920 and who had a great taste for luxury and the high life, as you can imagine that he would. Here, you see his house on Fifth Avenue, and you can see how different it was from everybody else's houses, both on the streets and on the avenue itself. It looked like it sort of trotted out of the Loire Valley and was built in New York for Mr. Vanderbilt.

And, of course, what he gave are works of art that look like this. After his death, he gave the great Boucher *Toilet of Venus*, from 1751. He gave the extraordinary portrait by Reynolds of Captain George Coussmaker, a military man, a sort of dandy, a man who's comfortable with his wealth. And [he gave] the great portrait of Mrs. Grace Dalrymple Elliott by Gainsborough, showing one of the wealthiest, and best bred, and most perfectly dressed women in late-18th-century London, who is here walking in from her country house, and who did so in his Fifth Avenue mansion, and is now doing that in the Metropolitan Museum.

And you also have sort of people who—the Havemeyers, this wonderful couple, H. O. Havemeyer, who made his money with sugar. He was the great sugar magnate of America. His second wife was Louisine Elder Havemeyer, and they married and became—she was really interested in art, and one sees her here as a beautifully dressed young woman, looking perfectly demure and wonderful. This is my favorite photograph of her when she's a suffragette later in life, going down the streets in New York with the torch of the Statue of Liberty, wanting liberty for women. Good for her. And when she died in 1929, in early 1929, the collection that came to the Met was extraordinary. This is a Japanese screen that we haven't seen in the lectures which came from her collection, a Momoyama screen from the late 16th century. We have seen this wonderful print by Hokusai, and she gave all of the prints of Hokusai and many, many hundreds of prints by other Japanese Ukiyo-e artists to the Metropolitan Museum in her bequest in 1929.

The great Rembrandt set of portraits of a woman and a man—and this is the portrait of a woman. I show it to you because, of course, she [Louisine Havemeyer] believed so much in feminism. We don't know her [the subject's] name, but this is a major early Rembrandt portrait in the Metropolitan Museum, thanks to the Havemeyers. Or, as we've seen, the *View of Toledo*, the only important landscape by

El Greco, either in Spain or in the United States; the great Ingres portrait of the postmaster in Napoleonic Rome, one of the great Roman Ingres portraits in America; the Manet, Mademoiselle Victorine dressed as an Espada, from 1862, one of the most shocking pictures of the early 1860s—all of these things came to the Met at the same time. Cézanne: It was very rare in American museums in 1929 to have a Cézanne in the permanent collection. This superb landscape with Mont Sainte-Victoire in the background, and the railway bridge, and the great pine in the foreground—one of the greatest paintings he made—came into the Metropolitan Museum as a result of her [Louisine Havemeyer]. And her Degas's were extraordinary because she knew Degas through Mary Cassatt.

Now, the Havemeyers gave a lot, and there are other people who were much richer than the Havemeyers who gave in much more strategic ways. I'm showing you John D. Rockefeller, one of the great titans of America, a man who made his money, and his early house, and his early fortune in Cleveland and moved to New York with his family later in life as he became a kind of national financier rather than a regional financier. Here, one sees him toward the end of his life with his family in the background, reading his book, looking very thoughtful.

I wanted to show you one work of art that came through him to the museum because it's so extraordinary that one can't imagine going into the Department of Ancient and Near Eastern Art without looking at these huge relief panels from the 9th century B.C., from the city of Nimrud, one of the great cities of the ancient Near Eastern world. When you see these works of art, these enormous works of art, you imagine cities that are even larger than they, and they create a sort of sense of the spectacle of urban life in the 9th century B.C. in the ancient Near East which no smaller work of art, no portable work of art, can convey. It was John D. Rockefeller who had the economic power and the foresight to make that possible for the Met.

Now, there are a lot of people who love Old Master paintings, and I just want to show you one. You could do the Marquands or Benjamin Altman. There are a lot of people whose collections form, collectively, the European Paintings collection, but I want to show you Jules Semon Bache because he owned one of my favorite paintings in the museum—and I hope it has become one of your favorite paintings, too—the Petrus Christus portrait of the

Carthusian, the lay Carthusian monk. We don't know who he is, and it's another painting that's tiny. And what you learn—what I would actually love is to have known Mr. Bache, and to have seen this painting in his New York apartment or house, and to have seen him with it, and to have him hand it to me or hand it to a class of students from the Institute of Fine Arts, and have a sense of his own relationship with this object. Because in his generosity, it just sits on the wall at the Met, and you count the hairs in the beard, and you look at the fly on the parapet, and you think about what pleasure this painting gave to Mr. Bache.

Now, Nelson Rockefeller was one of the great forces of New York. He was, of course, governor of New York. He had this tumultuous personality, and you see him here in a photograph which I love. He's looking at an Oceanic object. He's actually looking at the camera, but there's an Oceanic [object] in between him and Princess Beatrix from the Netherlands, who became Queen Beatrix of the Netherlands. And he's taking her and not showing her Dutch art, which you'd think that he would, but showing her primitive art, what was then called primitive art, because he owned and ruled the Museum of Primitive Art, which came into the Metropolitan Museum and became its Departments of African, Oceanic and Ancient American Art, and one sees him here.

The museum would be so poor without his belief in these kinds of works of art. This is a very rare, and early, and important shield, overmodel shield, from the Solomon Islands, which I've already talked about, but which came from Nelson Rockefeller, [as did] this wonderful Benin mask, one of the greatest pieces of ivory carving from Africa. Africa is absolutely known for its carving in elephant ivory, and this is an absolute masterpiece, coming to the Met as a result of Nelson Rockefeller and the only surviving masterpiece of lowland Maya wooden art, an art that absolutely was lost because these objects don't survive in a jungle culture. It, too, this rare object from Maya, came to the Met through him.

The last donor I want to tell you about is Jayne Wrightsman. Jayne Wrightsman is standing here, beautifully dressed in her superb apartment, and in back of her is one of the works of art that she gave. It's by Vermeer, the rarest artist in America. It was given in memory of Theodore Rousseau, who was the curator of European Paintings for years at the Met and whom she adored. There is this sense in which her connection was not merely to the artist but also to the staff of the museum. And this great Rubens—Rubens himself, and his wife, Helena Fourment, and their son, Peter—from the 1630s was given to the museum in honor of Sir John Pope-Hennessy, who was also one of the greatest curators of European Painting in the history of the Met. What she does is, in her gifts, she recognizes the importance of the staff. One can't imagine the collection of 18th-century Venetian art without this superb Giambattista Tiepolo, this equally superb Giandomenico Tiepolo, and this wonderful painting by Canaletto—all three works of art given to the Met by Jayne Wrightsman.

Now, all these people and literally hundreds of others—both the hundreds of people who are on the staff of the Met and the hundreds of people who have been donors and trustees of the Met—have made the Met. It is an institution which was made by individuals, some of whom were enormously successful financially; others of whom were enormously successful in terms of what they learned about art, their art expertise. It's the bringing together of those two worlds that creates such an extraordinary museum. You need great curators, and great directors, and great donors, and great collectors to make a great museum in America because the state doesn't buy it for you. We don't have our grand dukes and our kings who go out of fashion and give us their collections.

What I want to talk about now is the way in which, when you come into a great museum—and we've seen that great museums are organized by art historical principles. When you go into a series of galleries, it's with all these objects that are arranged in chronological and cultural order. And you spend so much time thinking about this style and that style, and this culture and that culture, and this religion and that religion that sometimes it's easy to forget that all art is human. It's made by people for people. It's made by individuals or groups of individuals for other individuals or groups of individuals. There are extraordinary lessons to be learned from works of art when you go through a museum, and this is what I hope has become clear to you as a result of these lectures.

When you think even about life and the life cycle—we've talked about the relationships between mothers and children in the history of art. All through the history of art, in virtually every culture, there are works of art that are about that bond between mothers and children. And in this case, in this wonderful early Italian painting by Berlinghiero—which was the first painting I talked about in the European paintings lectures—one sees this rather adult-looking child and his kind of worried mother who looks off to the side, and one kind of worries about Christ and Mom in looking at this image. You can sort of think about, in all of these Virgin's and Child's in the museum, what the psychological relationships are between mother and child and between the mother and child unit and you as the viewer. But you can also do that in other parts of the Met, [as] we've seen in this *Yashoda and Krishna*, an earthly mother. This is a surrogate mother in this case and another divine child, Krishna, who is suckling at his mother's breast. These two objects were made about 100 years apart but literally thousands of miles apart and in cultural traditions which have almost nothing to do with each other.

We can look at babies in the history of art. Here's an Olmec baby given by Nelson Rockefeller, [dated] between the 12th and the 9th century B.C., in its wonderful chubby form, and it's looking up at its parent or something that's looking at it. And we can look at another ceramic baby, this one by Andrea della Robbia, and this one, of course, with Mom, the Virgin. But this little kid is pretty independent, and he's also made of the same material, the similar white slip over him, as the Olmec baby from a millennium, more than a millennium, earlier. And there is a sense that we're linking with these children when we think about them as children.

Or little children: You could do a whole book about infants and little children in the Met. This is a grave stele for a young girl, a little girl who died, like so many little girls have died throughout human history. Here, she's memorialized in this marvelous Greek tomb relief with her two birds, and one of them is pecking at her, and the other one looks like it might fly off. And then you can go into another gallery and see this painting of a little boy, who's probably not so different in age from that little girl, and he has his pet, too, but this is a pet squirrel tied to a string. And he looks out at us, and we know that he wants to play. There's this wonderful mischievousness about him and his wise eyes.

Or young men who have made it, and this is a young man who has made it. His name is Elijah Boardman. He was painted by Ralph Earl, and he's shown with all of his learning down below and all of his stuff that he makes his money from at the door, looking directly into our eyes. And then you can go to the European Paintings gallery and see this very elegant young man who's totally full of himself, about the same age as that fellow, also equally confident in his gaze at us, allowing us both to gaze at him and gazing at us. One can see that he doesn't care so much about his attributes, and we don't need to know how he made his money and what he is because he is so self-possessed.

And then the images of age: There are many, many images of age and aging throughout the history of art in every culture. And [you can] think about that when you go through—the wonderful late Rembrandt self-portrait of 1660 (he dies nine years later, in 1669)—we can see, we can feel, every crevice in his face. And one sees here, when one goes into the Pre-Columbian galleries, a work of art where this lined, sort of haggard, weird, emaciated old man is emerging from the earth, and his eyes are buggy, and he has wrinkles all around him, and one thinks of the representation of the wise old man or the god. We don't know whether he's human or a deified person. [We get] the sense that one can investigate the human understanding of the life cycle simply by going to a museum and deciding to do it by the age of human figures.

Now, all of us live in nature, and Central Park is a great museum in nature. We think a lot, and we think a lot today particularly, since we imagine our planet to be in peril, and we worry about the future of the natural world, and we realize our effect upon the natural world. Well, [people have] always realized that their effect upon the natural world is strong and that the effect of the natural world on them is strong. One can go through department after department after department at the Met, whether you're thinking about costumes, cloaks, and hats, and shawls, and whatever, to protect you against bad weather or wind; works of art that tell you about the power of the sea; works of art that tell you about the abundance of the land.

These works of art are everywhere in the museum. And thinking about that; I mean, deciding that well, I really don't know very much about art, but I'm very interested in nature, and I'm very interested in the ways in which mankind has decided to make imprints with art materials about nature. That kind of way of seeing the Met is another way of seeing the Met. You can see the great screens in the Japanese galleries by Ogata Korin, which make sort of decorative patterns out of the power of the waves that surround an island nation. Or when you're in the European Paintings galleries, there are literally scores of landscapes, some pure—in other words, having no figural subject, like this one by Ruisdael—and other ones where landscapes are serving as settings for the rest on the flight into Egypt or a scene from antiquity which is set in a natural scene. The relationship between human action and nature can be measured by looking at works of art. Works of art are a kind of clue to the ways that our ancestors in every culture thought about these issues.

Now, living today, probably the most pressing issue—the issue that we hear about the most when we read the newspapers and we think about the traumas of our civilization—has to do with the relationship between religion and history. I know of no better place to gain not just a sense of tolerance about world religion but knowledge about world religion. You don't have to read the entire Koran; you don't have to read all of the books about Buddhism; you don't have to read all those long and incredibly difficult books about Hinduism, which I've actually tried to read. You can go to the museum; and you can look at works of art; and you can read the very well-focused and very interesting labels identifying the various deities, and their systems, and what they mean to people, and the humans within the realms of the divine; and think very, very clearly—and on your own and independently—about the relationship between religion and culture in all human cultures, in Oceania, in Africa, in the ancient New World, in China, in the Greek world, in the Roman world, in the Egyptian world. There is not a place [left out]. The European Paintings galleries are [also] filled with works of art that tell us about Christian religion, both Protestant and Catholic.

In a certain way, as one goes through the Met looking at objects and using it as a way to open up your own sense of the power of world religions, that is one of the most important functions in the museum. I show you three objects [some] of my favorites. This is a gilt bronze altarpiece dated 524 A.D., which is Chinese. It's in the Chinese galleries, and it shows the Buddha Maitreya, or the Bodhisattva Maitreya, standing in the middle surrounded by all these things. I've already analyzed it, but it's a work of art that has donors and has got all sorts of subsidiary figures. You stand in the center in front of it. You worship it in a certain way. There would have been candles. There would have been chanting and music, and you think about what you would have done in front of this object if you lived then and if you believed in that system of religion.

And then you go upstairs to the European Paintings galleries and stand in front of the Raphael given by J. P. Morgan, and you can see another scene. There are no donors in this picture, but there are saints, some historical—actually, all historical—related to the divine figures in the center, and then completely deified figures. This is the realm that is at once divine and human, below. And this realm above is completely divine in the lunette, and you stand centered in front of it, even though it's a painting—it's in a paintings gallery—and you arrange yourself, and you think about it in a certain way whether you're a Catholic or a Buddhist or Muslim. There's a kind of sense in which, as you think about how these objects communicate, you learn something profound about religion.

And the same with this wonderful *mihrab* or prayer niche from Isfahan, from the 14th century. This is an empty object, and I analyzed the texts all around it that teach you life lessons. And, of course, most of us can't read Arabic, so most of us can't understand this object. But when you read the label and when you think about it, you can understand something that's so much more profound than simply reading an article about Islamic extremism or Islam in the newspaper. There is a sense in which the incredible complexity and the incredible peace of Islam [are] made clear from this object, and these are lessons you learn at the Met. The Metropolitan Museum is literally inexhaustible, and it is for that reason that one should go to it throughout one's life.

Works Discussed

Notes:

The format and content of the entries in the Works Discussed list and on screen may vary somewhat depending upon the requirements of the organization that supplied the image. The titles of these works appear as listed in museum catalogues and may vary slightly from titles as used by the professor during a particular lecture.

Artists' names are shown in bold in the following list. If no name is cited, the artist is unknown. Works are listed in the order in which they first appear in the course; if a particular work reappears in another lecture, it is not cited again. Unless otherwise noted, all works of art are located in The Metropolitan Museum of Art in New York City.

Lecture Thirteen

Antonio Rossellino. *Madonna and Child with Angels.* 15th century. Marble, gilding on halo and dress, 28¾ × 20¼" (73 × 51.4 cm).

Andrea della Robbia. *Virgin and Child.* 15th century (c. 1470–1475). Glazed terracotta relief, 37¼ × 21¾" (94.9 × 54.9 cm).

Gian Lorenzo Bernini. *Bacchanal: A Faun Teased by Children.* c. 1616–1617. Marble, H 52" (132.1 cm).

Giovanni Battista Foggini. *Grand Prince Ferdinando de' Medici (1663–1713).* 17th century (c. 1683–1685). Marble, H (including base) 39" (99.1 cm).

————. *Cosimo III de' Medici, Grand Duke of Tuscany (1642–1723).* Marble, H (with base) 39".

Jean-Louis Lemoyne. *La Crainte des Traits de l'Amour (The Fear of the Arrows of Cupid).* 1739–1740. Marble, H 72" (182.9 cm).

Jean-Antoine Houdon. *Sabine Houdon.* 1788. White marble on gray marble base, overall (without base) 11 × 8½ × 6" (27.5 × 21.6 × 15.2 cm), H (with base) 13½" (44.5 cm).

Augustin Pajou. *Madame de Wailly.* 1789. Marble, base of gray marble, overall (without base) 24½ × 20½ × 10½" (62.2 × 52.1 × 26.7 cm), H (with base) 30¼" (76.8 cm).

Antonio Canova. *Perseus with the Head of Medusa.* 1804–1806. Marble, overall 92¼" (234 m). Fletcher Fund, 1967.

Apollo Belvedere. c. 350–320 B.C. Marble copy (Roman), H 88" (230 m). Museo Pio-Clementino, Vatican Museums, Vatican City.

Jean-Baptiste Carpeaux. *Ugolino and His Sons.* Modeled c. 1860–1861, executed in marble 1865–1867. Saint-Béat marble, H 78" (195.6 cm).

Edgar Degas. *The Little Fourteen-Year-Old Dancer.* Executed c. 1880, cast in 1922. Bronze, partially tinted, with cotton skirt and satin hair-ribbon, wood base, H (without base) 39" (99.1 cm).

Auguste Rodin. *Honoré de Balzac.* Probably 1891. Terracotta, H 9¼" (23.5 cm).

Lecture Fourteen

Feather Box. New Zealand, Maori. c. 18th century. Wood with shell inlay, 17¾" (44.7 cm).

Mask (Buk, krar, or kara). Australia, Torres Strait, Mabuiag Island. Mid- to late 19th century. Turtleshell, wood, feathers, coconut fiber, resin, shell, paint, 17½ × 25 × 22¾" (44.5 × 63.5 × 57.8 cm).

Standing Male Figure (Tiki). Mangareva (Gambier Islands), Mangarevan people. 18th–early 19th century. Wood, 38¾ × 10 × 7½" (98.4 × 25.4 × 19.1 cm).

Male Figure (Moai Tangata). Chile, Easter Island (Rapa Nui), Rapanui people. Early 19th century. Wood, obsidian, bone, 16 × 4 × 2½" (40.6 × 9.9 × 6.4 cm).

Shield (Grere'o [?]). Solomon Islands, possibly Santa Isabel Island. Early to mid-19th century. Cane, mother-of-pearl, pigments, fiber, 33¼ × 11 × 1½" (84.5 × 27.9 × 3.8 cm).

Helmet Mask (Temes Mbalmbal), Vanuatu, Malakula Island, Mbotgote. Mid-20th century, wood, vegetable fiber, pig tusks, glass, metal, paint, 26 × 15½ × 19" (66 × 39.4 × 48.3 cm).

Skull Hook (Agiba). Papua New Guinea, Kerewa, Pai'ia'a, Kikori Delta. 19th–early 20th century. Wood, paint, 56 × 29½ × 5" (142.2 × 74.9 × 12.7 cm).

Bis Poles. New Guinea, Irian Jaya, Faretsj River Asmat people, Omandesep. Mid-20th century. Wood, paint, fiber, 210 × 39 × 63" (538 × 99 × 16 cm).

Seated Figure. Mali, Djenné. 13th century. Terracotta, 10 × 11¾" (25.4 × 29.9 cm).

Pendant Mask. Iyoba, Nigeria, Edo, Court of Benin. 16th century. Ivory, iron, copper (?), 9½ × 5 × 3¼" (23.8 × 12.7 × 8.3 cm). Gift of Nelson A. Rockefeller, 1972.

Figure: Seated Couple. Mali, Dogon. 16th–19th century. Wood, metal, 28¾ × 9½" (73 × 23.7 cm).

The Buli Master (Ngongo ya Chintu possibly). Prestige Stool: Female Caryatid. Democratic Republic of Congo, Luba/Hemba. 19th century. Wood, metal studs, H 24" (61 cm).

Power Figure: Male (Nkisi). Democratic Republic of Congo, Kongo. 19th–20th century. Wood, pigment, nails, cloth, beads, shells, arrows, leather, nuts, twine, H 23 × 10¼ × 10" (58.8 × 26 × 25.4 cm).

Mask (Kpeliye). Côte d'Ivoire, Senufo. 19th–20th century. Wood, horns, fiber, cotton cloth, feather, metal, sacrificial material, 30¼ × 13 × 9" (76.8 × 33 × 22.9 cm).

Reliquary Head (Nlo Bieri). Gabon, Fang, Betsi group. 19th–20th century. Wood, metal, palm oil, 18½ × 9¾ × 6¾" (46.5 × 24.8 × 16.8 cm).

Lecture Fifteen

"Baby" Figure. Mexico, Olmec. 12th–9th century B.C. Ceramic, cinnabar, red ochre, H 13½ × 12½ × 5¾" (34 × 31.8 × 14.6 cm).

Mask. Mexico, Olmec. 10th–6th century B.C. Jadeite, H 6¾ × 6½ × 6½" (17.1 × 16 × 16 cm).

"Smiling" Figure. Mexico, Remojadas. 7th–8th century. Ceramic, 18¾ × 11¾ × 6¼" (47.5 × 29.9 × 15.9 cm).

Mirror-Bearer. Mexico or Guatemala, Maya. 6th century. Wood, red hematite traces, 14 × 9 × 9" (35.9 × 22.9 × 22.9 cm). Bequest of Nelson A. Rockefeller, 1979.

Vessel with Mythological Scene. Guatemala, Maya. 8th century. Ceramic, H 5½" (14 cm), Diameter 4½" (11.4 cm).

Seated Standard Bearer. Mexico, Aztec. Second half 15th–early 16th century. Laminated sandstone, H 31¾" (80.5 cm).

Frog Pendant. Costa Rica, Chiriquí. 11th–16th century. Cast gold, H 4" (10.5 cm).

Lime Container (*Poporo*). Colombia, Quimbaya. 1st–7th century. Cast gold, H 9" (22.9 cm).

Seated Figure. Colombia or Ecuador, Tolita/Tumaco. 1st century B.C.–A.D. 1st century. Ceramic, 25 × 14½ × 13" (63.5 × 36.8 × 33 cm).

Feline-Head Bottle. Peru, Tembladera. 9th–5th century B.C. Ceramic, postfired paint, H 12¾" (32.4 cm), W 8" (20.5 cm).

Feline Incense Vessel. Bolivia, Tiwanaku. 6th–9th century. Ceramic, H 10" (25.7 cm), W 8¼" (21 cm).

Double-spout bottle. Peru, Nazca. 2nd–4th century. Ceramic, H 6¼" (15.9 cm).

Funerary Mask. Peru, Sicán (Lambayeque). 10th–11th century. Gold, copper overlays, cinnabar, H 11½" (29.2 cm), W 19½" (49.5 cm).

Deer Vessel. Peru, Chimú. 14th–15th century. Silver (hammered), 5 × 3¼ × 7½" (12.7 × 8.3 × 19.1 cm).

Deity Figure (Zemí). Dominican Republic (?), Taino. 15th–16th century. Ironwood, shell, 27 × 8¾ × 9" (68.4 × 21.9 × 23.2 cm).

Dance Mask. Alaska, Yup'ik. Early 20th century. Wood, paint, feathers, H 24 × 23¾ × 6½" (61 × 60.3 × 16.5 cm).

Lecture Sixteen

Sallet. Italian. 1470–1480. Steel, copper-gilt, glass, polychromy, H 11¾" (30 cm), Weight 8 lb. 4 oz. (3.7 kg).

Burgonet with Falling Buffe. French. c. 1555. Steel, blued, and gilded, H 14" (35.5 cm), Weight 5 lb. 6 oz. (2.4 kg).

Justus Sustermans (Workshop). *Cosimo II de' Medici (1590–1621), Grand Duke of Tuscany.* Oil on canvas, transferred from wood, 78 × 48" (198.1 × 121.9 cm).

Armor of George Clifford, Third Earl of Cumberland. English. c. 1580–1585. Steel, etched, blued, and gilded, H 67" (176.5 cm), Weight 60 lb. (27.2 kg).

Lucas Cranach the Elder. *The Judgment of Paris.* Possibly c. 1528. Oil on panel, 40 × 28" (101.9 × 71.1 cm).

Armor (*Gusoku*). Edo period, Japanese. 16th and 18th century. Lacquered iron, mail, silk, copper-gilt, H 67" (176.5 cm).

James Morisset. Presentation Smallsword. English. 1798–1799. Silver-gilt, enamel, paste jewels, steel, L 41½" (105.4 cm), Weight 1 lb. 3 oz. (539 kg).

Saber. Ottoman period, Turkish. 19th century. Steel, jade, gold, assorted jewels, L 39¾" (100.97 cm).

Ambrosius Gemlich (etcher) and Peter Pech (maker). Double-Barreled Wheellock Pistol of Emperor Charles V. German. c. 1540–1545. Wood (cherry), steel, staghorn, L (overall) 19½" (49.2 cm), Weight 5 lb. 10 oz. (2551 gm), Caliber (each barrel) .46.

Samuel Colt (manufacturer) and Gustave Young (engraver). Colt Third Model Dragoon Percussion Revolver. American. c. 1853. Steel, gold, and walnut, L 14" (35.56 cm), L (barrel) 7½" (19.05 cm), Caliber .44.

Tournament Shield (*Targe*). German. c. 1450. Wood, H 22" (55.88 cm), W 16" (40.64 cm).

Girolamo da Treviso (attributed). Shield. Italian. c. 1535. Wood, Diameter 24¾" (62.53 cm).

Hans Ruckers the Elder. Double Virginal. Antwerp, Flanders. 1581. Wood, metal, L 19½" (49.5 cm), W 71¾" (182.2 cm).

Michele Todini. Harpsichord. Italian. c. 1675. Wood, various materials, inner instrument 106 × 34 × 7½" (269 × 87 × 19 cm).

Bartolomeo Cristofori. Grand Piano. Italian. 1720. Various materials, L (of case perpendicular to keyboard) 90" (228.6 cm), W (parallel to keyboard) 37½" (95.6 cm) D (of case without lid) 9" (23.5 cm), H (total) 34" (86.5 cm).

Matteo Sellas (attributed). Guitar. Italian. c. 1630–1650. Wood, bone, various materials, L 37¾" (96.5 cm).

Antonio Stradivari. Violin. Italian. 1693. Wood, L 23¼" (59 cm), W 7¾" (19.7 cm).

Mayuri (Peacock). Northern India. 19th century. Wood, parchment, metal, feathers, L 44" (112 cm).

Rag-Dung. Ming Dynasty, China. 1368–1644. Brass, copper, cloisonné, L 72" (188 cm), Diameter 12" (30.6 cm).

Sho. Early Tokugawa period, Japan. 19th century. Bamboo, wood, metal, L (longest pipe) 18" (45.4 cm), L (shortest pipe) 7" (18.1 cm).

Charles Joseph Sax. Clarinet in B-flat. Brussels, Belgium. 1830. Ivory, brass, L 26¾" (68 cm), L (of mouthpiece) 35" (89 cm), L (of barrel) 27½" (70 cm), L (of upper body section) 8¾" (22.1 cm), L (of lower body section) 10" (25.7 cm), L (of bell) 4¾" (11.8 cm), Diameter (of bell) 33½" (85 cm).

Bondjo. Democratic Republic of the Congo. c. 1915. Ivory, wood, polychrome, L 55" (139.5 cm), Diameter (greatest) 8¼" (20.8 cm).

Kodenji Hayashi (?). *O-daiko.* Tohshima?, Aichi Prefecture, Japan. c. 1873. Wood, metal, cloisonné kankodori, hide, silk, padding, H (of drum) 19" (48.3 cm), Diameter 22" (55.8 cm), H (of stand) 29" (73.7 cm), H (total) approximately 62" (approximately 158 cm), L (of drum) approximately 21" (approximately 53 cm), Diameter (of heads) approximately 17" (approximately 43 cm).

Lecture Seventeen

Doublet. French. Early 1620s. Silk, L (at center back) 19¾" (50.2 cm).

Shoes. French. 17th century. Silk, leather, L 10" (25.4 cm).

Court Dress. British. c. 1750. Silk, metallic thread, L (at center back): a. 49" (124.5 cm), b. 37" (94 cm); L (at c.) 11" (27.9 cm).

Coat. British. c. 1833. Silk, L (at center back) 38½" (97.8 cm).

Dress. American. 1855–1865. Silk, L (at center back): a. 30¾" (77.8 cm), b. 38¼" (97.2 cm), c. 59¼" (150.5 cm), d. 25" (63.5 cm).

Paul Poiret. Costume (Fancy Dress). 1911. Metal, silk, cotton, L 50¼" (127.6 cm), Diameter 8" (20.6 cm).

Caroline Reboux. Cape. 1920s. Silk, L (at center front) 47" (119.4 cm).

Gabrielle "Coco" Chanel (designer). Coat. c. 1927. Silk, metal, L (at center back) 44" (111.8 cm).

————. Suit. 1938. Silk, L (at center back): a. 22" (55.9 cm), b. 29" (73.7 cm).

Salvatore Ferragamo. Sandal. 1938. Leather, cork, 5½ × 9" (14 × 22.9 cm).

Yves Saint Laurent (designer). *"L'Eléphant Blanc."* Spring/summer 1958. Silk, metallic thread, glass, plastic, L (from shoulder to hem) 41¾" (106 cm).

Rudi Gernreich. *Ensemble.* 1967. Wool, plastic, nylon, L (at center back): a. 29" (74.5 cm), b. 8½" (22.5 cm), c. 22" (56.5 cm), d. 22" (56.5 cm), e. 23" (58.5 cm).

Miguel Adrover. *I Love New York.* 2000. Cotton, cotton/silk blend, synthetic, L (at center back) 27½" (69.9 cm).

Sheet of Royal Linen. Dynasty XVIII, Egyptian. c. 1466 B.C. Linen, W (greatest) 5'2" (161 cm), L (greatest) 16'11" (515 cm), Weight

2.9 oz. (140 g), 118 warp per square inch (46 warp per square cm), 77 weft per square inch (30 weft per square cm).

Mantle. Ocucaje, Peru. 2nd–1st century B.C. Camelid hair, 74 × 54" (118.9 × 137.8 cm).

Personification of Luna, the Moon, or Head of Diana, Goddess of the Hunt. Coptic period. Late 3rd–4th century. Linen, wool, 22 × 25" (56 × 63 cm).

Fragment with Printed Lions. Persian. 10th–11th century. Cotton and other fibers, 17¾ × 39" (45.1 × 99.1 cm).

Mandala. Yuan dynasty. c. 1330–1332. Silk, metallic thread, 96 × 82" (245 × 209 cm).

Length of Velvet. Italian. Late 15th century. Silk, metal thread, W 23" (58.4 cm), L 12'4" (375.9 cm).

Lecture Eighteen

The Hart Room. From the Thomas Hart House, in Ipswich, Massachusetts. 1680.

The Marmion Room. Small parlor from a plantation house in King George County, Virginia, home of the Fitzhugh family. 18th century. Walnut, pine, sienna marble and paint, 21' × 16'5" × 11' (6.42 × 5 × 3.32 m).

The Verplanck Room. Parlor from the Cadwallader Colden, Jr., house in Coldenham, New York. 1767.

The Richmond Room. Drawing Room from the Williams House, Richmond, Virginia. 1810.

Turned Armchair. 1640–1680. Ash, 44¾ × 23½ × 15¾" (113.7 × 59.7 × 40 cm).

Chest of drawers. c. 1762–1775. Mahogany, tulip poplar, yellow pine, 91 × 45 × 24" (233 × 113 × 62 cm).

Paul Revere, Jr. Teapot. c. 1782. Silver, overall 6½ × 9½" (16.5 × 23.8 cm), Weight 539.2 g (17.336 troy ounces), Diameter (of base) 4" (10.5 cm).

Rudolph Christ. Sugar Bowl. 1789–1821. Earthenware with slip decoration, 12¾" (32.4 cm), Diameter 10" (25.4 cm).

Emanuel Gottlieb Leutze. *Washington Crossing the Delaware.* 1851. Oil on canvas, 12'5" × 21'3" (378 × 647 cm).

John Trumbull. *The Sortie Made by the Garrison of Gibraltar.* 1789. Oil on canvas, 72 × 108" (180 × 271 cm).

Matthew Pratt. *The American School.* 1765. Oil on canvas, 36 × 50¼" (91.4 × 127.6 cm).

John Vanderlyn. *The Palace and Gardens of Versailles.* 1818–1819. Oil on canvas, 12 × 165' (365 × 5,029 cm).

Charles Willson Peale. *George Washington.* c. 1779–1781. Oil on canvas, 96 × 60" (241 × 156 cm).

Gilbert Stuart. *George Washington.* Begun 1795. Oil on canvas, 30¼ × 25¼" (76.8 × 64.1 cm).

John Singleton Copley. *Daniel Crommelin Verplanck.* 1771. Oil on canvas, 49½ × 40" (125.7 × 101.6 cm).

Ralph Earl. *Elijah Boardman.* 1789. Oil on canvas, 84 × 51" (210 × 129 cm).

James Peale. *Still Life: Balsam Apple and Vegetables.* c. 1820s. Oil on canvas, 20¼ × 26½" (51.4 × 67.3 cm).

Edward Hicks. *The Falls of Niagara.* c. 1825. Oil on canvas, 31½ × 38" (80 × 96.5 cm).

Thomas Cole. *View from Mount Holyoke, Northampton, Massachusetts, after a Thunderstorm–The Oxbow.* 1836. Oil on canvas, 50 × 74" (130.8 × 193 cm).

Frederic Edwin Church. *Heart of the Andes.* 1859. Oil on canvas, 5'6" × 10' (168 × 302 cm).

Albert Bierstadt. *The Rocky Mountains, Lander's Peak.* 1863. Oil on canvas, 72 × 102" (182 × 259 cm).

Lecture Nineteen

Eastman Johnson. *The Hatch Family.* 1870–1871. Oil on canvas, 48 × 74" (121.9 × 186.4 cm).

Alexander Roux. Cabinet. c. 1866. Rosewood, tulipwood, cherry, poplar, pine, 53 × 72 × 18" (135.6 × 186.4 × 46.7 cm).

Herter Brothers. Library Table. 1882. Rosewood, brass, mother-of-pearl, 31¼ × 60 × 35¾" (79.4 × 152.4 × 90.8 cm).

Augustus Saint-Gaudens. Vanderbilt Mantelpiece. c. 1881–1883. Marble, mosaic, oak, and cast iron, 15'4" × 13' × 3'1" (468 × 393 × 94 cm).

Louis Comfort Tiffany. Loggia from Laurelton Hall, Oyster Bay, New York. c. 1905. Limestone, ceramic, glass, 21 × 23' (640 × 701 cm).

Augustus Saint-Gaudens. *Hiawatha.* Modeled 1871–1872, carved 1874. Marble, 93 × 33 × 37" (236 × 87 × 94 cm).

———. *Diana.* 1893–1894, this cast 1894 or after. Bronze, 28¼ × 16¼ × 14" (71.8 × 41.3 × 35.6 cm).

Daniel Chester French. *The Angel of Death and the Sculptor* from the *Milmore Memorial.* 1889–1893, this version 1926. Marble, 93 × 100 × 32" (237 × 255 × 82 cm).

Thomas Eakins. *The Champion Single Sculls (Max Schmitt in a Single Scull).* 1871. Oil on canvas, 32¼ × 46¼" (81.9 × 117.5 cm).

Mary Cassatt. *The Cup of Tea.* c. 1880–1881. Oil on canvas, 36½ × 25¾" (92.4 × 65.4 cm).

John Singer Sargent. *Madame X (Madame Pierre Gautreau).* 1883–1884. Oil on canvas, 81 × 43" (208 x 109 cm).

James Abbott McNeill Whistler. *Arrangement in Flesh Colour and Black: Portrait of Théodore Duret.* 1883. Oil on canvas, 76 × 36" (193.4 × 90.8 cm).

John Henry Twachtman. *Arques-la-Bataille.* 1885. Oil on canvas, 60 × 78" (152 × 200 cm).

Childe Hassam. *Celia Thaxter's Garden, Isles of Shoals, Maine.* 1890. Oil on canvas, 17¾ × 21½" (45.1 × 54.6 cm).

William Merritt Chase. *At the Seaside.* c. 1892. Oil on canvas, 20 × 34" (50.8 × 86.4 cm).

Winslow Homer. *The Gulf Steam.* 1899. Oil on canvas, 28 × 49" (71.4 × 124.8 cm).

Lecture Twenty

Pablo Picasso. *Harlequin.* 1901. Oil on canvas, 32¾ × 24" (82.9 × 61.3 cm). Gift of Mr. and Mrs. John L. Loeb, 1960.

———. *Gertrude Stein.* 1906. Oil on canvas, 39½ × 32" (100 × 81.3 cm).

Jean-Auguste-Dominique Ingres. *Louis François Bertin.* 1832. Oil on canvas, 45¾ × 37½" (116 × 95 cm). Musée du Louvre, Paris.

Pablo Picasso. *Girl Reading at a Table.* 1934. Oil and enamel on canvas, 63 × 50" (162.2 × 130.5 cm).

Henri Matisse. *Nasturtiums with the Painting "Dance."* 1912. Oil on canvas, 74 × 44" (191.8 × 115.3 cm).

————. *Dance (I).* Early 1909. Oil on canvas, 8'6½" × 12'9½" (259 × 390 cm). Museum of Modern Art, New York.

Salvador Dalí. *The Accommodations of Desire.* 1929. Oil and cut-and-pasted printed paper on cardboard, 8¾ × 13¾" (22.2 × 34.9 cm).

Umberto Boccioni. *Antigraceful.* 1913, cast 1950–1951. Bronze, 23 × 20½ × 20" (58.4 × 52.1 × 50.8 cm).

Constantin Brancusi. *Bird in Space.* 1923. Marble, H (with base) 56¾" (144.1 cm), Diameter 6½" (16.5 cm).

Bastis Master (Attributed). Marble female figure. Early Cycladic II, late Spedos type. c. 2600–2400 B.C. Marble, H 24¾" (62.79 cm).

Gaston Lachaise. *Standing Woman (Elevation).* 1927. Bronze, 72 × 31 × 17" (185.1 × 81.3 × 45.1 cm).

Charles Demuth. *The Figure 5 in Gold.* 1928. Oil on cardboard, 35½ × 30" (90.2 × 76.2 cm).

Grant Wood. *The Midnight Ride of Paul Revere.* 1931. Oil on masonite, 30 × 40" (76.2 × 101.6 cm).

Georgia O'Keeffe. *Cow's Skull: Red, White, and Blue.* 1931. Oil on canvas, 40 × 36" (101.3 × 91.1 cm).

Balthus. *The Mountain.* 1936. Oil on canvas, 8' × 12' (248 × 365 cm).

Charles Rennie Mackintosh. Washstand. 1904. Oak, ceramic tile, colored and mirror glass, lead, 62 × 50 × 20" (160.7 × 130.2 × 51.8 cm).

Josef Hoffmann (designer). *Tea Service.* c. 1910. Silver, amethyst, carnelian, ebony. Various dimensions.

Ludwig Mies van der Rohe. "MR" Armchair. 1927. Tubular steel, painted caning, 31½ × 22 × 37" (80 × 55.9 × 94 cm).

Frank Lloyd Wright. Living room from the Little House, Wayzata, Minnesota. 1912–1914. 13'8" × 46' × 28' (4.17 × 14 × 8.53 m).

Lecture Twenty-One

Alberto Giacometti. *Three Men Walking (II).* 1949. Bronze, 30 × 13 × 12¾" (76.5 × 33 × 32.4 cm).

Max Beckmann. *Beginning.* 1949. Oil on canvas, 5'9" × 10'5" (175 × 318 cm).

Clyfford Still. *1947-8-W-No. 1(PH-114)*. 1947–1948. Oil on canvas, 92 × 71" (233 × 179.7 cm).

Willem de Kooning. *Attic*. 1949. Oil, enamel, and newspaper transfer on canvas, 61 × 81" (157 × 205 cm).

Battle between Romans and Barbarians. The Portonaccio Sarcophagus. c. 180–190. Museo Nazionale Romano, Rome.

Jackson Pollock. *Autumn Rhythm (Number 30)*. 1950. Enamel on canvas, 8'9" × 17'3" (266 × 525 cm).

Mark Rothko. *No. 13 (White, Red on Yellow)*. 1958. Oil and acrylic with powdered pigments on canvas, 96 × 80" (242 × 206 cm).

Ellsworth Kelly. *Blue Green Red*. 1962–1963. Oil on canvas, 90 × 81" (231 × 208 cm).

Roy Lichtenstein. *Stepping Out*. 1978. Oil and magna on canvas, 84 × 69" (218 × 177 cm).

Fernand Léger. *The Three Musicians*. 1944 (after a drawing of 1924–1925; dated on painting 1924–1944). Oil on canvas, 68 × 56" (173.9 × 145 cm). The Museum of Modern Art, New York.

Andy Warhol. *Self-Portrait*. 1986. Acrylic and silkscreen on canvas, 79 × 79" (203 × 203 cm).

James Rosenquist. *House of Fire*. 1981. Oil on canvas, 6'6" × 16'6" (198 × 502 cm).

Romare Bearden. *The Block*. 1971. Cut and pasted printed, colored, and metallic papers, photostats, pencil, ink marker, gouache, watercolor, and pen and ink on masonite, overall 4' × 18' (121 × 548 cm), each of six panels 48 × 36" (121.9 × 91.4 cm).

Red Grooms. *Chance Encounter at 3 A.M.* 1984. Oil on canvas, 8'3" × 13' (254 × 393 cm).

Lecture Twenty-Two

Bernardo Daddi and The Assistant of Daddi. *The Assumption of the Virgin*, fragment of an altarpiece. c. 1340. Tempera on panel, gold ground, 42½ × 54" (108 × 136.8 cm).

Osservanza Master. *Saint Anthony the Abbot in the Wilderness.* c. 1435. Tempera and gold on panel, overall 18¾ × 13¾" (47.6 × 34.6 cm), painted surface 18½ × 13¼" (47 × 33.7 cm).

Sano di Pietro. *Saint Anthony Abbot Tormented by Demons.* c. 1435. Tempera and gold on panel, 18¾ × 13½" (47.5 × 34.3 cm). Yale University Art Gallery, New Haven, Connecticut.

Giovanni di Paolo. *The Creation of the World and the Expulsion from Paradise.* 1445. Tempera and gold on panel, 18¼ × 20½" (46.4 × 52.1 cm).

———. *Paradise.* Tempera and gold on canvas, transferred from wood, overall 18½ × 16" (47 × 40.6 cm), painted surface 17½ × 15" (44.5 × 38.4 cm).

Sandro Botticelli. *The Annunciation.* c. 1485. Tempera and gold on panel, 7½ × 12½" (19.1 × 31.4 cm).

Neroccio de' Landi. *Annunciation.* c. 1475–1480. Tempera on panel, 19½ × 50½" (49 × 128.5 cm). Yale University Art Gallery, New Haven, Connecticut.

Leonardo da Vinci. *Annunciation.* c. 1473–1475. Oil on panel, 39 × 84" (98 × 217 cm). Galleria degli Uffizi, Florence.

Hans Memling. *The Annunciation.* 1480–1489. Oil on panel, transferred to canvas, 30 × 21½" (76.5 × 54.6 cm).

Petrus Christus. *A Goldsmith in His Shop, Possibly Saint Eligius.* 1449. Oil on oak panel, overall 39½ × 33¾" (100.1 × 85.8 cm), painted surface 38¾ × 33½" (98 × 85.2 cm).

Quentin Metsys. *The Moneylender and His Wife.* 1514. Oil on board, 28 × 26¾" (71 × 68 cm). Musée du Louvre, Paris.

El Greco. *Saint Jerome as Cardinal.* c. 1610–1614. Oil on canvas, 42½ × 34¼" (108 × 87 cm).

Rembrandt van Rijn. *Portrait of Gérard de Lairesse.* 1665. Oil on canvas, 44½ × 34½" (112.7 × 87.6 cm).

———. *Self-portrait.* 1660. Oil on canvas, 31¾ × 26½" (80.3 × 67.3 cm).

Gerard de Lairesse. *Apollo and Aurora.* 1671. Oil on canvas, 80 × 76" (204 × 193 cm).

Francisco de Goya y Lucientes. *Condesa de Altamira and Her Daughter, María Augustina.* 1787–1788. Oil on canvas, 77 × 45" (195 × 115 cm).

Albrecht Dürer. *Self-portrait, Study of a Hand and a Pillow* (recto). 1493. Pen and brown ink, 11 × 8" (28 × 20 cm).

————. *Self-Portrait with Sea-Holly*. 1493. Oil on parchment on canvas, 22 × 17" (56.5 × 44.5) cm. Musée du Louvre, Paris.

————. *Six Pillows* (verso of *Self-portrait, Study of a Hand and a Pillow*). 1493. Pen and brown ink, 11 × 8" (28 × 20 cm).

Rogier van der Weyden. *The Annunciation*. c. 1435. Oil on panel, 34 × 36¾" (86 × 93 cm). Musée du Louvre, Paris.

Rembrandt van Rijn. Sketch after Leonardo da Vinci's fresco *The Last Supper*. c. 1635. Red chalk on buff prepared paper, 5 × 8" (12.4 × 20.9 cm).

Leonardo da Vinci. *The Last Supper*. 1498. Tempera on plaster, 15 × 29" (38.1 × 73.6 cm). S. Maria delle Grazie, Milan.

Canaletto. *Warwick Castle: The East Front*. 1752. Pen and brown ink, gray wash, 12½ × 22" (31.6 × 56.2 cm).

————. *Warwick Castle, East Front from the Courtyard*. 1752. 29½ × 48" (75 × 122 cm). Birmingham Museums & Art Gallery, Birmingham, Great Britain.

Domenico Tiepolo. *The Burial of Punchinello*. c. 1800. Pen and brown ink, brown and yellow wash, over black chalk, 14 × 18¾" (35.3 × 47.3 cm).

Bernaert van Orley (designer), Pieter de Pannemaker (probable weaver). *The Last Supper*. c. 1520–1530. Wool, silk, silver-gilt thread, 52' × 54'3" (1,584 × 1,653 cm).

Albrecht Dürer. *The Last Supper*. 1510. Woodcut, 15¾ × 11" (40 × 28 cm).

Lecture Twenty-Three

Jean-Auguste-Dominique Ingres. *Princesse de Broglie*. 1851–1853. Oil on canvas, 47¾ × 35¾" (121.3 × 90.8 cm).

Jean-Baptiste Camille Corot. *Diana and Actaeon*. 1836. Oil on canvas, 24'3" × 17'6" (739 × 533 cm).

Claude Monet. *Landscape at Zaandam*. 1871–1872. Oil on canvas, 18 × 26½" (45.7 × 67 cm).

Pierre-Auguste Renoir. *Two Young Girls at the Piano*. 1892. Oil on canvas, 44 × 34" (111.8 × 86.4 cm).

Henri Matisse. *Olive Trees at Collioure*. 1906. Oil on canvas, 17½ × 21¾" (44.5 × 55.2 cm).

André Derain. *Houses of Parliament at Night.* 1905–1906. Oil on canvas, 31 × 39" (78.7 × 99.1 cm), framed 40½ × 47½ × 3" (102.5 × 121 × 7.6 cm).

Claude Monet. *The Houses of Parliament (Effect of Fog).* 1903–1904. Oil on canvas, 32 × 36½" (81.3 × 92.4 cm).

Pierre Bonnard. *Before Dinner.* 1924. Oil on canvas, 35½ × 42" (90.2 × 106.7 cm).

Balthus. *Nude Before a Mirror.* 1955. Oil on canvas 75 × 64½" (899 × 772 cm).

Statue of an Offering Bearer. c. 1985 B.C. Dynasty 12, Middle Kingdom, Egyptian, Western Thebes. Gessoed and painted wood, H 44" (112.1 cm).

Jean-Auguste-Dominique Ingres. *Study of a Female Figure (Study for "Raphael and the Fornarina" [?]).* c. 1814. Pencil on white woven paper, 10 × 7¾" (25.4 × 19.7 cm).

———. *Raphael and the Fornarina.* 1814. Oil on canvas, 25½ × 21" (64.77 × 53.34). Fogg Art Museum, Cambridge, Massachusetts.

Raphael. *Madonna della Seggiola ("Madonna of the Chair").* c. 1516. Oil on panel, Diameter 28" (71 cm). Galleria Palatina, Palazzo Pitti, Florence.

Jean-François Millet. *Women Carrying Fagots.* c. 1858. Charcoal heightened with white gouache, charcoal border, on heavy gray-blue laid paper, 13½ × 10¾" (34.3 × 27.6 cm).

Edgar Degas. *Study of a Ballet Dancer* (recto) c. 1873. Oil paint heightened with body color on prepared pink paper, 17½ × 12½" (44.5 × 31.4 cm).

———. *A Woman Ironing.* 1873. Oil on canvas, 21½ ×x 15½" (54.3 × 39.1 cm).

———. *Two Dancers.* 1873. Dark brown wash and white gouache on bright pink commercially coated wove paper, now faded to pale pink, 24 × 15½" (61.3 × 39.4 cm).

Adolph von Menzel. *Studies of a Young Woman.* 1870 or 1879. Graphite on paper, 6¼ × 9½" (15.9 × 24.1 cm).

Pierre-Auguste Renoir. *Young Girl in a Blue Dress.* c. 1890. Watercolor with gouache highlights on thick cream wove paper, 8¼ × 6½" (20.8 × 16 cm).

Georges Seurat. *Study for "Les Poseuses."* 1886. Conté crayon on laid paper, 11¾ × 9" (29.7 × 22.5 cm).

Odilon Redon. *Pegasus and Bellerophon.* c. 1888. Charcoal, charcoal with water wash, white chalk, erasure highlighting on buff papier bueté, darkened, 21 × 14" (53.7 × 36.1 cm).

Felix Vallotton. *Street Scene in Paris.* 1895. Gouache and oil mounted on cardboard, 14 × 12" (36 × 30 cm).

Lecture Twenty-Four

Whose Sleeves? (Tagasode). Late 16th century. Ink, color, and gold on gilded paper, 22'5" × 53'8" (365 × 1,635 cm).

Rembrandt van Rijn. *Portrait of a Woman.* 1632. Oil on canvas, 44 × 35" (111.8 × 88.9 cm).

Paul Cézanne. *Mont Sainte-Victoire and the Viaduct of the Arc River Valley.* 1882–1885. Oil on canvas, 25¾ × 32" (65.4 × 81.6 cm).

Edgar Degas. *The Dancing Class.* Probably 1871. Oil on panel, 7¾ × 10¾" (19.7 × 27 cm).

Timeline

July 4, 1866 .... Paris meeting of Americans at the Bois de Boulogne in Paris, where they decide to create a "national institution and gallery of art" in America.

c. 1865 .... The Union League Club of New York, under the leadership of John Jay, works with political leaders, philanthropists, and art collectors to create the museum.

April 13, 1870 .... New York City leaders founded The Metropolitan Museum of Art; the museum's first accession, the Roman sarcophagus from Tarsus, donated.

1872 .... The museum opens to the public for the first time in the Dodworth Building at 681 Fifth Street.

1872 .... Artist John Kensett dies, leaving 38 paintings to the museum's collection.

1873 .... Museum moves to the Douglas Mansion at 128 West 14th Street; the museum purchases the Cesnola Collection from excavations in Cyprus.

1880 .... The museum moves to Central Park at 82nd Street and Fifth Avenue; Vanderbilt donates 670 Old Master drawings.

1886 .... The Department of Paintings established.

1889 .... Lucy W. Drexel and Mrs. John Crosby Brown make a large donation of musical instruments; the museum acquires two paintings by Édouard Manet.

1901 ....$7 million gift by Jacob S. Rogers creates a fund for the purchase of art.

1902 ....The Central Wing is finished and opens to the public.

1906 ....Museum starts undertaking archaeological expeditions to Egypt, financed by J. P. Morgan; the Department of Egyptian Art established; the George A. Hearn Fund created to purchase art from living artists.

1907 ....The museum acquires its first Renoir painting; the Department of European Sculpture and Decorative Arts established.

1909 ....The Department of Greek and Roman Art established.

1910 ....The museum becomes the first to include Matisse in its collection.

1911 ....The North Wing, designed by McKim, Mead and White, is completed.

1912 ....The Department of Arms and Armor established.

1913 ....The South Wing, designed by McKim, Mead and White, is completed; Benjamin Altman donates his collection of European paintings.

1915 ....The Department of Far Eastern Art is established.

1916 ....The Department of Prints created, with William M. Ivins, Jr. as its first curator.

1917 ....J. P. Morgan donates a large gift instrumental in developing the museum's medieval collection; a gift by Isaac Fletcher creates the Fletcher Fund for acquisitions.

1925 ....John D. Rockefeller purchases sculpture from The Cloisters in order to donate it to the museum.

1926 ....The Beaux Art style facade and additions by Robert Morris Hunt are completed and open to the public.

1929 ....The H. O. Havemeyer bequest of Old Master and Impressionist paintings.

1931 ....The Michael Friedsam bequest.

1933 ....The Department of Medieval Art and The Cloisters established.

1934 ....The American Decorative Arts Department established.

1938 ....The Cloisters opens in Fort Tryon Park.

1946 ....The Stieglitz collection of photographs donated; the Museum of Costume Art merges with The Metropolitan Museum of Art.

1948 ....The Department of American Paintings and Sculpture established; the Department of Musical Instruments created.

1949 ....The Jules Bache collection of European painting is donated to the museum.

1956	The Department of Ancient Near East Art established.
1963	The Department of Islamic Art created.
1967	The Department of Contemporary Art established.
1969	Robert Lehman dies and leaves his art collection to the museum.
1970	Department of Contemporary Art incorporated into the new Department of 20th Century Art [Dept. of Modern Art].
1971	Approval of the museum's comprehensive architectural plan by architectural firm Kevin Roche, John Dinkeloo and Associates.
1975	The Lehman Wing housing the Lehman Collection opens to the public.
1978	The Sackler Wing is completed and the Temple of Dendur is installed; the Treasures of Tutankhamun temporary exhibition.
1980	The completion of the American Wing with 24 period rooms.
1981	The Astor Court and the Douglas Dillon Galleries of Chinese paintings open to the public; the Mr. and Mrs. Charles Wrightsman bequest.
1982	The Rockefeller Wing opens; the Department of the Arts of Africa, Oceania, and the Americas established.

1987	The Lila Acheson Wallace and Henry R. Kravis wings created; the Ford Motor Company and John C. Waddell donate their large photograph collection.
1991	The completion of the museum's comprehensive architectural plan.
1992	The Department of Photographs established.
1993	The Department of Drawings and Prints established; the Blanche and A. L. Levine Court opens.
1994	The Florence and Herbert Irving Galleries open.
1996	The Robert and Renée Belfer Court opens.
1997	The Gilman Gallery opens, dedicated to displaying photographs.
1998	The Arts of Korea gallery installed.
1999	The renovated galleries of the Department of Near Eastern Art reopen.
2000	The Cypriot Galleries open.
2007	The reinstalled Greco-Roman galleries reopen.

Glossary

altarpiece: A piece of art—in most cases a series of paintings or sculpture on panel—to be positioned behind or above an altar.

Annunciation: The biblical narrative in which the angel Gabriel announces the miraculous incarnation to the Virgin Mary.

avant-garde: French for "fore guard" (referring to soldiers who advanced at the front of an army unit). A term used to describe art or artists that are at the front of a movement or that are experimental and innovative.

calligraphy: Specialized decorative hand lettering using a brush or pen.

composition: A principle of design referring to the arrangement or placement of elements in a work of art.

cuneiform: Pictographic writing elements inscribed in clay tablets; typically created in ancient Mesopotamia.

diptych: A two-paneled piece of art often joined together by hinges and used as an altarpiece.

donor: An individual or single business entity that financially supports or donates to an institution such as a church or a museum.

engraving: A printing method in which an incising tool or graver is used to cut an image into the surface of a metal plate. Ink is applied to the incised surface and wiped off, leaving ink in the wells of the incisions; a print is then created using this inked plate.

etching: A type of print where an image is drawn with an etching needle onto a chemically treated metal plate, which is then put into a chemical acid bath that etches or bites into the lines of the drawn image. Ink is then placed into these etched depressions, and the plate is used to create a printed impression.

genre: The term used to describe the depiction of ordinary, common life and activities.

icon: Considered sacred in and of itself, an icon is a pictorial representation of a sacred figure or event painted on a wooden panel or surface.

iconography: The study of the pictorial representation of the collected images or representations of a particular subject or subject matter.

illumination: Images or decorations, typically with brilliant colors and metals, used to enrich the text and letters of manuscripts or writings.

kouros: Greek for "young man," this term refers to the idealized youth depicted in classical sculpture.

krater: A large bowl from ancient Greece or Rome with a wide mouth and two vertical handles, normally used for mixing wine and water.

manuscript: A handwritten document or book typically created before the invention of printing.

mihrab: A niche in the wall of an Islamic mosque that indicates the direction of Mecca.

oil painting: The art or technique of painting with oil colors, which are pigments suspended in a drying medium (such as linseed oil).

parable: An allegorical story or statement meant to teach a moral lesson or religious principle.

Passion: The theological term referring to the narrative of Christ's sufferings from the Last Supper through the Crucifixion.

pietà: The visual representation of the Virgin Mary holding and mourning over the dead body of Christ.

plein air: The type of painting executed outdoors and directly responding to what is in front of the artist.

polychrome: An object such as a statue, vase, or mural in which a variety of colors has been used.

reliquary: A receptacle or repository for sacred relics.

sarcophagus: A stone coffin, typically having inscriptions or decorative sculpture.

stele: An upright slab or stone bearing inscriptions upon its surface, used as a monument or a commemoration.

still life: The visual representation of an inanimate object or series of inanimate objects.

tempera: A type of water-based paint in which ground pigment is suspended in egg yolk.

terracotta: Latin for "earth cooked," this term refers to a hard, semi-fired, waterproof, brownish-orange clay used in pottery.

triptych: Greek for "threefold," this term refers to a series of three panels of paintings usually hinged together.

woodcut: A type of print where an image is cut in relief onto the "plank" part of a piece of wood; ink is applied to create an image from this matrix.

Biographical Notes

Altman, Benjamin (1840–1913): An early donor to the museum who bequeathed important paintings by artists like Boticelli and Rembrandt.

Annenberg, Walter and Leonore (1908–2002; b. 1918): Long supporters of the museum, their gifts include the Annenberg Collection of Impressionist and Postimpressionist Paintings and a $20 million grant to purchase art works.

Bache, Jules (1861–1944): Donated important works of art in 1949, including works by Crivelli, van Dyck, and Goya.

Cesnola, Luigi Palma di (1832–1904): The museum's first director.

Clark, Stephen (1882–1960): Former trustee and donor who gave works including Seurat's *Circus Sideshow* and Degas's *The Singer in Green* (c. 1884).

de Montebello, Philippe (b. 1936): The museum's current director. He has improved the quality of both the museum and its galleries and has made a series of extraordinary acquisitions.

Havemeyer, H. O. and Louisine (1847–1907; 1885–1929): Generous donors to who gave paintings such as El Greco's *View of Toledo* and a very large and important collection of Impressionist paintings in 1929.

Hoving, Thomas (b. 1931): The museum's director from 1966 until 1977.

Hunt, Richard Morris (1828–1895): Architect of the museum's 1926 Beaux Art façade and additions.

Jay, John (1817–1894): Proposed that a "national institution and gallery of art" be created. His later efforts brought together New York City leaders and art enthusiasts, eventually giving birth to the museum.

Johnston, John Taylor (1820–1893): Railroad tycoon and the museum's first president. His personal art collection was the core of the museum's collection.

Lehman, Robert (1891–1969): New York banker who donated about 3,000 works of art to the museum that are housed in the Lehman Wing.

Morgan, J. P. (1837–1913): Philanthropist and museum trustee from 1903 to 1913, he generously donated art work to the museum including period rooms and the Raphael's *Madonna and Child Enthroned with Saints.*

Mould, Jacob Wrey (1825–1886): The architect of the original red brick building along with Calvert Vaux, which housed the museum's collection along Fifth Avenue in Central Park.

Putnam, George Palmer (1814–1872): The New York publisher who became the museum's founding superintendent.

Rockefeller, John D. (1839–1937): Philanthropist and early supporter of the museum who acquired and donated many works of art, including The Cloisters.

Rockefeller, Michael C. (1938–1964): An anthropologist and the youngest son of Nelson A. Rockefeller, he was memorialized in the Michael C. Rockefeller Wing dedicated to the arts of Africa, Oceania, and the Americas.

Rockefeller, Nelson A. (1908–1979): Benefactor who donated over 3,000 pieces of art to the museum in memory of his son, Michael C. Rockefeller.

Rorimer, James J. (1905–1966): Director of the museum from 1955 to 1966.

Sage, Mrs. Russell (1828–1918): Collector of early American furniture and objects whose donation of almost 900 pieces established the core of the museum's Department of American Decorative Arts.

The Vanderbilts: Various members of the Vanderbilt family have contributed many works of art to the museum, including Cornelius Vanderbilt (1794–1877), who donated 670 old master drawings, and William K. Vanderbilt (1878–1944), who donated Rembrandt's 1632 painting, *Man in Oriental Costume ("The Noble Slav").*

Vaux, Calvert (1824–1895): The museum's architect who designed the red brick Central Park building along with Jacob Wrey Mould.

Wrightsman, Charles and Jayne: Recent museum donors who gave paintings by artists such as Vermeer and Rubens in honor of the museum's curators.

Bibliography

Aldred, Cyril. *Temple of Dendur*. New York: Metropolitan Museum of Art, 1978.

Allen, James P. *The Heqanakht Papyri: Publications of the Metropolitan Museum of Art Egyptian Expedition, 27*. New York: Metropolitan Museum of Art, 2004.

Auchincloss, Louis. *J. P. Morgan: The Financier as Collector*. New York: Abrams, 1990.

Avery, Kevin J., and Peter L. Fodera. *John Vanderlyn's Panoramic View of the Palace and Gardens of Versailles*. New York: Metropolitan Museum of Art, 1988.

Baetjer, Katharine. *European Paintings in the Metropolitan Museum of Art by Artists Born Before 1865: A Summary Catalogue*. New York: Metropolitan Museum of Art, 1980.

Barnhart, Richard. *Asia (The Metropolitan Museum of Art Series)*. New York: Metropolitan Museum of Art, 1987.

Bean, Jacob. *100 Drawings in the Metropolitan Museum of Art*. New York: Metropolitan Museum of Art, 1964.

Behrendt Kurt A. *The Art of Gandhara in The Metropolitan Museum of Art*. New Haven: Yale University Press, 2006.

Bolger, Doreen. *American Pastels in the Metropolitan Museum of Art*. New York: Abrams, 1989.

Brettell, Richard, Francoise Forster-Hahn, Duncan Robinson, and Janis Tomlinson. *The Robert Lehman Collection at the Metropolitan Museum of Art, Volume IX: Nineteenth- and Twentieth-Century European Drawings*. New York: Metropolitan Museum of Art, 2002.

Brooks, Sarah T. *Byzantium: Faith and Power (1261–1557): Perspectives on Late Byzantine Art and Culture: The Metropolitan Museum of Art Symposia*. New York: Metropolitan Museum of Art, 2007.

Caldwell, John, Oswaldo Rodriguez Roque, Dale T. Johnson, and Kathleen Luhrs. *American Paintings in The Metropolitan Museum of Art, Vol. 1*. New York: Metropolitan Museum of Art, 1994.

Capistrano-Baker, Florina H. *Art of Island Southeast Asia: The Fred and Rita Richman Collection in the Metropolitan Museum of Art*. New York: Metropolitan Museum of Art, 1994.

Clark, Kenneth. *Masterpieces of Fifty Centuries: Metropolitan Museum of Art*. New York: E. P. Dutton, 1970.

Collins, Lisa Gail, and Lisa Mintz Messinger. *African-American Artists, 1929–1945: Prints, Drawings, and Paintings in The Metropolitan Museum of Art*. New York: Metropolitan Museum of Art, 2003.

Cone, Polly. *The Jack and Belle Linsky Collection in The Metropolitan Museum of Art*. New York: Metropolitan Museum of Art, 1984.

D'Alton, Martina. "The New York Obelisk, or How Cleopatra's Needle Came to New York and What Happened When It Got Here" *The Metropolitan Museum of Art Bulletin*, 4.72 (Spring 1993).

Danziger, Danny. *Museum: Behind the Scenes at the Metropolitan Museum of Art*. New York: Viking, 2007.

Dean, Bashford. *Helmets And Body Armor In Modern Warfare: The Metropolitan Museum Of Art*. New York: Metropolitan Museum of Art, 2007.

de Montebello, Philippe. *Met and the New Millennium: Chronicle of the Past and a Blueprint for the Future*. New York: Metropolitan Museum of Art, 1994.

———. *The Metropolitan Museum of Art Guide Revised Edition*. New York: Metropolitan Museum of Art, 2007.

———, and Barbara Burn. *Masterpieces of the Metropolitan Museum of Art*. New York: Metropolitan Museum of Art, 1993.

Dorman, Peter F. *The Metropolitan Museum of Art: Egypt and the Ancient Near East*. New York: Metropolitan Museum of Art, 1987.

Douglas, Newton. *Art of Africa, the Pacific Islands, and the Americas*. New York: Metropolitan Museum of Art, 1980.

Druesedow , Jean L . "Celebrating Fifty Years of the Costume Institute." *The Metropolitan Museum of Art Bulletin*, 4.64 (Fall 1987).

Frelinghuysen, Alice Cooney. *Splendid Legacy: The Havemeyer Collection*. New York: Metropolitan Museum of Art, 1993.

Galitzn, Kathryn Calley, and Gary Tinterow. *Masterpieces of European Painting in the Metropolitan Museum of Art, 1800–1920*. New York: Metropolitan Museum of Art, 2007.

Gardner, Albert Ten Eyck, and Stuart P. Feld. *American Paintings: Catalogue of the Collection of the Metropolitan Museum of Art I: Painters Born by 1815*. New York: Metropolitan Museum of Art, 1965.

Grancsay, Stephen V. *Loan Exhibition of Mediaeval and Renaissance Arms and Armor from the Metropolitan Museum of Art*. Los Angeles: Los Angeles County Museum, 1953.

Grinnell, Isabel Hoopes. *Greek Temples*. New York: Metropolitan Museum of Art, 1943.

Hambourg, Maria Morris. "Photography between Wars: Selections from the Ford Motor Company Collection." *The Metropolitan Museum of Art Bulletin*, 4.56 (Spring 1988).

Hartt, Frederick. *The Metropolitan Museum of Art: Renaissance in Italy and Spain*. New York: Metropolitan Museum of Art, 1987.

Heckscher, Morrison H. *American Furniture in the Metropolitan Museum of Art: Late Colonial Period: The Queen Anne and Chippendale Styles*. New York: Metropolitan Museum of Art, 1986.

———. *The Metropolitan Museum of Art: An Architectural History*. New York: Metropolitan Museum of Art, 1995.

Hibbard, Howard. *Metropolitan Museum of Art*. New York: Metropolitan Museum of Art, 1980.

Hindman, Sandra, Mirella Levi D'Ancona, Pia Palladino, and Maria Francesca Saffiotti. *The Robert Lehman Collection at the Metropolitan Museum of Art*. Princeton: Princeton University Press, 1998.

Hoving, Thomas. *The Chase and Capture: Collecting at the Metropolitan*. New York: Metropolitan Museum of Art, 1975.

———. *Making the Mummies Dance: Inside the Metropolitan Museum of Art*. New York: Simon and Schuster, 1993.

Howard, Kathleen, ed. *Metropolitan Museum of Art*. New York: Metropolitan Museum of Art, 1983.

Ivins, William Mills. *Prints and Books: Informal Papers*. New York: Metropolitan Museum of Art, 1926.

Kisluk-Grosheide, Danielle, Wolfram Koeppe, and William Rieder. *Highlights of the European Furniture Collection*. New Haven: Yale University Press, 2006.

Kjellgren, Eric. *Oceania: Art of the Pacific Islands in The Metropolitan Museum of Art*. New York: Metropolitan Museum of Art, 2007.

Koda, Harold, Andrew Bolton, and Mimi Hellman. *Dangerous Liaisons: Fashion and Furniture in the Eighteenth Century*. New York: Metropolitan Museum of Art, 2006.

LaGamma, Alisa. *Art and Oracle: African Art and Rituals of Divination*. New York: Metropolitan Museum of Art, 2000.

———. *Echoing Images: Couples in African Sculpture*. New York: Metropolitan Museum of Art, 2004.

———. *Eternal Ancestors: The Art of the Central African Reliquary*. New York: Metropolitan Museum of Art, 2007.

Lerman, Leo. *Museum: One Hundred Years and the Metropolitan Museum of Art*. New York: Viking Press, 1969.

Libin, Laurence. *Our Tuneful Heritage: American Musical Instruments from The Metropolitan Museum of Art*. New York: Metropolitan Museum of Art, 1998.

Lieberman, William S. *Painters in Paris: 1895–1950*. New York: Metropolitan Museum of Art, 2000.

———, Lisa Mintz Messinger, Sabine Rewald, and Lowery S. Sims. *20th Century Art Painting 1945–85: Selections from the Collection of the Metropolitan Museum of Art*. New York: Metropolitan Museum of Art, 1987.

Liebling, Roslyn, Christine Lilyquist, Thomas J. Logan, and Karen Briggs. *Time Line of Culture in the Nile Valley and Its Relationship to Other World Cultures*. New York: Metropolitan Museum of Art, 1978.

Liedtke, Walter. *Dutch Paintings in The Metropolitan Museum of Art*. New York: Metropolitan Museum of Art, 2007.

———. *Flemish Paintings in the Metropolitan Museum of Art Two Volumes*. New York: Metropolitan Museum of Art, 1984.

Little, Charles T. *Set in Stone: The Face in Medieval Sculpture*. New Haven: Yale University Press, 2006.

Luhrs, Kathleen, ed. *American Paintings in the Metropolitan Museum of Art*. New York: Metropolitan Museum of Art, 1980.

Marandel, J. Patrice. *Europe in the Age of Enlightenment and Revolution (The Metropolitan Museum of Art Series)*. New York: Metropolitan Museum of Art, 1987.

Martin, Richard. *Our New Clothes: Acquisitions of the 1990s*. New York: Metropolitan Museum of Art, 1999.

McCann, Anna Marguerite. *Roman Sarcophagi in the Metropolitan Museum of Art*. New York: Metropolitan Museum of Art, 1978.

Mertens, Joan. *Greece and Rome*. New York: Metropolitan Museum of Art, 1987.

Milleker, Elizabeth J., and Joseph Coscia. *Light on Stone: Greek and Roman Sculpture in The Metropolitan Museum of Art: A Photographic Essay*. New York: Metropolitan Museum of Art, 2004.

Miller, R. Craig. *Modern Design in the Metropolitan Museum of Art, 1890–1990*. New York: Metropolitan Museum of Art, 1990.

Moffett, Charles S. *Impressionist and Post-Impressionist Paintings in the Metropolitan Museum of Art*. New York: Metropolitan Museum of Art, 1998.

Muscarella, Oscar White. *Bronze and Iron: Ancient Near Eastern Artifacts in the Metropolitan Museum of Art*. New York: Metropolitan Museum of Art, 1988.

Naef, Weston J. *The Collection of Alfred Stieglitz: Fifty Pioneers of Modern Photography*. New York: Metropolitan Museum of Art, 1978.

Nickel, Helmut, Stuart W. Pyhrr, and Leonid Tarassuk. *Art of Chivalry: European Arms and Armor from the Metropolitan Museum of Art: An Exhibition*. New York: Metropolitan Museum of Art, 1982.

Norris, Michael, Carlos A. Picon, Joan R. Mertens, and Elizabeth J. Milleker. *Greek Art from Prehistoric to Classical: A Resource for Educators*. New York: Metropolitan Museum of Art, 2001.

O'Neill, John P., ed. *20th Century Art: Selections from the Collection of the Metropolitan Museum of Art*. New York: Metropolitan Museum of Art, 1986.

———. *Mexico: Splendors of Thirty Centuries*. New York: Metropolitan Museum of Art, 1990.

Peck, Amelia. *Period Rooms in the Metropolitan Museum of Art*. New York: Metropolitan Museum of Art, 1996.

Phipps, Richard, and Richard Wink. *Invitation to the Gallery: An Introduction to Art.* New York: Metropolitan Museum of Art, 1987.

Picón, Carlos, and Richard De Puma. *Art of the Classical World in the Metropolitan Museum of Art: Greece, Cyprus, Etruria, and Rome.* New York: Metropolitan Museum of Art, 2007.

Pittman, Holly. *Art of the Bronze Age: Southeastern Iran, Western Central Asia, and the Indus Valley.* New York: Metropolitan Museum of Art, 1984.

———. *Egypt and the Ancient Near East.* New York: Metropolitan Museum of Art, 1987.

Pope-Hennesy, John. *The Study and Criticism of Italian Sculpture.* New York: Metropolitan Museum of Art, 1980.

Pyhrr, Stuart W., Donald J. LaRocca, and Morihiro Ogawa. *Arms and Armor: Notable Acquisitions 1991–2002.* New York: Metropolitan Museum of Art, 2003.

Quodbach, Esmee. *The Age of Rembrandt: Dutch Paintings in The Metropolitan Museum of Art.* New York: Metropolitan Museum of Art, 2007.

Richardson, Joy. *Inside the Museum: A Children's Guide to the Metropolitan Museum of Art.* New York: Harry N. Abrams, 1993.

Roque, Oswaldo R. *The United States of America (The Metropolitan Museum of Art Series).* New York: Metropolitan Museum of Art, 1987.

Rousseau, Theodore. *Guide to the Picture Galleries.* New York: Metropolitan Museum of Art, 1954.

Russell, John Malcolm. *From Nineveh to New York: The Strange Story of the Assyrian Reliefs in the Metropolitan Museum and the Hidden Masterpiece at Canford.* New York: Metropolitan Museum of Art, 1997.

Salinger, Margaretta. *Masterpieces of American Painting in the Metropolitan Museum of Art.* New York: Metropolitan Museum of Art, 1986.

Scully, Vincent Joseph. *New World Visions of Household Gods & Sacred Places: American Art and the Metropolitan Museum of Art, 1650–1914.* New York: Metropolitan Museum of Art, 1988.

Sims, Lowery Stokes, Sabine Rewald, and William S. Lieberman. *Still Life: The Object in American Art, 1915–1995: Selections from the Metropolitan Museum of Art*. New York: Metropolitan Museum of Art, 1996.

Snyder, James. *The Renaissance in the North*. New York: Metropolitan Museum of Art, 1987.

Stauffer, Annemarie, Marsha Hill, Helen C. Evans, and Daniel Walker. *Textiles of Late Antiquity*. New York: Metropolitan Museum of Art, 1995.

Szabó, George. *Masterpieces of Italian Drawing in the Robert Lehman Collection, the Metropolitan Museum of Art*. New York: Metropolitan Museum of Art, 1983.

―――. *The Robert Lehman Collection: A Guide*. New York: Metropolitan Museum of Art, 1975.

Thompson, Nancy. *Roman Art: A Resource for Educators*. New York: Metropolitan Museum of Art, 2007.

Tinterow, Gary. *Modern Europe*. New York: Metropolitan Museum of Art, 1980.

―――. *The New Nineteenth-Century European Paintings and Sculpture Galleries*. New York: Metropolitan Museum of Art, 1993.

Tomkins, Calvin. *Merchants and Masterpieces: The Story of the Metropolitan Museum of Art*. New York: Dutton, 1970.

Valenstein, Suzanne G. *Handbook of Chinese Ceramics*. New York: Metropolitan Museum of Art, 1975.

Von Bothmer, Dietrich. *The Metropolitan Museum of Art Guide to the Collections: Greek and Roman Art*. New York: Metropolitan Museum of Art, 1964.

Von Sonnenburg, Hubert. *Rembrandt/Not Rembrandt: In The Metropolitan Museum of Art—Aspects of Connoisseurship*. New York: Metropolitan Museum of Art, 1995.

Watt, James C. Y., An Jiayao, Angela Falco Howard, and Boris I. Marshak. *China: Dawn of a Golden Age, 200–750 AD*. New York: Metropolitan Museum of Art, 2004.

Weitzenhoffer, Frances. *Havemeyers: Impressionism Comes to America*. New York: Metropolitan Museum of Art, 1986.

Welch, Stuart. *The Islamic World*. New York: Metropolitan Museum of Art, 1987.

Winlock, Herbert Eustis, and Harry Burton. *The Tomb of Queen Meryet-Amun at Thebes: The Metropolitan Museum Of Art Egyptian Expedition.* New York: Metropolitan Museum of Art, 1972.

Zeri, Federico, and Elizabeth E. Gardner. *Italian Paintings: A Catalogue of the Collection of the Metropolitan Museum of Art, North Italian School.* New York: Metropolitan Museum of Art, 1986.

———. *Italian Paintings: A Catalogue of the Collection of the Metropolitan Museum of Art, Sienese and Central Italian Schools.* New York: Metropolitan Museum of Art, 1980.

Recommended Web Sites:

The general information website for The Metropolitan Museum of Art is www.metmuseum.org. It contains a variety of information including free downloadable podcasts of select objects in the museum's collection, a visitor site with all the useful information for planning a visit, and a link to sign up for a membership to receive regular mailings and special member benefits.

Notes